The Natural Laws of Business

Applying the Theories of Darwin, Einstein, and Newton to Achieve Business Success

Richard Koch

CURRENCY
DOUBLEDAY

NEW YORK LONDON TORONTO SYDNEY AUCKLAND

A Currency Book
published by doubleday
a division of Random House, Inc.
1540 Broadway, New York, New York 10036

Currency and Doubleday are
trademarks of Doubleday, a division of Random House, Inc.

First published in 2000 as *The Power Laws* in Great Britain and the Commonwealth by Nicholas Brealey Publishing

Book design by Lee Fukui

Library of Congress Cataloging-in-Publication Data

Koch, Richard, 1950–
[Natural laws of business]
The natural laws of business: applying the theories of Darwin, Einstein, and Newton to achieve business success / Richard Koch.
p. cm.
Originally published: The Power Laws: the science of success. 2000.
Includes index.
1. Success in business. 2. Management. 3. Science—Methodology. I. Title.
HF5386 .K763 2001
658'.001—dc21 00-065886

ISBN 0-385-50159-5

Printed in the United States of America
August 2001
First Edition in the United States of America

Currency Books are available at special discounts for bulk purchases for sales promotions and premiums. Special editions, including personalized covers, excerpts of existing books, and corporate imprints, can be created in large quantities for special needs. For more information, write to Special Markets, Currency Books, 280 Park Avenue, 11th floor, New York, NY 10017, or e-mail specialmarkets@randomhouse.com

10 9 8 7 6 5 4 3 2 1

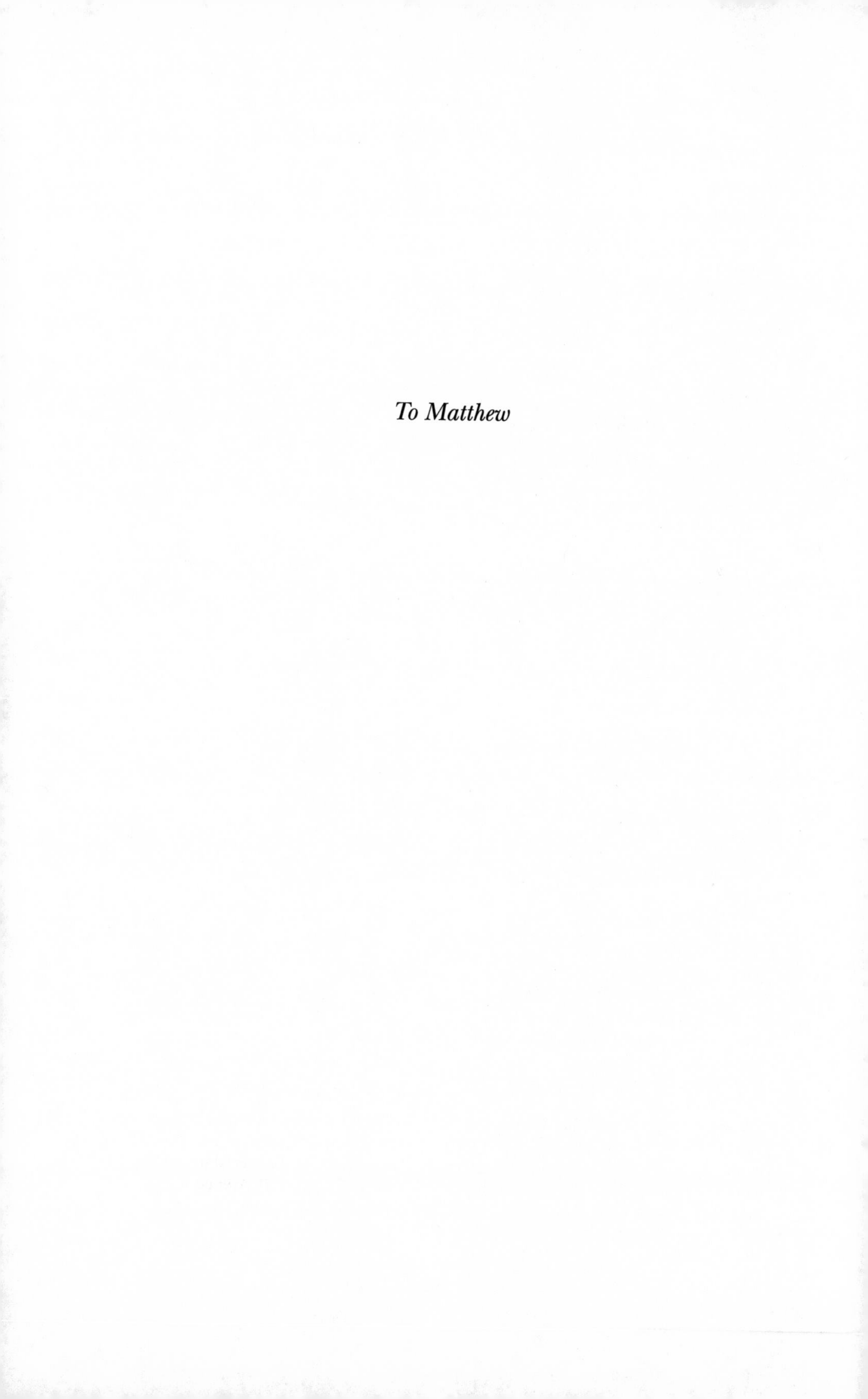

To Matthew

Acknowledgments

The greatest scientists since the seventeenth century deserve my first thanks: I have appropriated and interpreted their insights. Though several dozen scientists have been useful, particular thanks are due to Sir Issac Newton, Charles Darwin, Gregor Mendel, Vilfredo Pareto, Albert Einstein, and G. F. Gause, the Soviet biologist.

My greatest debts to contemporaries are to Richard Dawkins, a brilliant scientist whose combination of Darwin and modern genetics is an unforgettable marvel, and who writes like an angel; and to Matt Ridley, a science writer who generates more intriguing juxtapositions and insights per page than anyone else I know. Their ideas have helped immeasurably in the development of my theory of business genes—a particular subspecies of the "memes" invented by Dawkins.

Very late in the writing of this book, I was given an advance copy of Jane Jacobs's excellent short book, *The Nature of Economies* (Random House, New York, 2000), which I found extremely useful, highly congruent with my own argument, but also extremely helpful for refining some of this book's themes.

I would also like to thank all my friends who have made useful comments on various large manuscripts, and especially Mark Allin, Dr. Richard Burton, Robin Field, Anthony Hewat, Dr. Peter Johnson, Clive Richardson, and Patrick Weaver, who have been extremely generous with their time and added many insights, and, at least as important, subtracted many of my "insights" that were insufficiently grounded in the natural laws. Dr. Marcus Alexander of the Ashridge Strategic Management Centre gave me a rigorous review and also access to his exciting research on "boundaries." In a class all of his own is Dr. Chris Eyles, a vet turned Internet strategist, who has encouraged and badgered me throughout the process, adding his own blend of wisdom and knowledge. Chris also supplied the structure for the book when this issue was driving me nuts—thanks, Chris, now get on with proving that the Internet really can make money.

Two absolutely crucial partners in this enterprise have been my researcher, Andrej Machacek, of Balliol College, Oxford, and Nicholas Brealey, the British publisher. Andrej did all the difficult initial research, telling me what to read, dredging up obscure monographs on some important subjects, and summarizing hundreds of natural laws with amazing brevity and accuracy. He has also been a charming and valuable foil as we have debated the ideas in the book, and while reviewing all six drafts has made wise comments, some of which I have incorporated into the text. Anyone who wants a terrific researcher could not do better than to contact Andrej.

Nicholas is a phenomenon and it is wonderful working with him. Sally Lansdell and Sue Coll also made major contributions to structuring the book and making it easier to use. Eileen Fallon, of the Fallon Literary Agency in New York, provided a terrifically valuable critique of the penultimate draft of the book. Many thanks, Eileen. I also am extremely grateful to my assistant, Aaron Calder, who has greatly speeded up the production process.

RICHARD KOCH

Contents

Preface: **Appreciating a Wonky World**

In Search of a Few Universal Principles

You don't see something until you have the right metaphor to let you perceive it.

THOMAS KUHN

I can never forget the excitement I first felt, as an undergraduate at Oxford University, when I realized that science could be used to make life fuller and richer. While some of my contemporaries were turned on by Karl Marx, my hero was Vilfredo Pareto, the Italian economist who, in 1896, discovered that incomes and wealth, regardless of country or era, followed a certain predictable pattern. This pattern, eventually called the Pareto Rule, helped economists to prove that the great majority of results flowed from a small minority of causes: to simplify, 80 percent of what happens flows from 20 percent of inputs (hence the Pareto Rule is generally known today as the "80/20 Principle").

The young Richard Koch found that the 80/20 principle had all sorts of useful applications. It helped me get ahead in my business career, not by working hard (though that played no small part in my success), but by teaching me to concentrate on the few things that were really powerful and important. Applying the same rule to the stock market helped me make a lot of money.

I find it astonishing and literally wonderful that a simple scientific discovery—one that can be described in a single paragraph—has so much universal power, reaching well beyond the scientific application in which it originated. More important, understanding the premise of the 80/20 principle helps me spend my leisure time on things that I truly enjoy.

Since that moment of discovery in Oxford's Bodelian library, I have been on the lookout for other universal scientific principles that illuminate the nature of life generally, and can help us lead more fulfilling lives.

Science has, over time, revealed universal patterns which predict and explain how the world *really* works, not just within specific scientific disciplines, but also outside them. I have identified the most important and relevant of these patterns, rules, and relationships, which I have called "natural laws."

To be a natural law of business, a principle must satisfy three criteria:

- It must be a coherent theory of how things work, with wide acceptance among scientists.
- It must transcend the discipline where it originated, and cross over to more than one scientific discipline.
- It must be capable of application to business.

As it turns out, there are many sciences which can be applied toward the third criterion.

I have tried to avoid well-trawled areas, seeking fresh perspectives not currently available in management literature, and have generally avoided management concepts, even where they claim (usually spuriously) scientific validity. I have also done my best to avoid facile comparisons. There is nothing worse than half-baked business conclusions drawn from quarter-understood scientific ideas.

My researcher, Andrej Machacek, and I examined over a thousand scientific theories and principles which, on first inspection, appeared possibly relevant, before winnowing the list down. We have included not only theories well supported by data, but also empirically observed facts and a few resonant concepts that, though unverifiable, make such good sense we felt they deserved a mention. We even allowed for a handful of ideas that offer insight without having *any* scientific validity, such as Murphy's and Parkinson's laws. The vast majority of the natural laws, however, are scientifically respectable.

Applying Scientific Insight Toward Business Success

Science is an attempt to explain the world around us. Business is part of this world. Physicists know that the universe is unitary: the same laws apply everywhere, all the time. Scientists working in different disciplines have often been helped by theories developed elsewhere. What works in biology also works in economics, in physics, and in psychology, and vice versa. Interdisciplinary sciences such as chaos and complexity observe the same phenomena and the same patterns—equally relevant to meteorology, financial markets, geology, physics, chemistry, or many other disciplines—which are usually capable of similarly mathematical expression within all these areas.

The reason that insights and theories from one science work in another is that the universe is more basic than our scientific taxonomy. In trying to understand and study things we break them down, but all we are doing is glimpsing, from different angles, the same universal principles. My quest has been for natural laws that transcend scientific boundaries and defy artificial barriers between science and business.

In trying to gain insight from science, I have first tried to understand the science properly, in its own terms, before applying it to business. This is exactly what a chemist does, for example, in seeking to understand and apply an idea from physics.

From Order to Chaos

Nineteenth-century science was solid and dependable. Twentieth-century science was surreal, often incomprehensible, and pretty incredible. At the start of the twenty-first century, most of us feel at home with the scientific world of the late nineteenth century. It was the culmination of three centuries of progressively increasing degrees of understanding and confidence: educated people felt that they understood how the world worked and that there would soon be few limits to humanity's dominion over nature.

The twentieth century changed all that. As scientists learned more, the universe seemed less predictable, less ordered, more mysterious and frightening. Defense mechanisms set in. The universe just *couldn't* be that random, that pointless, that out of sync with reason. And so began an intellectual reaction that is still with us. Most of our mental models are still those of nineteenth-century science.

Let's see how the world became so much easier to understand from the sixteenth to the nineteenth centuries, and how much more difficult thereafter.

In Praise of the "Incomparable Mr. Newton"

Perhaps the most important science book ever—Sir Isaac Newton's *Principia Mathematica*—was published in 1687. Newton linked together knowledge that had been simmering for centuries and was then coming to a boil: from the ancient Greeks, from Roger Bacon (a late-thirteenth-century Oxford scholar), from Leonardo da Vinci, Galileo, and Kepler, from French philosopher René Descartes, and from many other sources. Newton was both the father of modern empirical science and the codifier of the most powerful intellectual framework the world has ever seen—the idea of the clockwork universe.

The Newtonian world was simple and easily understood. Everything could be related to everything else, on earth and in the heavens. Reality was comprised of machines and parts of machines, all behaving in accordance with a few basic, universal, reliable laws.

Science as a total system made sense. God was relegated to the role of a wise clockmaker, the guy who wound up the clock—the universe—and then left it to operate on its own according to certain standard operating procedures.

You can see the clockwork universe manifested in the work of Adam Smith and all the classical economists; in Thomas Robert Malthus's thoughts on population and sustainability; in the ideas of the French enlightenment on the "perfectibility of man," an idea encapsulated by British historian Edward Gibbon, who wrote in 1776 that "we cannot be certain to what heights the human species may aspire";[1] in Charles Darwin's theory of evolution by natural selection; in Sigmund Freud's mechanical model of the mind and consciousness; and in all political and social writers from Thomas Hobbes to Karl Marx, John Stuart Mill, Auguste Comte, Vilfredo Pareto, and Max Weber. Although many of these thinkers added a teleological or dialectical perspective—which is at odds with a simple, static, clockwork world—their views are all mechanistic and rational. Everything is a machine, everything obeys simple laws, everything fits together and can be understood, analyzed, and reduced to its basic elements. Everything works and has a purpose. People can aspire to control the world, society, and their own nature, because everything is mechanical and intelligence can control mechanical things.

The Newtonian ideology gave people confidence that they could understand and control the world, and so they did. The explosion of science, industry, technology, and wealth that followed in the next three hundred years, which was well beyond any historical precedent and which took us to the brink of material utopia, would have been impossible without faith in the clockwork Newtonian universe.

It is therefore difficult to overstate Newton's impact on business. One route of influence is directly through engineering and machinery, and the productivity revolutions from 1750 to 2000. Another is through the influence of mechanical models on economics and the way that "organizations"—a modern word, but a very Newtonian concept—are structured. A third is through the power of numerical analysis: accounting systems, calculators, and computers, all of which depend on Newtonian methods.

Nearly all executives and management writers still base their work on conclusions made in the nineteenth century. Yet science has moved forward.

Weird and Wonderful Twentieth-Century Science

Danish physicist Niels Bohr (1885–1962) was one of the great minds of the twentieth century and perhaps the most important developer of quantum physics, which must rank as one of the most sublime (and counterintuitive) scientific theories of all time. Bohr used to tell a story about a Jewish theological student who attended three lectures by a famous rabbi. The first lecture was splendid, and the student understood it all. The second lecture was even better; the rabbi clearly understood every word, but it was so subtle and deep that the student couldn't follow it entirely. The third lecture, though, was the crowning achievement; it was so brilliant that even the rabbi didn't understand it. Bohr said that quantum theory was "weird": it made him feel like the rabbi at the third lecture.[2]

Quantum theory is positively subversive. As we'll see in Chapter 8, the microworld of atoms "chooses" which state to leap into entirely at random; the precise positions or velocities of electrons cannot be measured; light is both like a wave and like a particle—nothing is real, nothing is predictable; everything is uncertain, and everything is related, mysteriously, to everything else.

The first two decades of the twentieth century also gave us Einstein's theories of relativity, which are extraordinarily difficult to understand. Einstein himself said that only twelve people in the world would understand his general theory. As a result of relativity, we know that space is curved, that gravity is the warping of space and time by physical mass, that time and space are not two dimensions, but one linked frame of reference, and that time is part of the physical universe.

The scientific theme that there is no objective reality was reinforced in 1931 by the brilliant Austrian scientist Kurt Gödel, who was eccentric to the point of madness. Nonetheless, his incompleteness theorem proved beyond doubt that, even within a simple, formal system like mathematics, you could make statements that could never be either proved or disproved within the terms of that system. Reality is thus an invention, not a given.

Systems thinking and the development of chaos and complexity theories in the last third of the twentieth century revealed even more difficult concepts. It turns out that most things in the world, and certainly some of the most important—including the weather, the brain, cities, economies, history, and people—are "nonlinear systems," which means that they don't behave in the straightforward way assumed by Isaac Newton and all scientists up to the end of the nineteenth century.

Nonlinear systems don't have simple causes and effects. They don't behave like mechanical objects. Everything is interrelated, equilibrium is elusive and fleeting, small and even trivial causes can have massive effects, control is impossible, prediction is hazardous, simple systems can demonstrate incredibly complex behavior, and complex systems can give rise to very simple behavior. In this weird and wonky world, intelligence, common sense, and good intentions are no guarantee of good results. Instead, unwelcome and unintended consequences are endemic.

So the twentieth century is a topsy-turvy world where classical Newtonian cause-and-effect logic seems to have no place. Yet scientists have discovered remarkably consistent laws and patterns that can explain "chaotic" behavior. Beauty, method, and order do exist within the apparent madness and disorder.

A New Gestalt for Business?

If we accept the world revealed by modern science, we can better understand the laws that dictate business success or failure.

We will learn, for instance, why individuals are badly programmed to work effectively in large organizations, and why—for good and ill—organizations have a will of their own.

A slight but crucial change in perspective will demonstrate that the fundamental unit of value in business is economic information; that the market in economic information is highly imperfect, allowing us to appropriate huge value; that technology drives growth; that entrepreneurs, not scientists, are the main drivers of technology.

We'll see that a struggle for existence is at the heart of business, but that the struggle is primarily between ideas, not between corporations. We'll also examine how corporate competition is marginal to our economies and to our personal success. We'll learn that business is not at all like war.

The natural laws of business tell us that innovation is mandatory, but also predictable, following a seamless process of variation, frequent failure, infrequent success, and further variation—a process eerily reminiscent of natural selection. Experimentation is essential and yet most experiments have to fail, but business is not generally structured for experimentation, foolishly preferring the architecture of the cathedral to that of the bazaar.

The new gestalt holds that growth is not difficult to find but is extremely difficult to perpetuate, that less is more, and that influence is generally superior to control. We are moving into an era where return on management effort (ROME) is more important than return on capital employed (ROCE), and where corporate ownership has more downside than upside.

The new science explains that most of business is nonlinear and unpredictable, yet that different branches of business each follow discernible and distinctive patterns. There are always a few powerful forces that we can use to our advantage or that will upset our plans, and success usually emerges when we are looking the other way. But unexpected successes, if we deign to notice them, can be deliberately nurtured into explosive bonanzas.

We'll see that while business often obtains diminishing returns from extra effort and investment, the most important economic phenomenon at the start of the twenty-first century is increasing returns, where additional investment and command of intellectual property throw off exponentially increasing cash.

We'll learn that either/or thinking is a trap, that trade-offs can be eluded, and that a both/and attitude is the handmaiden of creativity. There are an infinite number of ways to fail, but there are always multiple routes to success, and the opposite of a great business truth is . . . another great business truth.

Finally, the natural laws of business reveal that business is a book of bets, that only skillful gamblers can consistently win. Yet business is also a series of related transactions linked together by cooperation, loyalty, networks, serial reciprocity, and reputation, where the richest results—and the satisfaction of our own selfish ends—require us to forgo our own short-term self-interest in order to cooperate with the best cooperators. It is not the meek who shall inherit the earth, nor the aggressive, but rather the cooperative.

These are not random opinions or tentative interpretations of science, nor are they wild extrapolations from it. They are well-grounded inferences from scientific theory and from the observation of business within the rather novel framework of the natural laws. This framework is superior because it fits both dominant scientific insights and business reality, and because it prescribes a set of actions that work, that lead to success. A final key advantage of the new framework is that it can also accommodate the traditional "mechanical" view of science and business which, after all, has proven its worth.

The Old Régime Has Its Place

If by some impossible trick we had only twentieth-century science and nothing from the Newtonian heritage, we would all be incomparably poorer in the depth and power of our thinking, and in our wealth. Newton's science would have been enough to send men to the moon and back, and for most practical purposes the inaccuracies in his physics can be safely ignored. It is true that tiny, inanimate particles don't behave at all in a Newtonian way, but this doesn't stop us from building bridges as we did in the days before quantum theory. A world whose science was confined to relativity, quantum theory, modern genetics, systems theory, and chaos and complexity theory would be a strange, inhospitable place.

We need the "old stuff" in science. We need engineers and chemists and old-style physicists and doctors. We need mechanistic thinking, analysis, and faith in reason.

And we need these things in business too. We need our balance sheets and budgets, our old-fashioned management by objectives, our planning and monitoring, and our faith—illusory or otherwise—in our ability to control our own fate.

The new scientific view has the merit of greater accuracy and understanding of how the universe works. It is a less appealing view, but no reason to behave like ostriches. However, there is a downside to comprehension and awareness: it can paralyze. It can make us give up before we start. The great thing about Newtonian science was that it was activist and optimistic: it drove, and drives, huge numbers of ordinary people to achieve extraordinary results. Control was the watchword. The universe could be understood, and it could be controlled.

We now know that control is *not* possible. The universe has a mind of its own and will defeat our attempts to order and subdue it. And yet, it's still important to try.

Let me illustrate this by jumping ahead to one of the concepts to emerge from complexity theory, "self-organization." The theory reveals a stunning and irrefutable tendency of complex systems, like cities or economies or human bodies, to organize themselves from simpler parts and earlier stages. They do this according to certain typical patterns that are repeated, with minor variations, over and over again.

It is undeniable that a business organization is a similar sort of entity: it is a self-organizing system. The simplistic, modernist prescription might therefore be that we should leave organizations to organize themselves. Anyone who has tried to organize a team from a preordained plan with prescribed rules for each team member knows the limitations of this approach. It's far better to tell the team what to do and let the team members work it out on their own.

Yet the extrapolation of this liberal approach to a whole organization—on the implicit grounds that if this is how nature arranges things, this is how we should do it too—is deeply flawed. If it is left alone, the organization will organize itself effectively—for its own ends. It won't do what its owners or leaders want it to do. Nor will it function from society's viewpoint. The self-organizing organization will end up larger and fatter than it needs to be to achieve any given economic objective. This criticism, it is true, comes from an old-fashioned, Newtonian, mechanistic view of the world. It is part of an ideology of control and rational objectives. But if I am accused of harboring this ideology, I gladly plead guilty. The ideology of control and objectives is one price of progress.

Escaping Obsolete Mental Models

Scientists working with relativity, or quantum theory, or modern mathematics, or systems theory, or chaos, or complexity are at the top of their fields. They may not reach absolute truth, but they are closer to knowing what happens and, to a large extent, how and why. But what about the rest of us, trying to pilot our way through life in general and our business affairs in particular? We're bound to misunderstand what is happening, to see most of our efforts lead nowhere much, to pull levers that don't work, and to do things that may lead precisely to the outcomes we most want to avoid. We work in the twenty-first-century world using nineteenth-century mental models and governed by genes that have not changed essentially since the Stone Age.[3]

Yet if we understand a handful of natural laws, and *if we act to exploit those laws,* we can multiply our effectiveness.

The natural laws of the universe are like the winds. If we're sailing, we have to use the winds because there is no other source of power on a yacht. But a good sailor doesn't allow the wind to blow her off course. Even against a head wind, she makes progress. She has a map. She has an objective. She tacks and turns, following a zigzag course that, however tortuous and slow, will bring her safely to port.

We have no other sources of power than those provided by the universe, our own brains and instincts included. We need to understand the natural laws, whether these control tiny particles, huge planets, or our own behavior. But that's not all. We have to respect the laws. We must recognize when they can undo our plans. And when we can harness their power in creative ways.

We need a good dose of Newtonian mechanics, Cartesian faith in reason, Gibbonian faith in the perfectibility of man, Darwinian faith in evolution, Marxian faith in our ability to arrange society, and Freudian belief in our ability to control our emotions—all faiths that are intellectually untenable, at least in their extreme forms—while simultaneously understanding and using the weirder and subtler reaches of our more recent knowledge.

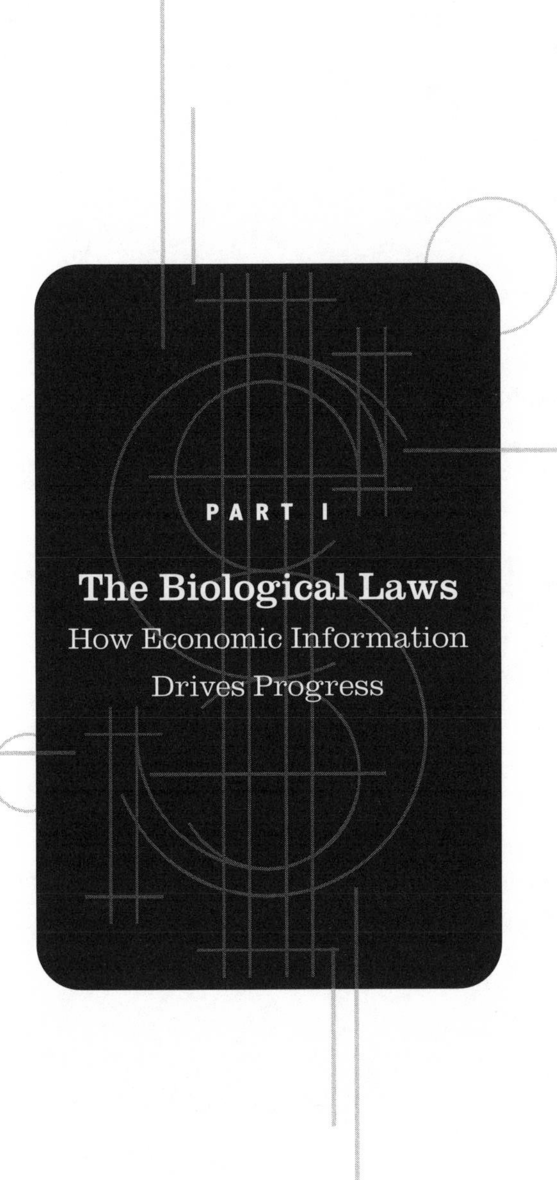

PART I

The Biological Laws

How Economic Information Drives Progress

The Universe Is Run by Selection

Evolution by Natural Selection

If I could give an award for the best idea ever I would give it to Darwin, because his idea unites in a stroke these two completely disparate worlds, until then, of the meaningless mechanical physical sciences, astronomy, physics and chemistry on the one side, and the world of meaning, culture, art and biology.

DANIEL DENNETT

In the material world, nothing is more important than *evolution by natural selection.* Without natural selection, our species could not exist. If selection did not apply to ideas, technologies, markets, companies, teams, and products in precisely the same way as it applies to species, we would all be working on the land struggling to avoid malnutrition and famine. Selection drives all material progress.

The Origins of Darwinism

In the 1830s, both during his long trip around the world and when back in England, Darwin observed the behavior of animals that favored the survival of themselves and their offspring. For example, when in the Galápagos archipelago in the South Pacific in 1835, Darwin noted that a certain white bird would calmly sit by while the first of its hatchlings killed the second. Why did the bird not intervene—

or, if she wanted only one hatchling, why bother to lay more than one egg? Repeated observation gave Darwin the answer: he determined that a single egg gave only a 50 percent survival rate (survival being defined as that of at least one hatchling), that two eggs raised the survival rate to 70 percent, but that three eggs brought the survival rate below 50 percent. Further, if there were two live hatchlings, the probability of one of them surviving was lower than if there was only one hatchling. Hence the mother's apparently perverse behavior was actually conducive to the survival of her family.

Darwin combined observations from his field research with two ideas that had been around for many decades in different academic disciplines, and fused them together with explosive effect. The two ideas were competition and evolution. Darwin first thought of natural selection in 1838 while reading Thomas Robert Malthus's *Essay on Population,* a dire prophecy of the effects of competition between individuals for food. Malthus in turn had been influenced by Adam Smith's theories of economic competition in *The Wealth of Nations,* the first volume of which had been published in 1776. Smith's thinking had been influenced by a writer another century or so earlier, namely the political philosopher Thomas Hobbes, who had in 1651 described society as "the war of all against all."[1] This means the idea of competition was common currency among intellectuals almost two hundred years before Darwin published *On the Origin of Species by Means of Natural Selection; or, the Preservation of Favoured Races in the Struggle for Life.*

Evolution had also been widely discussed in the early nineteenth century. Fossils showed that species had evolved from earlier, more primitive species. K. E. von Baer (1792–1876) revealed a major key to the process when he stated that "less general characters are developed from the most general, until the most specialised appear."[2] Evolutionists talked about "heterogeneity emerging from homogeneity."[3] What no one before Darwin had explained satisfactorily was how evolution worked.

Natural Selection

Darwin's theory of natural selection is elegant and extremely economical, resting on three plain observations.

First, creatures systematically overproduce their young. "There is no exception to the rule," Darwin states, "that every organic being naturally increases at so high a rate, that if not destroyed, the earth would soon be covered by the progeny of a single pair." He observes that cod produce millions of eggs. If they all survived, the oceans would be solid cod within six months. Elephants are the slowest breeders of all known animals, yet within five centuries, if unchecked, "there would be alive fifteen million elephants, descended from the first pair." Survival is a numbers game, with the odds stacked against most creatures. "A struggle for existence," Darwin concludes, "inevitably follows from the high rate at which all organic beings tend to increase."

Second, all creatures vary. We are all unique.

Third, the sum of that variation is inherited. We are more like our parents than we are like other people's parents.

Darwin put these three obvious facts together to derive the rudiments of natural selection. Competition among siblings means that only a few can survive. As Darwin wrote with feeling in *On the Origin:*

> . . . all organic beings are exposed to severe competition . . . Nothing is easier to admit in words the truth of the universal struggle for life, or more difficult—at least I have found it so—than constantly to bear this conclusion in mind. Yet unless it be thoroughly engrained in the mind, I am convinced that the whole economy of nature, with every fact on distribution, rarity, abundance, extinction, and variation, will be dimly seen or quite misunderstood.[4]

Which individual plants and animals will survive? Clearly, those that exploit or fit in best with what Darwin called "the conditions of life." Darwin coined the phrase "natural selection" as the "preservation of favourable variations and the rejection of injurious variations." This means plants and animals that have been naturally selected will have had the most successful parents—those who in turn had survived and came from a long line of survivors—and in turn will have more offspring than other organisms. So in each generation there is improvement, driven by the natural selection of the survivors and by the relative reproductive success in that generation of the survivors: *"The slightest advantage in one being . . . over those with which it comes into competition, or better adaptation in however slight a degree to the surrounding physical conditions, will turn the balance."*[5]

Darwin keeps hammering home his point that natural selection depends on variation. When the "conditions of life," such as climate, change, he says: *". . . this would manifestly be favourable to natural selection, by giving a better chance of profitable variations occurring; and unless profitable variations do occur, natural selection can do nothing."*[6]

For most of Darwin's contemporaries, the really controversial aspect of *On the Origin* was not the original part—natural selection—but rather the support that Darwin gave to the general idea of evolution, and especially humanity's descent from animal species. But although he collected (rather inconclusive) data between 1838 and 1859, his main contribution was the flash of insight that he had in 1838: that there was competition for life between individuals and that traits were conserved through their relative adaptability to life's conditions.

The process is thus very simple: variation, then selection, then further variation. Then more variation, more selection, more variation. And so on back to the start of life and forward to eternity. This is how species evolve.

Variation Leads to "Better Adaption"

Intrinsic to improved congruence with the conditions of life, therefore, is variation. If there were no differences between parents, there would be no differences between offspring. If there were no differences, even between the offspring of the same parents, there would be no basis for differential success. And success means fitting the "conditions of life." There will thus be a continual process of improvement or better adaptation to the environment. Although, of course, the environment may change, producing different winners and losers.

Variations and improvements occur continually within species, but occasionally a mutation occurs when an individual has a new characteristic. This mutation may improve or worsen the odds of survival. If the latter, the mutation will die out. If the former, the individual mutant will prosper and leave plenty of offspring, who will inherit and pass on the advantage.

Over time, therefore, most species will evolve positively. And they will respond to any change that the environment brings. When conditions change, new characteristics are required—and encouraged.

Diversity Leads to Efficient Use of Resources

Darwin suggested that the more species there were on a piece of land, the more efficiently the land would be used. A number of recent experiments have confirmed his hypothesis. Research reported in 1984 on 147 plots of Minnesota prairie, for example, demonstrated that the greater the number of species in a plot, the more biomass the plot produced and also the more nitrogen the soil produced; with fewer species, nitrogen leached out of the soil and was wasted.[7]

What does this prove? That if a species is diverse, it can survive and prosper; if a species is homogeneous, it is vulnerable.

In the Pacific Northwest of the United States, where wild salmon were disappearing, scientists bred huge numbers of hatchery salmon and dumped them into the rivers. But these hatchery salmon had little diversity. They were vulnerable to a slight change in the ecosystem. Too many riverside trees had been cut down for logs. Result: less shade and therefore a slight rise in river temperatures. Further result: an increase in certain diseases that couldn't flourish in colder water. Final result: the hatchery salmon nearly all died from disease. On reflection, the scientists realized that lack of diversity was the root problem—had the salmon been gradually interbred, allowing mixing and mutation, a diverse adult population would have contained some salmon resistant to the new diseases.

The same applies to computers. More than nine out of ten computers today have the Windows operating system. These computers have the same core internal components. And every computer with Microsoft software is vulnerable to the same computer viruses. Early in 2000, a hacker took advantage of this vulnerability by releasing a virus disguised in the message "I love you," which infected computers worldwide and disrupted thousands of e-mail systems from private homes to the Pentagon. The "Love Bug" virus drew strength from the homogeneity of software.

It's not fanciful to see the same process at work in cities. In the 1950s and 1960s, town councils and private developers alike, both in America and Europe, built massive tower blocks, all the same shape and pattern—oblong, high, undifferentiated. Like Malvina Reynold's "Little Boxes," "they're all made out of ticky-tacky and they all look just the same." Result: misery, alienation, crime. In her fascinating book, *The Death and Life of Great American Cities,* Jane Jacobs shows that when street lengths, building shapes, sizes, ages, and areas within cities are more diverse, then the cities are not only more beautiful, but also more energetic and wealthier.

Diversity, therefore, always leads to even greater diversity, and to sustainable growth. If we want to sum up the theory of evolution by natural selection in two words, which have great relevance for all societies and businesses, we should simply remember: *diversity works.*

Does Evolution Imply Progress?

According to Darwin, competition and blind chance drive improvement.

> The inhabitants of each successive period in the world's history have beaten their predecessors in the race for life, and are, in so far, higher in the scale of nature; and this may account for that vague and yet ill-defined sentiment, felt by many palaeontologists, that organisation on the whole has progressed . . . old forms having been supplanted by new and improved forms of life, produced by the laws of variation acting round us, and preserved by Natural Selection.[8]

Modern biologists are usually extremely careful to stress that there is no implicit evolutionary process leading naturally to improvement; evolution, to scientists, does not imply any imminent purpose or historical progress. Organisms adapt themselves to the conditions of life, but the fact that "better adapted" organisms thrive at the expense of the "less adapted" implies no value judgment: better means more likely to survive and multiply, not superior.

Six Universal Principles Implied by Evolution by Natural Selection

Jane Jacobs[9] identifies three themes that were common to all the "evolutionists" of the nineteenth century:

- ***Differentiation emerges from generality.*** One original species leads to all others. New species are formed from an existing species. This is a universal principle: in knowledge, one branch gives rise to one or more new branches through specialization; in the economy, the same thing happens when one industry gives rise to more specialized branches thereof, or when one firm spawns spin-offs, each of which develops its own particular variations. Variation is the key to development.

- ***Differentiations become generalities from which further differentiations emerge.*** In other words, variation never stops and inevitably gives birth to increasing complexity and diversity.

- ***Development depends on codevelopment.*** "All forms of life," said Darwin, acutely aware of nature's web of interdependent species, "make together one grand system." Jane Jacobs's *The Nature of Economies* provides a perfect illustration of this:

  > A horse requires more than its ancestors. A horse implies grass. Grass implies topsoil. Topsoil implies breakup of rocks, development of lichens, worms, beetles, compost-making bacteria, animal droppings—no end of other evolution and lineages besides that of the horse.[10]

Does this theory apply only to organic species? Absolutely not. Today's global economy, as we'll explore later in greater detail, demonstrates the same pattern of codevelopment and intricate interdependence.

In addition to these three evolutionary themes, Darwin's theory of natural selection contains another three crucial twists:

- ***The odds against survival are high, leading to a struggle for life.*** In nature, in ideas, and in economies, so much is produced that only a small fraction can survive. Failure is the normal condition. This implies that only organisms producing many offspring and generating a stream of new variants can hope to beat the odds.

- ***The conditions of life determine whether species and individuals survive or not.*** In contrast to the French naturalist Jean Lamarck (1744–1829), who claimed that species adapted to the demands of the environment, Darwin held that the environment was the determining factor. In Lamarck's opinion, species evolve to survive; Darwin argued that species naturally evolve, and the environment decides whether or not they survive.

  This may sound a subtle distinction, but it is crucial. Darwin implies that species, and to an even greater degree individuals, cannot hope to control their own destiny. This is a key insight that can be applied to business, and in life. If a business or a career is failing, there are only two remedies: change the environment or change the character of the business or the individual.

  In evolution by natural selection, the environment is more powerful than the species, and the species is more important than the individual. In economic development, the market is more important than any particular industry, and the "species" of producers or consumers is more important than any individual firm or consumer. It follows that if any business enterprise or individual is not succeeding, a radical change of environment or behavior is necessary.

- ***The process of natural selection contains high degrees of luck, randomness, and arbitrary development.*** Natural selection is a process of experimentation in which luck is paramount. So is business.

Darwin and Business

According to Bruce Henderson, the founder of the Boston Consulting Group, "Darwin is a better guide to competition than economists."[11] This is an important observation, although perhaps hardly surprising: Darwin's idea of natural selection was, as we have said, in part analogous to the theories of competition of Thomas Malthus and Adam Smith. So, in applying the lessons of natural selection to business, we are in a sense coming home to a common intellectual heritage.

Differentiation Emerges from Generality

The development of economies, industries, corporations, and individual careers follows the same evolutionary path described by Darwin and earlier evolutionists. Differentiation emerges from generality. What was previously one market develops into more than one, resulting in specialization.

The computer industry, for example, forks into the hardware industry and the software industry. Then the hardware industry forks into the personal computer (PC) industry and the market for larger machines. Subsequently, the PC industry forks into the retail store market and the market for direct delivery (via phone and the Internet). The PC industry also forks into a large number of individual product segments.

This endlessly repeated process results in a richer world. It explains why the richest economies are the most diverse, with the greatest degrees of subdivision and specialization. Any business or individual wishing to own a new market should create a new segment based on greater specialization. Take one market or industry and make it two. The opportunity always exists—it is the way that markets must evolve—and all that is required to realize a new segment is imagination allied to the following simple method.

Focus on a subgroup or new group of customers that has some homogeneity internally and some differentiation from the rest of the current market. Next, decide how you can serve that customer group better, so that extra value is created for them, but without a proportionate increase in the cost to supply them, and ideally with a decrease in cost. Typically, this can be done by cutting out or downgrading elements of the product or service that are important to the market as a whole but not to your target customer group.[12] Once you have found your new market, identify techniques and partners from other markets and industries who embody the highest standards of value delivery, who are "highly evolved" economic species. Then appropriate their ideas or make them partners. Finally, aim to become and remain the standard, the model, and the leader in your new market segment.

The Ford Model-T, at the start of the twentieth century, is a case in point. Before the Model-T, cars were a conspicuous luxury, only for very rich people. Henry Ford's genius was to imagine a whole fresh market: not-so-rich people, including the more skilled workers who made up his own work force. To tap this market, cars had to be made a fraction of the price they were before. To make this possible, Ford stripped the specifications down to the bare essentials, painted them all black, and invented the assembly line to make them as cheaply as possible. In doing so, he created a new market and set the standard for automobile production for the best part of a century.

The same strategy was followed in the 1970s and 1980s by Japanese producers of VCRs. The technology was invented by Ampex in the United States. Initially, the only competition Ampex faced was from RCA, and from the Dutch firm Philips. All three firms made pretty much the same product for the same market: broadcasting studios and other high-end industrial applications. VCRs cost just over a thousand dollars and were sold for upwards of fifteen hundred dollars.

The Japanese had a different idea. Victor, Sharp, and Sony-Betamax imagined a massively enlarged market of consumers who might like to record TV programs. Like Henry Ford, the Japanese needed to reengineer the product to cut costs: first to five hundred dollars, later to below two hundred dollars. Once this was done, Ampex was first confined to the sophisticated studio market, and then challenged even there by the Japanese.

It doesn't matter whether you go for a larger or smaller market, whether you go "up-market" or "down-market"—the key is to go for a *different* market, and to set the standards for the new market. This is how evolution works. As an example of *narrowing* the focus, look at Toys "Я" Us. It started as a children's furniture store. Then founder Charles Lazarus thought he should sell toys. These sold so well that he threw out everything except toys. Then he opened up larger stores that just sold discount toys. Today, in the United States, Toys "Я" Us has 618 stores, selling over a fifth of the nation's toys.

Marketing guru Al Ries describes five steps to evolutionary success:

1. Narrow the focus
2. Stock in depth
3. Buy cheap
4. Sell cheap
5. Dominate the category.[13]

Think of a market that you could evolve using the same principles.

We can go even further. Darwin's particular genius was to build on earlier evolutionary theories, none of which was very specific, and describe the way that natural selection operates. We can now parallel this process in thinking about our own business world.

Where Does Evolution by Selection Work in Business?

Depending on how good the economic information inside a product is, how well the product packages the information for customers, and how well adapted (relative to competing products) the product is to its market, products will either prosper or die young.

Products live in families, both vertically (over time) and horizontally (at the same time). Products exist within generations. All products will eventually die, but the most successful ones will live long enough to generate at least one "offspring," a next-generation product or a same-generation variant. The most successful products will generate many of both. For every successful product, however, there will be many that never got off the drawing board, never survived the test market, died shortly after launch, or never produced any offspring.

Successful products will all be able to say: not one of our progenitors died in infancy. But progenitors are rare. Most products die before they reproduce. Some $160 billion is spent each year on research and development, but only 5 percent of that money succeeds in generating a product or service. And even for the few products that are born, there is a high death rate in the early months and years.

For a technology, a unit of economic information, or a product to succeed, they must beat the odds against selection, have many offspring, and gain currency—either intellectual currency or dollars.

But what is success for the owners of a technology or of a product? Surely, to make the largest possible long-term profit from selling the technology or product in one form or another. This requires making the product or technology proprietary to the owners. This also tends to produce more variation, more experimentation, more products, more losers and more winners. Recognition of intellectual property rights does not restrict the evolution of economic information, it tends to speed it up, because it encourages variation to justify or to avoid that intellectual property, and to convert it to currency.

Four Lessons of Economic Selection for Products and Marketing

First, *product ideas will be stronger—more likely to survive and reproduce—if they have emerged from a struggle for life, from substantial competition.* This does not necessarily mean that you should launch a multitude of products, just that you should consider and test a large number, so that those that do emerge have faced genuine competition.

Suppose the publisher of this book, for example, has a policy of only publishing twenty books a year. This may be very sensible: it ensures that each book can be properly structured and edited, marketed and promoted. But it would not be wise for him to accept the first twenty books that came along that he felt were acceptable. He should carefully consider perhaps one to two hundred potential books, and set up some competitive process between them, before choosing his twenty. If he selects the wrong twenty, another publisher will gain the market's support.

For some firms and markets, putting out a lot of products and letting the market decide which ones survive is a sound procedure. When Sony introduced the Walkman, it flooded the market with hundreds of variants, letting the market decide which few would survive. Capital One is a very successful credit card firm that regularly generates a large number of new ideas, puts them to the market test, and mercilessly kills off the majority that fail. It relies heavily on direct mailings to attract new customers, puts out perhaps three hundred different "products"—varying the letter, the color of the envelope, the position of the address, and so on—then uses the response rates from its test markets to decide which mailing will be the standard one. The company is currently taking a risk with a major new project, trying to parlay its data mining and direct marketing competencies into the sale of mobile phones. If the experiment works, great; if not, it will be swiftly terminated.

One of the world's most successful consumer goods firms, Procter & Gamble, took the revolutionary and apparently wasteful step, back in 1930, of allowing direct competition between its own brands. This provided challenges that often didn't exist elsewhere in the marketplace. Brands couldn't rest on their laurels. Discomfort stimulated improvement and cut complacency. Although this formula worked extremely well, it took almost thirty years for rival firms to copy it. Even though it is our best route to success, we still hate competition.

Procter & Gamble also has an extremely rigorous and structured product development process, including mandatory test marketing to see whether product concept expectations are met and whether product sales are sustainable. Few concepts make it through to production. Even successful products are subject to routine and ongoing consumer research, to aid in further product refinement and innovation. P&G has a far higher ratio of potential products to actual products than most of its competitors, and a far greater propensity to produce new generations of successful products.

The second lesson is that *new product variants will arrive sooner or later, whether you introduce them or not.* Natural selection does not care which organism mutates or does not mutate, lives or dies. Economic selection does not care who owns the new product; it just wants to see it arrive. The market doesn't care whether Bic or Schick or Gillette is the market leader in disposable razors, but it does want to see new razors emerge. The market doesn't care whether the big brewers or new specialists supply light beer, imported beer, Mexican beer, or microbrew beer, but it does want to see new eruptions of product variants.

The third lesson, therefore, is to *scatter new breeds around your core product: fill up the potential product spaces so that newcomers can't move into these niches.* You might not think that a new type of product—cherry cola, for example, or healthier versions of mainstream food products—has much chance of success. Still, have a go and let the market decide. In the late 1970s and early 1980s it was already clear that "healthier" food was a growing trend, yet in general the main food manufacturers stood back. The result? New specialists came in and filled the niches. In some cases, as with Schick and Gillette, neglecting to fill a niche can eventually mean a challenge to the core business itself. Fill up all your niches or potential niches. Reinvent your product.

The Internet supplies a great example of where leading firms have often failed to claim all the niches or potential niches. Whatever else it is, the Internet is clearly a channel of distribution that comprises a separate market segment. The leaders in most "real-world" businesses have been slow to become the leaders in online provision of their services: partly because they have been unfamiliar with the "virtual" world, and partly because they fear that the Internet will simply cannibalize their existing demand, and do so at lower prices. These fears are partly justified, but entirely beside the point. The leader of a new niche must dominate it, or inevitably a new leader will. Had Barnes & Noble, the leader in real-world bookselling, embraced the Internet opportunity at the outset, the word "Amazon" would still just connote a large river or a nation of female warriors. Now Barnes & Noble is stuck, probably forever, with having to share its market with the upstart.

The fourth lesson is that *product and service improvement can and should always be accelerated*. Competitive selection drives faster evolution, and evolution proceeds not just through new variants, but also through new and better versions of the old product. Tolerate, even encourage failure; it's an intrinsic part of the process. Plan to accept your own failures.

Procter & Gamble's experience with Olestra, a fat substitute, is a case in point. The company's original vision was to develop an easily digestible fat that would help premature babies gain weight. The problem was that the fatlike compound, composed of a fat molecule bonded to a sugar molecule, passed through babies unabsorbed. P&G redirected the project to develop a fat-substitute product. Although it took many years to perfect, the process resulted in Olean, a product that tastes and fries like fat but does not digest in the same way. Olean is now incorporated into Frito-Lay chips and fat-free Pringles.

Evolution is slow or nonexistent unless there is competition, unless the cycle of struggle for life, selection and improvement, or variation is allowed to operate. But evolution can be sped up—by you or by someone else.

Evolve your products by selection, or someone else may do it for you.

Winners and Their Sex Lives

Winners should breed prolifically. If the market proclaims a new initiative a stunning success, get the bandwagon going as fast and as far as possible. This means reproduction. It means new generations of improved versions of whatever is successful. It means backing the winners with cash and the best skills available from anywhere.

Too many industry leaders remain celibate. They while away their days pleasantly enough, fulfilling existing customers' needs in the same way that they always have, enjoying easy orders and fat margins. Then someone else invents something new, perhaps an improved version of the leader's current product or service—and they die. Winners who don't have sex—a lot of sex—will become extinct. Winners who have an ordinary sex life will horribly underperform in relation to their potential. Winners have an evolutionary duty to have a superabundant sex life that produces a large number of offspring.

What does this mean in business? It means taking the winning product or service as far afield geographically as you possibly can—so long as it will still be a winner in the new environment. It means adapting the winner to local markets. It means introducing new generations of product faster and more extensively than those with less successful products do. It means forming spin-off teams and companies that can take what is best and apply it to new products, new customers, and new geographic areas. It means squeezing the last particle of possible expansion out of what you have. It means taking a few risks.

This is counterintuitive. Surely, it is those who are less successful who should be trying harder to improve what they have? This is normal business reasoning. But economic selection implies that when we have something good and successful, it must be improved and spread, and the new generations improved and spread, as far and as fast as possible. Selection puts enormous pressure for improvement and reproduction on the organisms that are most successful to start with. Selection also gives winners the inbuilt mechanisms needed to keep winning. Use them.

Fisher's Fundamental Theorem of Natural Selection

R. A. Fisher published his *Fundamental Theorem of Natural Selection* in 1958. It was already known that the average fitness of a population grows from generation to generation. Fisher found that the larger the variance in fitness, the faster the average growth of the population. Greater variation implies greater improvement and therefore faster growth.

Technologies, products, teams, firms, and markets that experiment the most and produce the most variants will improve fastest, and faster improvement leads to faster market growth. That which adapts faster to the conditions of life gains market share and earns superior margins.

Fisher developed the mathematics describing how small variations cause big changes, bigger than one might expect. He showed that if a new "allele" (an alternative characteristic, explained in Chapter 2), produced by mutation, gives an animal just a 1 percent advantage in fitness, the allele will spread through the entire population within a hundred generations. The biological market works quickly and efficiently.

In business, it's difficult to measure something that customers prefer by a margin of just 1 percent. But imagine that there is a 10 percent advantage between one firm's product and another. This will translate into far more than a 10 percent difference in sales, market share, and profits.

Perhaps the most valuable insight from Darwin is that life, and business, cannot be understood properly in the present tense. Before Darwin established evolution as the key to life, biology had a short-term, "existential" orientation—animals and plants were dissected to see how they worked or to find magic potions. This is precisely what most businesspeople do—we analyze to find out what is happening to markets, to firms, or to products, and to uncover the secrets of business success.

Darwin made the present tense redundant. Mankind, he showed, could only be understood in the context of our billion-year evolution. If we want to know how to cure any particular disease, or to increase the productivity of grain, we need to trace the dynamics of evolution over very long time periods. Similarly, to understand the economy, we need to look at the long-term causes of growth, which, as we'll see in Chapters 10 and 11, lie in better ways of doing the same things while using fewer resources: "technology" in its broadest sense. To understand a market, we need to look at its evolution and the way it forks into several markets. To understand a company, we need to understand its history and its "DNA." To understand a product, we need to look at its forebears and its possible successors.

Pay close attention, therefore, to even so-called marginal customer preferences. Over time, they will count. When the customers vote you a loser compared to your most significant rival, even if it is by a tiny margin, expect trouble ahead.

Fisher's theorem predicts that markets, products, brands, technologies, companies, and individuals who improve their fit with the environment faster (than other markets . . .) will expand faster and be more profitable. The learning curve, and its derivative the *experience curve,* help to explain why. The Boston Consulting Group (BCG) found in the 1960s that there was a regular relationship between unit cost and accumulated experience, both for whole markets and for individual firms. As accumulated experience (the number of units of anything that has ever been produced) doubles, costs come down by a predictable amount—say by 20 or 30 percent.

It follows that in fast-growth markets, like semiconductors in the 1960s and 1970s, or software markets in the 1990s, or Internet-related markets today, accumulated production multiplies and costs plummet. As costs fall, new applications are opened up. So there is a tautological relationship between cost reduction and growth: cost reduction is both a cause and a result of growth.

Only by reducing costs or improving features or providing other forms of extra value can markets expand faster than other markets. Above-average growth is the reward for above-average improvement in delivering value.

What happens in whole markets also happens in relation to individual corporations. Firms that grow faster than the market can increase their accumulated production faster than the laggards and can therefore cut costs or increase value faster. By gaining market share, they actually also underpin the basis for defending and building further market share: they improve their relative cost position or relative value position. It is therefore an excellent strategy—in a profitable market—to build market share even at the expense of short-term profits. This is because by increasing market share the firm will increase its ability to offer customers a better deal. And this is particularly valuable in high-growth markets, because the improvement that is up for grabs is so much greater.

In evolutionary terms, markets, firms, technologies, brands, and individuals who gain experience at above-average rates are actually speeding up the evolutionary process. They are packing in more generations in a shorter time. Each generational change offers scope for improvement. Yet improvement only actually occurs if there is adaptive variation; that is, if each succeeding generation or version (of markets, firms, teams) produces something that customers like better, by doing something different that enables the market or firm to deliver better value—and to deliver improvement at a faster and faster rate.

On its own, growth does not necessarily represent success; many firms perversely choose to grow products and businesses that the market does not particularly like. The market typically takes its revenge by ensuring that the growth is profitless. Another caveat is that short-term growth, if not underpinned by the ability to sustain growth by providing real and continuously improving value, may subvert long-term growth or even lead to collapse. For a toy manufacturer to own the Cabbage Patch dolls, or for a publishing house to have a single smash-hit title, may be dangerous. There is an optimal short-run growth rate for every product. It may not be the highest available that will lead to maximum long-term growth—remember Darwin's white bird in the Galápagos, which maximized survival of her family by allowing one hatchling to kill another. Provided that there is innovation, a sustainable ability to add ever-increasing value, the culling of failures and less successful variants, and investment behind whatever the market judges best, growth is the ultimate enabler of business success.

Is Natural Selection Unfair?

Mathematician Stanislaw Ulam realized that his discipline spawns nearly two thousand new theorems every year. Very few of these survive, because funding to investigate them is not available. *Ulam's dilemma* was that no one either inside or outside the mathematical profession was qualified to decide which few new theorems should survive and which fall by the wayside. This, he thought, was unsatisfactory: *"There is no assurance of survival of the fittest, except in the tautological sense that whatever does in fact survive has thereby proved itself fittest, by definition!"*

In other words, theories don't win on their objective merits, but as a result of blind competition.

The parallels with business are clear. The "best" products (or companies, or executives) don't necessarily rise to the top. The standard QWERTY typewriter keyboard is far inferior to other forms, as it was designed to slow down typing. Yet I am using it now, on a brand new personal computer. English is less efficient than Esperanto. Betamax was probably a better video recorder technology than VHS. The market is not always fair and not always right.

The same is true in nature. Poor early mutations sometimes take hold. Nature is sometimes wasteful and produces unnecessary organs or allows them to remain (like the human appendix) long after they are redundant. Poor genes sometimes beat better genes. Sheer luck sometimes means that poor organisms reproduce while their better siblings suffer untimely death. In the short term, at least, nature is not always right.

Over time, selection tends to produce improvement. It is a weird and unfair system, and also imperfect, but on the whole it works extremely well.

Don't buck the market, even if you're sure that it's wrong. If the market feedback on a product or service is negative, get rid of it. If the capital markets appear foolish or bizarre, put aside your doubts and try to divine the markets' message for your strategy. Leave judgments on market sanity to investors. Remember the old motto: the customer is always right. So is the market, even when it is "unfair" or "wrong."

Evolving to Avoid Failure

In Darwin's theory, the "conditions of life" determine whether or not species survive. The environment disposes of or supports the species. The species does not determine the environment, nor does it even have the luxury of being able to adapt to it.

In natural selection, failure is endemic. Failure is dominant. Success is the lucky exception.

Is this too fatalistic and severe an insight to be useful in business? In one sense, yes. There are few second chances in nature. But in business there are usually multiple chances.

In a more profound sense, however, the lesson that failure is endemic is invaluable. If we realize that failure is normal, we come to view all business as an experiment, where success at the first attempt is not to be expected. Paradoxically, this is very good news. Whatever our failures, and however big they are, spectacular success may lurk around the corner—given certain conditions, and with a lot of luck. We would never have heard of Henry Ford if his first attempt at producing automobiles had been his last, or if his second attempt had quenched his determination. His third attempt succeeded because he finally hit on mass production as a way of lowering costs and standardization as a way of permitting mass production.

Natural selection tells us why failure is frequent, and therefore how it can be avoided. Failure implies a lack of fit between the environment and the product. Natural selection implies that failure is the natural course of events and that slight modification will not be enough for a turnaround. If a poor fit is to be turned into a good fit, at least one of two things must happen. Either the environment must change, or the failure must change—or, most likely, both must change.

Hoping that the existing environment will change is the prevalent strategy of failing businesses. This strategy nearly always fails, for reasons we learned from Darwin. Business has little or no control over the environment, but the reverse is not true.

The way out is to find a different environment and to change the character of the failure. If a company is losing out in one market, it had better find another market more attuned to its capabilities or change its character radically to serve the existing market in a different way. Since the existing capabilities were evolved to serve the existing market, it is extremely unlikely that there just happens to be another market perfectly suited for the failing business's capabilities. Variation is therefore probably required along both dimensions. The environment must be different—a different market segment, which implies at least one of the following: different customers, different location, different main business activity, different products or services, different competitors. And the firm's skills must change: different employees, different skill development, different business models, different suppliers, different partners, different standards.

In the 1930s, Caterpillar was one of many firms in the heavy construction equipment market struggling to survive. Most of its competitors eventually went bust. What saved Caterpillar was that it found a new environment and new skills, so that it set new standards for a new industry.

In 1941, the U.S. Department of War concluded that a world war required one worldwide supplier of heavy construction equipment to build roads, air strips, and army bases. After a brief "beauty parade," Caterpillar won this contract. With the Allies' help, Caterpillar built at very low cost a worldwide service and support network for heavy construction equipment.

After the war, Caterpillar continued to own and operate this network. It set new standards, guaranteeing the delivery of any part, any piece of Caterpillar equipment, to anywhere in the world within forty-eight hours. By creating this new skill for a new environment, Caterpillar dominated the industry globally for many decades.

Or take Firestone in the early 1980s. A new CEO, John Niven, took over a demoralized and failing company. Firestone's tires cost too much to make, its factories needed a fortune spent on them, its production processes resembled tangled spaghetti, and its customers were deserting in droves. U.S. and Japanese competitors were better at making tires. What could Niven do? In desperation, he decided to *stop making tires.* Since these comprised 80 percent of Firestone's sales, it was a bold step. Instead, Niven decided to re-create Firestone as a sales and service organization. He realized that this required new skills, but thought that he could set new standards in the servicing industry. In doing so, he saved the company.

Lou Gerstner pulled off the same trick for IBM in the 1990s. By 1993, IBM was coming apart at the seams. Gerstner saw that there was a terrific amount of business to be won in the service sphere, but that to succeed in service required a different approach. Out went high-pressure salesmanship. In came the IBM-er as problem-solving consultant. In its service business, IBM found a new market and new skills.

But most failing companies are not saved. This too is evolution at work. If a firm cannot be saved, it is distressing, but it is not the end of the world. It is time to start another business, using the best parts of the experience, contacts, and skills from the existing one.

The same principle applies to individuals. If your career is not making satisfactory progress, it is time to change your environment: leave your existing business for a new one. But realize also that the "market"—your previous environment—has given you some valuable feedback. You need to ensure that your character and skills are developed, so that the fit with the new environment will be dramatically better than before.

How to Use the Natural Laws

- ***Vary, reinvent, multiply, and vary again.*** Continuously evolve everything in your business life—your products and services, your ideas, your technologies, your teams, your corporation, your collaborators, yourself. Evolution requires experimentation, variation, rejection of inferior or less well-received variants, hard driving to multiply the successful variants, and a commitment to further cycles of experimentation, variation, selection, and multiplication of the few winners.

- ***Pursue evolutionary cycles repetitively,*** so that the quest for continual improvement via experimentation becomes routine.

- ***Expose product ideas and products to unrestricted competition.***

- ***Scatter product variants around your core products.*** Fill up the potential product space.

- ***Drive successes as hard and fast as possible.*** Ensure that they have prolific sex lives.

- ***Always accept the market's verdict, even when you consider it unfair.*** Don't give new projects, failing products, or businesses the benefit of the doubt.

- ***Only expect to have a few winners—but get the most out of them.*** Welcome your failures.

- ***If you are faced with a failing business or a failing career, quit!*** Find a different environment and change your character to fit the new environment better than any rival.

- ***Keep reminding yourself that diversity works.***

What Darwin Couldn't Explain

Mendel's Genes, Selfish Genes, and Business Genes

It is not success that makes good genes. It is good genes that make success.

RICHARD DAWKINS

People like to think that businesses are built of numbers (as in the "bottom line"), or forces (as in "market forces"), or things ("the product"), or even flesh and blood ("our people"). But this is wrong. Businesses are made of ideas—ideas expressed as words.

JAMES CHAMPY

As we saw in Chapter 1, Darwin's explanation of evolution by natural selection was brilliant and convincing. For the first time the mechanism of evolution was fully apparent and plausible. But there was one thing that Darwin couldn't explain. If traits were acquired, how did this work? And how were the acquired traits passed on?

Darwin went round in circles on this issue.[1] In *On the Origin,* he frankly admitted, "The laws governing inheritance are quite unknown." The problem for him lay in everyone's assumption that traits were blended from those of the parents. If this was the case, why didn't individual adaptations become watered down and disappear in a few generations?

Mendel's Laws of Heredity

From 1856 to 1863—spanning the period when Darwin's great work was published—Gregor Mendel (1822–84), a monk in the Austro-Hungarian empire, experimented with breeding and crossbreeding peas and other plants with distinctive traits. Mendel was surprised to find that the traits of the peas did not blend: a tall plant bred with a dwarf plant led to a tall plant, not a medium-sized one; a yellow pea crossed with a green one did not yield a greenish yellow pea, but rather a yellow one. When he went on to interbreed the hybrid plants produced by crossing a tall plant with a dwarf plant, although the hybrids were all tall, a quarter of their offspring were dwarf. Mendel correctly concluded that the alternative traits themselves or "factors," as he called them—whether short or tall, this shape or that—were inherited directly, apparently at random.

Mendel's "law of segregation" states that inherited traits are passed on directly and equally by each parent. Rather than blending, the traits remain separate, with the "dominant" trait determining appearance and the "recessive" trait lying dormant but capable of emerging in subsequent generations. Mendel also proposed the "law of independent assortment": pure chance determines which trait is passed on, with dominant traits no more likely to dominate in the next generation than recessive traits. The law of independent assortment also states that individual traits, not the whole complement of characteristics, are passed on in breeding. The seven traits that Mendel tested, each operated independently.

Nobody paid much attention to Mendel during his lifetime. Shortly before he died, when he had swapped crossbreeding his peas for less pleasant duties as abbot of his monastery, chromosomes were discovered, although at first nobody knew what they did. The significance of Mendel's findings only finally became apparent in the 1900s, when it was guessed that chromosomes carried genetic information. Mendel's "factors" were eventually renamed "genes," and it was realized that each pair of chromosomes in a cell carries a great deal of genetic data.

Between 1907 and 1915, American biologist Thomas Hunt Morgan (1866–1945) bred fruit flies, and was surprised to find that one had white eyes rather than the usual red. Even more surprising was that the white eyes were passed on, not in the next generation, but in the one after that. One-third of the fruit flies, all male, had white eyes, exactly as Mendel's laws predicted. In 1915, Morgan wrote *The Mechanism of Mendelian Heredity*, which showed that genes were physical entities located alongside chromosomes, and that it was the individual genes that were inherited according to mathematical probabilities.

This finally solved Darwin's dilemma. If inherited traits are not blended, they can be passed on undiluted. Natural selection operates through genetic inheritance. Morgan also shed new light on how mutations occur. He found that small variations enter the population as "alleles"—alternative characteristics—and the environment exerts selective pressure on their adaptability. In other words, alleles are different types of genes, like the brown eye and blue eye gene, competing for the same slot on a chromosome; the word "allele" therefore can be used loosely to mean rival or competitor. Strictly speaking, an allele is "one of the two alternative positions a gene can have on a chromosome."

Thus it is possible for there to be considerable variation within one species: mutations do not have to be large jumps. Specific traits can mutate, as well as new species. This is an important conclusion for understanding the nature of business progress.

DNA and Its Structure

DNA (deoxyribonucleic acid), a large molecule present in the nucleus of every cell of every organism, was discovered in 1869, named in 1899, and largely ignored until the late 1940s, when some scientists began to suspect that it could be the key to how bacteria reproduced. In 1948, the great chemist Linus Pauling used X rays to work out the shape of proteins, which turned out to be in the form of a helix. In 1953, Francis Crick and James Watson realized from X rays of DNA that it had a double helix structure, looking a bit like a twisted rope ladder, and in a paper in *Nature* they commented: *"the specific pairing we have postulated immediately suggests a possible copying mechanism for the genetic material.*"[2]

Our genes are made of DNA, a polymer that has a regular, repeating backbone with four kinds of side groups, "bases," sticking out at regular intervals. The order of the bases—the way in which the four letters of the DNA language are combined—comprises the genetic message, which can be astonishingly long in a complex organism. Human DNA is thought to contain more than 1 billion letters. Still, the structure is elegantly simple, and quite universal. All plants and animals share the same basic DNA structure. There are four different kinds of genetic building blocks, connoted A, T, C, and G. An A building block in a human is absolutely identical to an A building block in a butterfly. The difference between people and butterflies lies in the number and sequencing of the building blocks. Every human (except identical twins) has a different DNA sequencing code, yet shares the same structure of DNA with all forms of life.

The discovery of DNA vindicated Darwin's intuition in *On the Origin* nearly a century earlier:

> All living things have much in common, in their chemical composition, their germinal vesicles, their cellular structure, and their laws of growth and reproduction . . . Therefore I infer from analogy that probably all the organic beings which have ever lived on this earth have descended from one primordial form, into which life was first breathed.

Crick and Watson's discovery also upgraded the significance of genes, leading to "neo-Darwinian" theories, including the "selfish gene."

The Selfish Gene

Crick and Watson had shown that genes, even internally, are digital. Within a gene, everything is digital code, like a computer language—pure information in digital form. They also showed that the information transfer is irreversible: the gene passes on its information, and the information cannot be supplemented by anything that happens to the body within which the gene sits, although the gene can be damaged if its vehicle is (for example by toxins or radiation). Characteristics thus acquired, like a tan from spending time in the sun, are not passed on to any offspring.

Reflecting on these facts led Oxford biology professor Richard Dawkins to publish *The Selfish Gene* in 1976.[3] Instead of describing natural selection from the individual's angle, Dawkins sees it through the gene's eye. He says: *"The fundamental unit of selection, and therefore of self-interest, is not the species, not the group, nor even, strictly, the individual. It is the gene, the unit of heredity."*

According to Dawkins, in the beginning there were molecules. Then by chance, a remarkable molecule materialized: the replicator. The replicator could make copies of itself. But when copies were made, mistakes happened: the copies were sometimes not perfect. The primeval soup therefore began to fill up with several varieties of replicating molecules descended from the same replicator. But the primeval soup wasn't big enough to support all the replicators, so they had to compete with each other. The cunning replicators, the ones that survived, hit on the idea of building survival machines to live in. The survival machines, created by the replicators, got bigger, more varied, and more complex. Now the replicators "swarm in huge colonies, safe inside gigantic lumbering robots";[4] that is, inside plants and animals. These replicators, now called genes, "are in you and in me; they created us, body and mind; and their preservation is the ultimate rationale for our existence."[5]

Natural selection implies the differential survival of entities. Each gene wants to survive, to live a long time, perhaps even to become immortal. The gene survives by making an identical copy of itself. If it can house copies in a long succession of different survival machines (in animals, this means bodies), the gene may survive for a very long time. A gene is potentially near immortal, although it will only survive by collaborating with other genes inside the survival machines. Still, because all the genes can't survive, they are always in competition with each other. The gene is "selfish" because it has been selected only to advance its own cause: to be the survivor in the game of natural selection, where there are always more losers than winners. Genes selfishly compete with their alleles for survival. The genes that survive are the ones best fitted to their environment, which (in a subtle and important twist to Dawkins's argument) includes other genes. In a theme we will come back to in Chapter 5, cooperation turns out to be the highest form of selfishness, both for genes and for their most evolved vehicles, humans.

The Theory of Memes

Dawkins believes that the gene has come to dominate the earth, and the world of the selfish gene is one of savage competition, ruthless exploitation, and dastardly deceit. Yet Dawkins does not say that our genes control us. Certainly, the genes try to manipulate us, but we can choose to frustrate them, for example by using contraception.

Moreover, Dawkins offers hope that we can rebel against our genes. Our species is unique, he says, in being able to pass on knowledge in the form of culture: language, customs, art, architecture, science. Humans have invented a new form of replication, a new form of potential immortality, in the form of "memes," which is Dawkins's word for units of cultural transmission. A meme might be a book, a play, or an idea—like Darwin's idea of evolution by natural selection. Memes are anything that can be passed on from one person to another, or one generation to another, by means of learning or imitation. As Dawkins explains in *The Selfish Gene:*

> Examples of memes are tunes, ideas, catch-phrases, clothes fashions, ways of making pots or of building arches. Just as genes propagate themselves in the gene pool by leaping from body to body via sperms or eggs, so memes propagate themselves in the meme pool by leaping from brain to brain [*by*] . . . imitation.

Dawkins hints that a world of selfishness might conceivably be turned into something better, if memes with altruistic yet successful features were to replicate faster than genes.

The idea of memes is controversial. Some biologists do not accept the parallel with genes, or see the relevance of memes. But it makes perfect sense: memes are a human invention, yet once created they have a semiautonomous life of their own. Memes replicate, vary, adapt, and incorporate themselves in robust vehicles; memes produce ever more complex entities in a way that is very similar to genes.

We should note in passing that there is mounting evidence that humans are not the only animals for whom cultural evolution—meaning learned behavior rather than an increasing appreciation of opera—interacts with and transcends genetic evolution. Research by Dr. Lee Alan Dugatkin, a biologist at the University of Louisville, shows that even creatures with low intelligence can imitate the behavior of their peers. Simple marine bugs called isopods, that are scarcely a quarter-inch long, have devised a way of copying each other's choice of mates; female guppies (small West Indian fish) will change their minds about which male guppy to mate with if they see other females selecting a different male; and sage grouse shift what they think is sexy according to cultural idiosyncrasies that vary annually.[6]

A River Goes Out of Eden

In Dawkins's 1995 book *River Out of Eden*[7], the river of the book's title is DNA, flowing through geological time, occasionally branching to form a new species. Each species' river contains a mass of genes traveling downstream together as good companions. "It is a river of information," Dawkins says, that "passes through our bodies and affects them, but is not affected by them on the way through." Each river has steep banks, stopping the DNA of one species from getting into another species' DNA river.

Dawkins draws attention to two particular features of natural selection:

- ***Its "luxuriant diversity."*** There are tens of millions of different species. Each species has a different way in which its DNA makes a living and different ways of "passing DNA-coded texts on to the future."

- ***"Ancestors are rare, descendants are common."*** The vast majority of organisms die before they can breed. Only a few of those that do breed will have a descendant alive a thousand generations on. All organisms can therefore look back and say "none of our ancestors died in infancy," despite infant deaths being the general rule. It follows that the process of natural selection of genes is extraordinarily discriminating:

  > Each generation is a sieve: good genes tend to fall through the sieve into the next generation; bad genes tend to end up in bodies that die young or without reproducing . . . after a thousand generations, the genes that have made it through are likely to be the good ones.[8]

  The same selectivity applies to species as a whole. Although there may be about 30 million species on earth, these constitute only 1 percent of the species that have ever lived. Evolution's gate to the kingdom of life is indeed a very narrow one.

The Theory of Lifelines

The theory of the selfish gene is controversial among biologists. Professor Steven Rose, for example, denounces it as "ultra-Darwinism" and "genetic reductionism."[9] Although that may be unfair, Rose does make a convincing point that evolution happens at many levels, and that the "lifeline"—the progressive direction of life—includes the evolution not just of genes, but also of organisms and societies. I would add economies to the list; and no doubt Dawkins, if allowed to, would add memes.

The Theory of Business Genes

Building directly on genetic findings and on Richard Dawkins's theory of memes led me to develop a theory of business genetics that I have called the *theory of business genes.*

The DNA of business is "economic information." We may think

of units of useful economic information as "business genes." Business genes are a type of meme, which, as we've just seen, is Dawkins's word for a unit of cultural transmission. In my definition, a business gene is simply a meme that is related to business, a unit of economic transmission. We could call them "business memes" instead of "business genes," but I have opted for the latter because it makes the parallel with biological genes more explicit.

A characteristic of biological genes is that they tend to travel in packs, and their ability to work with a large number of other genes is crucial to their success. There are very large numbers of genes present in most animals. Biologists can separate out individual genes, but most economic information will comprise many different strands or units of information, many individual business genes.

Examples of these business genes, or groups of business genes, are ideas: the design behind a basic technology such as the steam engine or internal combustion engine, telephony, or computing; the design for a product component such as the script for a movie or an integrated circuit; the intellectual capital leading to a piece of software or the kernel thereof; or a formula, such as that for Coca-Cola or for a drug.

Business genes are the building blocks of know-how—of skills and technology in the broadest sense. They are the origin of economic life. They seek to replicate as widely as possible by incorporating themselves into what we may loosely call "commercial vehicles," all the visible apparatus of economic activity: the moving parts, including people, firms, and physical assets, products, and services. A business gene is anything intangible that comprises useful economic information and that, to attain its potential, must be incorporated, alone or alongside other business genes, either into a product or service, or into some vehicle that will then provide a product or service.

Animals and plants are the "vehicles," the survival machines, for biological genes. The vehicles do all the hard work to survive, prosper, and propagate the genes. The same is true for business genes and their vehicles. A business gene cannot survive or create value without some physical home; it must be embedded in something tangible. Even business ideas need some physicality before they can be sold or given away: they must be committed to paper or electronic record, or be communicated from one person to another.

Vehicles are likely to attract good business genes to the extent that they are the best available vehicles for those genes; and they are likely to be successful to the extent that they incorporate the best available genes. The vehicles are the physical expression of economic value and exist to multiply that value. Those best adapted to prevailing economic conditions will flourish; and if the nature of the vehicles, or economic conditions, changes in a way that alters this fit, then the vehicles will cease to flourish.

How Business Genetics Works

Business genes—successful units of economic information—are incorporated into, create, and manipulate many generations of vehicles. These business genes and their vehicles go through a process of evolution by selection, with the struggle for survival, variation, selection, and further variation leading to change. And, on the whole, via improved products and services, to a richer, more complex, and more specialized economy.

Think of how a technology develops: steam power, for example, or nuclear energy, or computing power, or something much simpler and more primitive, like the wheel or fire. The early, less successful versions of these were incorporated into a large number of new products and services. Any successful technology goes through many generations of experimentation, most of which fall by the wayside. They prove impractical, too expensive, or else they are supplanted by improved versions of themselves. A successful technology has ancestors that, by definition, survived long enough to give birth to a new technology.

The gene is—depending on which biologist you talk to—either the basic mechanism for evolution by natural selection, or the most basic level at which evolution occurs. The gene incorporates itself in plants and animals, in machines that are vehicles for its survival. Although they compete with other genes, successful genes have the ability to collaborate with fellow successful genes operating in the same survival machine.

You can see the parallel with technologies, units of economic information, or competencies (ways of doing useful economic things). The technologies incorporate themselves within products, which evolve because of the competition occurring between the other technologies, and between the products. The products with the best business genes survive and multiply to produce improved versions of themselves. Yet what is driving the process is not the actual products but the skills and technologies that spawned them. What ultimately survives is the useful economic information and technology that flows into and out through many generations of product. Although technologies compete with each other, as biological genes do, they also have to be able to coexist and collaborate with other successful technologies in order to adapt to the environment, just as biological genes must collaborate with many other genes.

And what constitutes the environment for technologies, useful economic information, or competencies? Other technologies, customers, and markets, where the business genes have to prove their right to survive by competing for other economic resources.

An Example of a Business Gene

The acid test of whether something constitutes a business gene is whether it is information or something tangible: information *constitutes* business genes, but tangible things such as recordings, robots, products, or machines are *vehicles* for business genes. What, for instance, comprises a movie's business gene? At one level, it may seem to be the digital master recording, from which many copies of the film can be made for movie theaters all around the world. The master recording can then be made into a video, a compact disc, or any other product that can accommodate it. But the digital master recording is itself a vehicle, not a business gene or collection of business genes.

In this case, the business genes are the information needed to create the movie and, subsequently, the information that it generates. This includes the skills and reputations of its actors, director, producer, and crew, all of which embody data of economic value that can be incorporated into future movies and other products. But the movie is not the only relevant vehicle for the economic information. The reputations of the actors are furthered by the people themselves as well as by the movie. For the same business genes, there are usually several vehicles, of similar types (various movies) and different types (the actors). At an even more basic level, the genetic information lies within the script itself. What really matters is not the physical script—the paper, tape, or disk on which it is written, which are vehicles—but the ideas it contains. Business genes are intangibles that have economic value, like stories, customs, ideas, ways of doing things, and the most basic levels of technology.

To qualify as a business gene, three conditions must be met. First, the business gene must be valued, either for its own intrinsic appeal or because it can help to deliver things that people want, or help to deliver them at a higher level of quality or using fewer resources. Second, the business gene must be capable of being replicated. Third, it must be intangible.

These three conditions have always been met for the ideas behind successful "scripts," like the *Book of Genesis,* or *Romeo and Juliet,* or indeed Newton's *Principia Mathematica.* All of these have been valued; and all have been copied, varied, and incorporated into a huge number of derivative products and other vehicles. The genetic code for novels, for instance, is the eight basic plots of which all others are said to be variants.

Humans and Business Genes

Where do we humans fit in this scheme of things? Can we *be* business genes, or are we always *vehicles* for business genes?

I've suggested three qualifications necessary for a business gene: it must add value, it must be capable of replication, and it must be intangible. Humans can pass the first two tests, but not the third. We can't be business genes. We are never ideas, technologies, ways of doing things, or economic customs. We can create ideas in the first place, and we can take ideas and capitalize on them. Either way, we are only vehicles for the ideas and for their replication.

But, you ask, if we can create ideas, create business genes, surely we are their masters rather than their servants. Doesn't this mean that here the parallel with biological genes breaks down? We cannot create biological genes, they create us. Yet we *can* create business genes, and they cannot create us.

You are right. Remember that what I have called business genes in fact form a subset of memes, Richard Dawkins's term for the social and intellectual replicators that humans have created as a new form of cultural evolution.

Humans also stand in a very interesting relation to business genes. We are both their creators and their vehicles, and the same is true for all memes. We use business genes, and are used by them. We can also propagate business genes that we did not invent. Indeed, this is the normal course of economic progress. For every human inventor of an idea, there can be hundreds or even millions of people who use and develop the idea. Most people who become rich through business do so by using other people's ideas, not their own. Perhaps they will elaborate the idea somewhat, and so create a few minor business genes, but the source of their fortune is mainly the powerful business gene or collection of business genes that they appropriated from elsewhere.

This is precisely the evolutionary process, where a few powerful business genes are replicating very successfully through a process of variation and continual better adaptation to the environment. We humans are occasional creators of the main business genes, more often the creators of minor business genes, and most frequently of all, our role is simply to orchestrate the replication of existing business genes.

Different Types of Vehicle for Business Genes

There are two different types of vehicle for business genes: the animate and the inanimate. The former, those that have a life of their own, comprise humans and systems that incorporate human endeavor, including teams, organizations, parts of organizations, cities, and economies. These are all self-organizing systems—a term that we shall meet later in this book—that come together (at least partly) of their own volition and create something that is more than the sum of their parts.

The latter, the inanimate vehicles, include machines, products, physical embodiments of technology like cables and telephone lines, buildings, offices, and trucks, and other "vehicles" in the usual sense.

The animate, self-organizing systems behave very differently from the inanimate objects, which will be discussed later, especially in Chapter 9. For our purposes as students of business genes, both the "live" systems and the inanimate objects are vehicles for the business genes, the only difference being that the human elements contained within the self-organizing systems can create business genes as well.

A New Perspective on Business

Instead of focusing on corporate competition, as in the old economic paradigm, business genetics posits several layers of economic value creation, which is driven by business genes and their struggle for life and reproduction. Humans have multiple roles in the process: as creators of business genes; as users of business genes to create better products and services; and as consumers of products and services and therefore arbiters of their survival, spread, and demise. Corporations are important intermediate vehicles, though there are many others which derive their power from being the best vehicles for business genes and for their creators, the entrepreneurs and knowledge workers.

Small companies go bust all the time. Although this is painful, it is a necessary part of economic progress. The companies that are better suited to the environment—which largely means the market—survive and are stronger for having to face competition. As the great economist Joseph Schumpeter said in 1942, capitalism progresses via a process of "creative destruction."[10] When a company is destroyed, it frees up resources for better use elsewhere.

There is nothing sacrosanct about corporations. As vehicles, they are only useful to the extent that they are the best possible incarnation of business energy and information. If that business energy and information would be better deployed elsewhere, we should throw away the old vehicle and use or create another one.

Large companies are less likely to go bust than small ones. They have become large companies by being part of a minority of small companies that have been very successful; the large companies have undergone a long process of selection for the privilege of being big. Yet large companies can set the cause of business evolution back if they use their size—as many do—to insulate themselves from competition. This may work for a time, but natural selection says that insulation from competition halts or at least slows down improvement in products and services (common sense and observation tell us the same). Selection also tells us that someone, somewhere, will be experimenting with new products or technologies that may eventually become a challenge to the sclerotic old firm. The reckoning can be postponed, but not averted, and when the firm eventually faces competition it may quickly crumble. Think of the near-collapse of IBM.

In 1982, IBM was lauded by Tom Peters and Robert Waterman's best-selling *In Search of Excellence.* Yet this "excellent" company was already in trouble by 1984. IBM lost a total of nearly $8 billion in 1991 and 1992, and another $8.1 billion in 1993. These losses were a sudden recognition of problems that had been brewing for two decades. IBM's problems had many causes. Some blame the management: Paul Carroll says IBM was "like a music publishing company run by deaf people." Some blame the powerful sales force, who blinded IBM to the microprocessor revolution because it threatened their profitable mainframe business. Some blame the decision to outsource two critical components of IBM personal computers: in the 1980s, in a bid to catch up, IBM engaged Intel to supply the chips and Microsoft to provide the operating system software. By the early 1990s, IBM was making more PCs than anyone else, yet its personal systems division was losing money, while Intel and Microsoft were coining it.

What really happened at IBM was all of these things but something more fundamental too. Because it had been so successful, man-

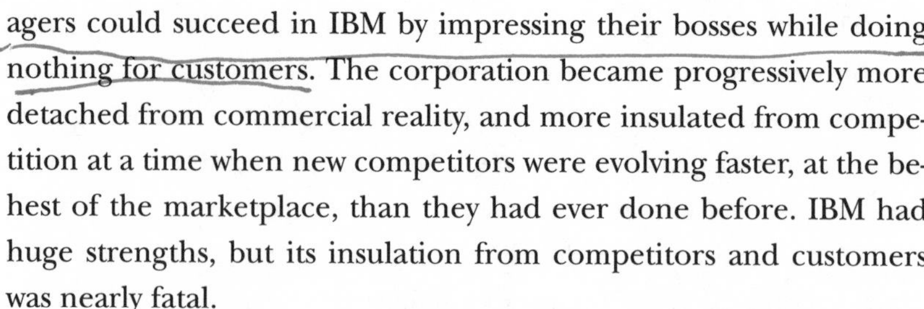

agers could succeed in IBM by impressing their bosses while doing nothing for customers. The corporation became progressively more detached from commercial reality, and more insulated from competition at a time when new competitors were evolving faster, at the behest of the marketplace, than they had ever done before. IBM had huge strengths, but its insulation from competitors and customers was nearly fatal.

If IBM *had* collapsed, the release of talent into more responsive companies would probably have done more for the industry and the economy than Lou Gerstner's revived IBM did. The process of killing off firms that have outlived their usefulness will be accelerated if we adopt the business gene view of corporations. Vehicles that are no longer working well should be abandoned by healthy business genes—and sooner rather than later.

Spin-offs

Spin-offs are growing in popularity, but are still not used enough. I use the term "spin-off" loosely, to mean not just firms that are still owned by the proprietors of the original firm, but also those where the key players come from a common "parent" and bring with them important parts of its knowledge or customer base.

Is it a coincidence that industries where there are many spin-offs also tend to grow faster than other industries—and also deliver faster increases in value to customers and investors? Silicon Valley is full of spin-offs. So is management consulting. And venture capital. And investment banking. Spin-offs and "team moves"—a sort of halfway house to a spin-off—are endemic in such industries. In more stagnant industries like cement or metal-stamping, where progress comes at an arthritic snail's pace, spin-offs are rare.

Natural selection predicts the progress of spin-offs. The new firm takes with it much that is good from the old firm—it inherits the latter's good genes—but it also adds new twists. If the innovations suit the market, the spin-off prospers. Spin-offs from the successful spin-off then repeat the process. No one will spin off from an unsuccessful firm.

Typically, the owners of successful firms do not benefit from spin-offs. The children go their own way and the parent gets no benefit. How much better for the owners of the successful firm if they can have a share of the spin-off. That this does not happen more often is due to a lack of foresight, combined with managers' natural reluctance to risk the creation of new, independent units that will not be under their control. Yet natural selection tells us that every successful firm should foster spin-offs. Owners who act in time to back promising spin-off ideas can then capture a share of the profits.

If you want to inherit healthy, thriving business genes, take part in a spin-off.

Business Genetics for Executives—Six Rules

- ***Use the best business genes available.*** There are three ways to deploy business genes. One is to create them from scratch: invent a new product or service, or a new business system. This is a rare event, and few of us have the originality required. A second way is to appropriate and use successful business genes. Remember, the genes want to multiply, so they are amenable to being used. But to do this effectively you must get there ahead of other people who might have the same idea. For instance, my friend Raymond Ackerman, who created the Pick 'n Pay supermarket giant in South Africa, used the idea—the business gene—of self-service supermarkets after it was already well established in the United States but before it had become so in Africa. A third way is to take an already successful business gene and modify it slightly: create a new variant of the business gene.

- ***Make yourself an optimal vehicle for successful business genes.*** To take advantage of healthy genes, you must further their purpose and help them multiply. This requires adaptation on your part. Adaptation requires exposure to competition. Don't insulate yourself from internal or external career competition; if you do, you'll stop developing. Compete in the major markets, not in the backwaters.

- ***Use the best vehicles available and drive them.*** You use economic information; you have valuable skills, including the skill to collaborate with successful business genes and other vehicles for them. The team or company you join and the other resources you commandeer are vehicles for you. They are there to advance your purpose, to provide protection, to incarnate your energy. Remember that the vehicles are just that, and the only reason to work through one is if it is *the best possible vehicle around for your purposes.* Continually ask yourself: am I driving or being driven? Am I driving the right vehicle? Is there anywhere else I could be more valuable?

- ***Career evolution requires variation.*** Start a project. Take on a new responsibility. Change the furniture. Get a new job. Identify new business genes that can provide you with fresh direction and for which you can be the best vehicle.

- ***Evolution requires continual experimentation and improvement.*** If you don't produce a new-generation version of yourself as quickly as your career competitors do, you'll fall behind. Experimentation and improvement require fresh combinations of new business genes—new skills, new ideas, new ways of working. Remember that your success requires you to be a vehicle for superior combinations of business genes, and to work within or alongside other successful vehicles, so constantly experiment all the time with new combinations.

- ***Evolution requires failure.*** The greatest and most abundant freedom that the universe offers is the freedom to fail. For most organisms this means an early death, and it is the species that benefits. Fortunately, when building our careers we always get another chance. But constructive mutation in your character and skills requires failure, as well as the maturity to recognize and accept this. Don't let your ego deny the necessity of failure in another form of competitive insulation. Failure is easier to accept and to reverse in the context of business gene theory. It results from being a good vehicle for poor business genes, or from being a poor vehicle for good business genes. Identify which is the case, and take appropriate corrective action. Failure allows us to compete.

How to Use the Natural Laws

- ***Identify business genes that are underexploited and that are having to make do with poor vehicles.*** Create the best new vehicles for existing powerful business genes—for valuable economic information, ways of working, and technologies.

- ***Join existing successful business genes into new combinations*** and provide appropriate vehicles for them.

- ***Make yourself the best vehicle for a winning and unique combination of business genes.***

- ***If you participate in running an organization, realize that its value derives from being a vehicle for successful business genes.*** Ensure that the organization is and remains the best vehicle for the genes. See that the organization's gene pool is continually replenished with new inputs that have already proven their success.

- ***Create spin-offs from existing organizations.***

3 Gause's Laws

> *Competitive strategy is about being different. It means deliberately choosing a different set of activities to deliver a unique mix of value.*
>
> MICHAEL PORTER, "What Is Strategy"

Gause's Principle of Survival by Differentiation

In the 1930s, Soviet scientist G. F. Gause did some very interesting experiments on small organisms. He put two protozoans of the same family but different species in a glass jar with limited food. The little creatures managed to cooperate and share the food, and they both survived.

Then Gause put two organisms of the same species in the jar, with the same amount of food as before. This time, they fought and died.

I call this *Gause's principle of survival by differentiation,* or PSD for short. Later in this chapter I'll explain why I think the PSD is so important, but for the moment, trust me. Try to keep Gause's organisms in your mind's eye, because if there is one image I'd like you to take away from this whole book, it's that of Gause's protozoans and the PSD.

Darwin anticipated the results of

Gause's experiment in Chapter III of *On the Origin of Species by Means of Natural Selection:*

> The struggle [for existence] almost invariably will be the most severe between the individuals of the same species, for they frequent the same districts, require the same food, and are exposed to the same dangers . . . As species of the same genus have usually . . . some similarity in habits and constitution, and always in structure, the struggle will generally be more severe between species of the same genus, when they come into competition with each other, than between species of distinct genera . . . We can dimly see why the competition should be most severe between allied forms, which fill nearly the same place in the economy of nature.

Gause's Principle of Competitive Exclusion

Gause's experiments also led to the conclusion that two competing species can only coexist if there is more than one scarce resource.

Two populations compete if one lowers the growth rate of the other. They may do this by eating each other's lunch, crowding each other's space, or blaring their Walkmans so loud that the other population runs away.

Coexistence, Dominance, and Bi-stability

Gause found three outcomes from the protozoan wars:

- Two species can equally well invade each other's territory. The boundaries between them break down; they end up *coexisting* in the same space.
- Only one species can invade the other's territory. It ends up *dominant.* The invaded species is wiped out.
- Neither species can invade the other's domain. Like the late, lamented arms race, there is a balance of power that ensures peace. Biologists call this *bi-stability.*

Ecological Niches and MacArthur's Warblers

In ecology, a niche is not just a place where a particular creature lives; it is also a way of making a living—a special way of obtaining resources, a specialized job, or, in Darwin's words, "a place in the economy of nature." Ecologist Robert MacArthur has shown that for warblers a spruce tree is not a spruce tree; it is actually several different niches for several different types of warblers. Each type of warbler has its own bit of the tree to which it does different things, like searching for insects. Each warbler has its own small and specialized ecological niche.[1]

It turns out to be quite difficult for ecologists to map the boundaries between ecological niches, but the principle is clear and very useful: *each separate niche sustains just one specialized type of plant or animal.* Note that the specializations are carried to a very high degree and that each creature does just one thing in one place. The warblers in the forests of the northeastern United States live according to Adam Smith's division of labor, the principle that specialization allows higher productivity.

Finding *Unique* Niches

The first business lesson to be gleaned from Gause's principle of survival by differentiation is that you want your competitors to be at least slightly different from you. They can be of the same family, but not of the same species. Remember that there are perhaps 30 million species on earth, so making your firm a separate species, if it isn't one already, shouldn't be impossible. If two organisms of the same species compete in the same space with a limited market (food), they fight and die. If they are different, they can cooperate and both live.

MacArthur's warblers chose to live in different parts of the spruce tree because they were different types of warbler. They had found unique niches, each warbler with its own bit of the tree.

Your firm too needs unique niches, places where no one else can go because they aren't exactly like you. The "places" can be particular customers, geographic markets, channels of distribution, products, technologies, or any other source of differentiation, but at least one of these must be unique to your firm. Otherwise you are the same species as your competitor, slugging it out in the market equivalent of Gause's glass jar.

Bruce Henderson, who found his unique niche as the founder of "intellectual" strategy consulting and also a keen student of biology, put it well:

> Competitors who prosper will have unique advantages over any and all competitors in specific combinations of time, place, products and customers. Difference between competitors is the prerequisite for survival in natural competition. These differences may not be obvious. But competitors who make their living in exactly the same way in the same place at the same time [won't prosper].[2]

Who Can Invade Whom?

Gause's principle of competitive exclusion highlights the symmetry or asymmetry in any competitive struggle. Your firm is in a very weak position if your rival can enter your space, but you can't enter his. If you are in this position, move! You must find a niche, a way of earning your living in a different way. If you can't do this, and the business is still profitable, sell it before it is too late.

Look at what happened to the British motorcycle industry in the 1970s. Honda had two unique markets that the British motorbike makers couldn't enter: it had the large Japanese market and the market for small bikes (clearly these overlap, but they are conceptually separate and, outside Japan, physically separate too). At first, the British had a separate market: that for larger bikes. But the relationship between the British and Honda was asymmetrical. The British couldn't enter Honda's markets, because British bikes were designed to be big and powerful, and were too expensive to downscale. But Japanese bikes were designed to use modular components and to be capable of upscaling. Honda's bikes were also cheaper and of better value (even after the cost of transport and distribution)—another reason for the asymmetry.

Before the Japanese entered the British bike market, the British industry felt secure. Even after the Japanese entered, they didn't feel threatened. They were only selling "toy" bikes, often to people who'd never bought a bike before. But if the British bike makers had read about Gause's protozoans, they would have foreseen their fate. Only by developing a unique niche which the Japanese couldn't enter—as BMW did with its ultracomfortable bikes for big bottoms—would the British have survived. By 1980 their bike industry was all but dead.

Of course, *if your firm can invade and the competitor can't,* you should. You can feel very confident of the outcome.

Bi-stability Is Better Than Coexistence

Gause's research makes the interesting contrast between bi-stability and coexistence. Coexistence is real competition, where either can invade the other. Bi-stability is when they can't; it's illusory competition.

Bi-stability implies that two populations are not really competitors. They are both excluded from each other's domain. This is very common in business. An industry may appear competitive, yet each competitor has different customers, different distribution channels, or some other differentiating factor that has barriers around it. Within each segment, different firms can enjoy high market shares and high profits. Whenever you see an industry that is very profitable, like high-end consulting, you find a market where competitors are very specialized and where each has a high share of its own niche. Smart players will keep it that way.

On the other hand, a market characterized by many coexisting competitors is probably in competitive stalemate. No one will have the edge. Market share will have little value. Here, the struggle between competitors for customers makes every supplier a loser.

The only hope within a coexistence game is to recognize it for what it is, and for all the competitors to signal to each other that they will live and let live. Price wars, aggressive marketing campaigns, or indeed vigorous activity of any kind must be avoided. To break out of a state of coexistence requires the development of a segment you can dominate, bringing us back to the fundamental point—that you need to be different.

Breaking into Bi-stability

If you're in a coexistence market, it may be possible to break out and make your own bi-stable market.

The airline industry is, in general, a good example of coexistence. Except where regulation restricts the number of competitors on any route, consistent profits are hard to come by. Without regulation, each airline can invade the others' customer base. Each innovation, such as free drinks in the cheapest class, can easily be copied. Only fare structures of byzantine complexity keep the airlines from taking losses, and fares are becoming increasingly transparent as sophisticated customers use the Internet to search for the lowest fares. Yet even in the airline industry, it's possible to escape coexistence by doing something radically different.

Southwest Airlines, for example. It doesn't follow the typical hub-and-spoke system based around large airports. It avoids long routes, in-flight meals, and ticketing bags to other destinations. It offers one-class, frequent flights between a few carefully selected cities, short check-in times, automated ticketing, and low fares. It has a standard fleet of 737s, cutting maintenance costs and delays. It encourages direct payment, cutting out commissions to travel agents. It appeals to a particular type of traveler who appreciates the trade-offs that it makes.

Other airlines can't copy Southwest: there's no room for two such airlines on any of its routes, and the competitors are not set up for this approach anyway. Southwest has therefore created a bi-stable market, and can enjoy high profits despite having low prices. The trick is to have higher utilization rates than is possible under coexistence.

The Danger of Having Only One Key to Success in an Industry

Gause's test-tube wars revealed one further fascinating fact. If only a single resource like food or air was scarce, one species always became dominant. Coexistence or bi-stability only occurred if there were more than one limiting factor.

The corporate equivalent? If price is all that matters, the corporation providing the lowest costs is bound to win. If quality reigns supreme, the supplier perceived to have the highest quality will dominate. If what counts is innovation, as in some fashion markets, then the trendiest will win.

If you're in a market where only one factor differentiates you from the competition, and that factor isn't enough to make consumers perceive your product or service as superior, you must create a new niche where that factor matters.

Differentiation Makes You Unique

Differentiation is not quite the same as specialization. It is actually more fundamental. Differentiation implies that you don't just specialize; rather, you accentuate the differences between you and your nearest competitor until you achieve a unique niche.

Think about how you could further differentiate your firm from your closest competitor (in each area where you face a different "closest competitor") in each of the following four dimensions:

- Customer type
- Type of product or service
- Geography
- Stage of value added

Extend the distance between yourself and your closest rival, until you no longer *have* a closest rival.

How to Use the Natural Laws

- ***Differentiate.*** Specialize. Put all your energy and resources into areas where you are substantially different from, and superior to, any rival.

- ***Systematically increase your difference from your closest rival,*** according to product or service type, customer type, geographic market, and value. Aim to become unique, to have no rivals.

- ***Get out of businesses where a competitor can invade your territory but you can't invade his.***

- ***If you can invade a competitor's territory, but he can't invade yours, do it.***

- ***Avoid businesses where there is coexistence:*** where everyone shares the same customers. If you're in a coexistence market, turn it into a bi-stable one by finding a distinctive approach that some customers like and competitors can't imitate. If you can't do this and are stuck with coexistence, make the most of it by trying not to overlap with competitors.

- ***In any business where a single criterion such as price, quality, or service is all that matters, and you are the best at satisfying that criterion, go all out for dominance.*** Widen the gap between yourself and competitors by using that criterion. If you are in such a business, yet are not the best at meeting the key criterion and cannot become the best at it, then find another area (within or outside your current niche) where only you can satisfy the need for that criterion.

4 The Neurology of Stone Age Man

Evolutionary Psychology

Behind every successful man stands a surprised woman.

MARYON PEARSON, wife of Canadian Prime Minister

One fascinating new scientific discipline that evolved in the last third of the twentieth century is *evolutionary psychology*, a mix of genetics, anthropology, paleontology, neuropsychology, and social psychology. A form of neo-Darwinism applied to the study of human behavior, evolutionary psychology holds some controversial but important lessons that can be applied to business.

Punctuated Equilibrium

In 1972, two evolutionary biologists, Stephen Jay Gould of Harvard University and Niles Eldredge of the American Museum of Natural History, proposed the idea of *punctuated equilibrium*. We will examine this theory in more detail in Chapter 11, but it's useful to introduce it here to help us understand why our genes may lag behind changes in society. The theory of punctuated equilibrium says that evolution proceeds by long periods of relative quiescence and stability punctuated by short periods of rapid change.

Man's Infrequent Punctuations and the Theory of Evolutionary Psychology

Business, society, and technology seem to operate via punctuated equilibrium, although on different time scales. Karl Marx divided history into three phases—feudalism, capitalism, and socialism—and hypothesized that the transition from the second to the third would be rapid. More conventional historians point to just two punctuation points during the whole of human history: the transition from hunter-gatherer Stone Age society to an agricultural one, and the relatively recent shift to an urban, industrial society.

The basic thesis goes like this. Humans emerged as hunter-gatherers, living in clans, about two hundred thousand years ago, and evolved traits suited to that life. Then, a mere seven thousand years ago, man developed agriculture, resulting in a vastly different society. A little over two hundred years ago, industry and commerce began to prevail over agriculture, and the conditions of human life were utterly transformed into an urban and generally prosperous society that harnesses machine and brain power.

But while the conditions of our life have changed radically since the Stone Age, we haven't. Evolutionary psychologists contend that we humans are still "hardwired" with the same circuits as our clan-living hunter-gatherer ancestors. We are still geared for living in the Stone Age. Seven thousand years is just not long enough time for human evolution to produce genetic traits that match our new surroundings. As Edward O. Wilson comments: *"The culture of the Kalahari hunter-gatherers is very distinct from that of* [modern-day] *Parisians, but the differences are primarily a result of divergence in history and environment, and are not genetic in origin."*[1]

Evolutionary psychologists point out that, despite our best efforts, we incorrigibly exhibit primitive behavior: we rely on first impressions, beat our breasts, develop clans, dislike outsiders, follow the herd, gossip, construct informal hierarchies, blindly follow confident leaders, and live up to sexual stereotypes. We may know that these behaviors are primitive, and we may understand intellectually that these actions belong to the Stone Age, not to the global world of twenty-first-century business. But we just can't help ourselves. We're hardwired to be what our genes make us: Stone Age animals.[2]

Four Human Characteristics

According to evolutionary psychology, we may summarize human characteristics under four headings:

- Dominance of emotion over reason
- Predictably primitive behavior
- Avoidance of risk
- Panic when seriously threatened

The Dominance of Emotion over Reason

Alert instincts were vital for survival during the Stone Age. Hunter-gatherers were vulnerable to predatory animals, rival enemy clans, and fiercely changeable weather. Those with good instincts, people quick to respond to fear or danger, passed on more of their genes than those who took too much time to analyze a situation.

Evolutionary psychologists contend that this is why our natural disposition is to react to everything emotionally, including people.

Predictably Primitive Behavior

One highly functional aspect of the hunter-gatherer was the tendency to live in fairly large groups and to cooperate with the rest of the clan. *Homo sapiens* emerged as a highly social animal, a bit like hyenas and lions, only much more so. Successful Stone Age people lived in large clans, containing up to one hundred fifty people, according to Robin Dunbar, a psychologist at the University of Liverpool.[3]

Sharing food was the basis for cooperative exchange among hunter-gatherers. The animals hunted were big, and successful hunts might be infrequent. It therefore made good sense to share the kill throughout the clan. Sharing reduced the risk of going hungry (because other hunters would reciprocate) at little cost, since there was plenty for everyone. The division of labor was important too, a supposition supported by evidence about modern tribes like the Ache of Paraguay, who are still hunter-gatherers—some men specialize in finding armadillos in their burrows, others in digging them out.

Cooperation, specialization, and trade require friendliness. Social skills, a propensity to trade information, to barter and do reciprocal favors are, to a greater or lesser degree, hardwired in us. The modern organization, which shares its largesse throughout the employee group, may therefore be going with the grain of human nature. We're programmed to cooperate, to be loyal and committed to each other, to be friendly to customers and collaborators. Yet we find it difficult to deliver bad news, to measure each individual's contribution accurately, or to remove deadweight. Perhaps, in the end, we are wired to favor equal treatment and fairness above efficiency and meritocracy.

On the whole, however, Stone Age friendliness and cooperation are highly appropriate to modern business. The same cannot be said of our other primitive characteristics.

Stereotyping on First Impressions

Evolutionary psychologists say that because the Stone Age world was threatening and complex, it was necessary to classify things immediately on the most basic data. Which berries could be eaten or would poison you? Which regions were good for hunting? Which strangers could you trust? How do you decide? You only had time to base your decision on a first impression. If people looked and acted friendly, they could probably be trusted. If not, they should be considered enemies.

Anthropologists have found nonliterate tribes that have classified every plant and animal in a similar way. This supports the theory that humans who carried successful Stone Age genes had developed the superior ability to make quick and mainly accurate decisions on first impressions. Taking time to analyze the data was not life enhancing.

In today's corporate world, however, first impressions are not as vital. Whether Jill is a good person to hire does not have to be decided in the first fifteen seconds of her initial interview. Wouldn't you be better served to fight your genetic instinct and delay forming your opinion of Jill until *after* the interview? Yet, as good salespeople know, a winning smile, a firm handshake, and a good opening line can be more important than the intrinsic characteristics of what is for sale.

It is highly probable that we make many poor decisions, or fail to weigh the evidence judiciously, because of our Stone Age programming. We also waste the time we have. If we're going to go on first impressions, we might as well keep all meetings down to five minutes in length.

Breast-beating

In the natural world, when life is unpredictable and terrifying, the person who appears least terrified and most confident is likely to attract followers, food, and sex. Genes for confidence are likely to proliferate and be reinforced.

But in today's business world, blind confidence doesn't work as well as on the savannah. Egotism and breast-beating used to impress, now they merely annoy. Excessive optimism used to be functional, now it filters out valuable reality. Our environment has changed, but much of our behavior hasn't.

Hierarchy

Everything known about hunter-gatherer societies suggests that ad hoc hierarchies flourished. Man has the desire to follow confident leaders and seeks security in a chain of status relationships. Food, shelter, and sex gravitated to the most powerful and confident, so for those who were weaker, the chances of security and an adequate living increased with attachment or deference to a leader.

If we are wired for hierarchy, this helps to explain why every revolutionary attempt to dispense with hierarchy—whether the French or Russian Revolutions or the modern single-status organization like Microsoft or Cisco—ends up creating new forms of hierarchy. Official hierarchy may be renounced or downplayed, yet unofficial pecking orders surface and flourish. Status is both sought and acknowledged.

The quote at the start of Robert Townsend's 1970 satire *Up the Organization*[4] reminds us:

> *And God created the Organization,*
> *and gave It dominion over man.*
>
> GENESIS 1, 30A, SUBPARAGRAPH VIII

The enduring taste for hierarchy may appear an anachronism in the age of the "knowledge worker," when the technical expert is meant to be more important than managers without specific expertise, but evolutionary psychology helps to explain why hierarchy abides.

Of course, hierarchy is sometimes extremely useful, like when the boss has some genuine insight about business that is not shared by his subordinates. Hierarchy without insight, on the other hand, subtracts value. Most successful organizations combine dictatorship with democracy. Evolutionary psychology explains why that balance is so difficult to maintain.

Conformism and Herding

Allied to hierarchy is the tendency for the clan to conform internally and be suspicious of outsiders. A sense of identification within the clan leads to a unified front in the face of danger. The individuals who thrived within any society were either leaders or docile followers, and the societies that thrived were those with the greatest internal cohesion.

Conformity still pays off. We have only to look at the strength of successive conformist ideologies—socialism, anti-Semitism, McCarthyism, fundamentalist religions of all kinds—and, less harmful but equally absurd, the fashion trend of bell-bottoms, the worship of rock stars or football teams, fads of political correctness, or the excesses of both bull and bear stock markets, to realize that following the herd is as popular as ever.

It's no different within a corporate organization. Only a brave, foolish, or unusually obstinate person usually goes against the grain in any firm. Robert Townsend's view of the workforce in 1970 was rather bleak:

> In the average company, the boys in the mail room, the president, the vice-president, and the girls in the steno pool have three things in common: they are docile, they are bored, and they are dull. Trapped in the pigeon holes of organization charts, they've been made slaves to the rules of private and public hierarchies that run mindlessly on and on because nobody can change them.[5]

Thirty years later, and after billions of dollars spent on gurus, consultants, and change programs, not much has changed. The management magazine *The Antidote* commented in 1999:

> The organisation built on the industrial model was sabotaging its own efforts to get more initiative . . . out of its people. Despite an ever-expanding tool kit, best practices and what-have-you, research found that managers . . . were disillusioned with these attempts at fine-tuning yesterday's model . . . most of the core beliefs associated with the industrial model and "organisation man" proved highly resistant to change.[6]

Richard Pascale argues persuasively that a key weakness of most large organizations is their inability to tolerate and harness questioning and conflict. In his book *Managing on the Edge: How the Smartest Companies Use Conflict to Stay Ahead,*[7] Pascale estimates that half the time that contention arises, its potential value is lost because the conflict is smoothed over and avoided. Our genetic predisposition to avoid confrontation can cause us to overlook problems within our midst.

Hostility to Outsiders

The strength of the clan and its conformity had the flip side of hostility to those outside. This, too, assisted survival, as Charles Darwin noted:

> A tribe including many members who, from possessing in high degree the spirit of patriotism, fidelity, obedience, courage and sympathy, were always ready to aid one another, and to sacrifice themselves for the common good, would be victorious over other tribes; and this would be natural selection.[8]

Matt Ridley's study of primitive man leads him to a similar conclusion:

> It is a rule of evolution . . . that the more cooperative societies are, the more violent the battles between them. We [humans] may be among the most collaborative social creatures on the planet, but we are also the most belligerent.[9]

Experience suggests that only trade and the weakening of exclusive national identities can lead to peace.

Within business, what are we to make of the preposterously popular military analogies? John Kay points out that we talk about the "cola wars" and yet that "not in Pepsi's wildest fantasies does it imagine that the conflict will end in the second burning of Atlanta [Coca-Cola's head office]."[10] Business competition is not at all like war. In war, the biggest combatant usually wins by destroying the opposition. In business, two or more competitors can flourish, and it is much more effective to avoid direct competition than to try to inflict direct damage on the competitor, a strategy that is rarely used and sometimes counterproductive even then. In business there is a third party, the customer, who decides which competitor will win: there is no such powerful third force in war. The idea that business is like war is so stupid that we can only explain the appeal of the analogy, like the continued appeal of war itself, by reference to our descent from

Stone Age man, when belligerent, macho, and destructive behavior paid off.

The only war analogy that works well in business is the phony war celebrated in George Orwell's novel *1984*. Here there are three superpowers. Two are always at war with the third. From time to time the sides switch. There is no evidence of actual conflict, yet the totalitarian governments of each superpower report victories perpetually, while also calling for home efforts to support the war to be redoubled. This is not a bad model for business. Competitors can be invoked as dire threats to encourage people within your organization to improve performance, while you meticulously avoid the inconvenience and expense of actual conflict with competitors.

Neolithic habits die hard. Cohesion within a function, division, or team is easy to build, but how often does manufacturing have a close relationship with marketing, or vice versa? The persistence of ancient rivalries should make us wonder whether an organization composed of several cohesive groups may not always be less effective, other things being equal, than one comprising a single homogeneous group.

The Avoidance of Risk

Evolutionary psychologists say that hunter-gatherers tended to take risks only when their world was falling apart. Their thesis is that our origins explain why today we are risk averse when we can afford risk, and yet risk takers when losses are endemic.

For hunter-gatherers, these conditions of security were rarely obtained. As long as they had about enough food and shelter, they wouldn't go hunting again until absolutely necessary. The risk of losing everything was just too great. Being attacked by one's prey wasn't an attractive risk to court deliberately. Because hunter-gatherers weren't secure, they generally avoided risk.

Risk aversion is built into most modern business. We talk about a "risk premium," where returns must be significantly higher to justify taking an extra risk. But given that the most important investors can afford to take risks, and can diversify their portfolios or hedge to keep risk within acceptable bounds, theoretically they should only care about the rate of return, not the risk-adjusted return. And if risk can be diversified away by holding a portfolio of investments, why should above-average volatility require a "risk premium"?

There is a false market in risk. Because we are risk averse, risk premiums are higher than they should be. Individual entrepreneurs take risks, it is true, but generally only when convinced that the upside greatly exceeds the downside in both quantum and probability. Organizations remain notoriously reluctant to take real risks, despite evidence that, increasingly, business fortune goes to the brave.

In high-growth markets, especially those involving networks, you have to place big bets to stand a good chance of winning. Up-front investment can be very high, because fixed costs are very high. Risk is also high, because each business segment will only support one substantial winner. But, equally, incremental costs are generally low (and sometimes virtually zero; on occasions, actually negative). The rewards from success can be astronomical and quite disproportionate to the cost, even to the total cost of all the contenders, winners and losers. There is usually a first-mover advantage, but regardless, the first player to establish a significant lead will usually be able to sustain its lead and move even further ahead. For an individual player, therefore, the risk of a low investment can actually be much higher than the risk of a high investment. Your best choice often lies between betting it all or betting nothing.

Writer Thomas A. Stewart, editor of *Fortune* magazine, advises firms not to try to avoid risk. He says that managing knowledge products is like holding a book of innovative bets. Companies should maintain a portfolio of ideas in which risk is both maximized and diversified. Don't put all your eggs in one basket, but do bet heavily.[11]

Panic

Primitive man did take risks and scramble furiously when his life was at stake. Panic often worked. The more successful scramblers survived more often, so that scrambling under threat is part of our genetic make-up.

Today, such scrambling behavior may not be so functional. When nonspecific layoffs are announced, and no one knows whether they'll keep their job, productivity often rises sharply. When a factory closes, certain employees may become hysterical or aggressive. When a normally sane person is under pressure while driving, "road rage" or sudden panic may take over. Higher productivity, screaming at managers, and attacking a fellow motorist are all examples of mad scrambling when threatened, but they rarely help the scrambler at all. What worked on the savannah doesn't apply anymore to the modern world.

Another interesting example is gambling. Those who win modestly in a casino cash in their chips early. Gamblers who start to lose often go beyond their preset limit of losses and gamble everything they have in a mad scramble to get back to where they started.

On the stock market, individual investors often display similar behavior. When their shares rise, they want to lock in the profit. If the shares fall heavily, novices will nearly always hang on, in an effort to avoid serious loss. They may even scramble to get funds enabling them to "average down" by buying more of the same shares at a lower price. Yet professional investors are trained to take the opposite approach. It normally pays to cut your losses, not to fight the market. Trading houses and fund managers often have strict rules to enforce such behavior; they need to, because human nature tends in the opposite direction. When we are losing badly, we are quite likely to gamble wildly. Further insight into our irrational attitudes to what we own, what we risk, and what we deserve are found in conventional psychology, biology, and game theory. I've picked three examples that can be applied toward business and that illuminate, and to a degree corroborate, some findings from evolutionary psychology.

Owners and Intruders

One fascinating insight from both biology and game theory relates to contests between owners or incumbents of territory and challengers or intruders. Being the owner confers a psychological advantage that is independent of relative strength.

Experiments with baboons show a pattern: the current owner of a territory is likely to keep it, even if it is the slightly weaker animal. There is strong incentive to hang on to what one already has, because taking new ground takes extraordinary effort.[12]

The Endowment Effect

Similar experiments on humans have shown what psychologists call the endowment effect. Say that someone has been offered two tickets to a top sporting event. A few days later she is offered two hundred dollars for the tickets. In experiments, most refuse the exchange. Reverse the experiment: give the subject two hundred dollars, and then offer the same tickets in exchange for the money. What do you think happens? Perversely, most still refuse the trade. The idea of ownership explains the apparent paradox: what people are given first, and hence what they own, is what they want to keep.

Game theory (see Chapter 5) has validated the ownership advantage. For "owners" and "intruders," there is a dominant strategy that works best in most cases. If you are the "owner" (or incumbent in a territory or market), you should raise the stakes to deter an intruder, to stop him entering your market. Under these circumstances, the intruder should retreat, knowing that success can only be bought at an excessive price. Eminent biologist John Maynard Smith called this pattern "bourgeois" competition, since respect for property rights ensures that conflict is not escalated. Bourgeois competition is implicit cooperation, with consent given to incumbents.

Clearly, this is useful knowledge in business. There is an in-built, apparently hardwired, genetic bias toward respect for incumbents that places challengers at a disadvantage. This bias is probably related to the risk aversion noted above: when hunter-gatherers had enough they would not fight for more, because it was too risky; they would, however, scramble to defend what they already had, because this was vital for their security. Consider these corollaries:

- The so-called "first-mover" advantage—the well-documented tendency for the first firm into a market to enjoy an advantage usually greater than it deserves on objective merit alone, independent of being first—may be rooted as much in the psychology of the challenger and the incumbent as it is in the effect on customers. The conventional explanation for first-mover advantage is that customers associate the new niche with the first firm holding it. Obviously, not much can be done about this by the challenger. If, however, much of the perceived advantage exists purely between challenger and incumbent, the advantage may not be as secure as it seems. If the challenger can somehow psych itself up to take the territory, and make it clear to the incumbent that it is no respecter of "bourgeois" rights, then the odds may shift significantly in its favor.

- If the incumbent and challenger are otherwise equally matched, the incumbent enjoys a clear advantage, if only in terms of motivation. If the incumbent comes under attack, even from a superior product or service, it should fight back with everything it's got, knowing that the odds are that the challenger will back down.

- Perceived ownership is what matters. If you want your firm to win in a particular market, you have to drill it into your people that you belong there, that it is rightfully yours. Bending the facts, as long as you can do so convincingly, can be very useful; propaganda can decide the contest. People will not easily concede space that they believe is theirs. On the other hand, they will not put their best foot forward if they think they are trespassing.

Take Xerox in the 1960s and 1970s as a case in point. At that time, Xerox was quite possibly the most technologically innovative and creative corporation on earth. At Xerox PARC in Palo Alto, California, scientists developed the personal computer, the mouse, Windows-type software, the laser printer, the paperless office, and Ethernet. Yet whatever the scientists invented, the Xerox Corporation, away from the campuslike ambience of the PARC, lacked the confidence to champion any of these new products. Xerox was about copiers. These new fields, the Xerox hierarchy felt, belonged to someone else. The Xerox bosses thought they were intruders, and they passed up the chance to become the most valuable corporation of the twentieth century.

Contrast this behavior with that of Bill Gates in 1995. Up to then, Gates and Microsoft had missed the significance of the Internet. Netscape, Sun Microsystems, and Yahoo! were all well ahead in Web applications. Belatedly, Gates realized his error. When it came to the Internet, the mighty Microsoft was the intruder, not the incumbent.

Yet Gates was not fazed. In a magnificent U-turn, he persuaded his people that the Internet was rightfully theirs. The Internet economy, Gates told his Microsoft troops, was the key extension of Microsoft's own markets and applications. Microsoft raised its R&D spending by half a billion dollars, entered a series of alliances with corporations providing Internet services, and acquired four firms with Web expertise. Before long, Microsoft was the incumbent, not the intruder, because Gates rejected the intruder psychology.

The Ultimatum Bargaining Game

Robert Frank, an economist interested in explaining why people do things using emotional as well as rational explanations, draws attention to the issue of fairness and the role it plays in negotiations. Psychologists use an experiment called the *ultimatum bargaining game.*

Alex is given $500 and told to share it with Justin. If Justin accepts what he's given, they both keep the cash. If Justin refuses the deal, neither gets anything. What should Alex offer Justin?

Rationally, Alex should offer Justin a very small cut, maybe $5, and keep the other $495. After all, Alex has the cash and Justin has the choice: $5 or nothing.

The thing is, in experiments where this happens, Justin tends to refuse the $5, and both players go away empty-handed. Apparently, our deep-rooted sense of fairness is offended by the inequality of the split, so that Justin looks at the *proportion* he's getting, rather than the absolute amount.

Usually, though, Alex doesn't go for the rational solution and offer a small share to Justin. By far the most common outcome in this experiment is that the person with the money offers $250, half the cash.

Does this reflect our ancestors' behavior on the savannah, where the hunters shared meat with those who didn't participate in the kill? Are generosity *and* socialistic envy hardwired by natural selection, where evolution has not had time to catch up with modern conditions?

At work, do we expect to have to share even where our colleagues have made no contribution? And do the latter get indignant if they don't get a "fair" chunk of the bonus pool, even if they've personally had a lean year? I've observed this behavior many times when advising bosses who have to decide bonuses. Justin may have brought no profit this year, but we don't want to demotivate him with a derisory bonus. Such thinking is deeply rooted and frustrates the very purpose of meritocratic rewards.

I believe that large organizations are inevitably socialistic, because they find it impossible to reward according to just desserts. In large multinational corporations, non-core workers, including those engaged in tasks such as cleaning, routine maintenance or clerical functions, are generally paid substantially more than they would be for the same job outside the multinational, because otherwise the wage gap between them and their more skilled colleagues would seem too large. The dilemma faced by those who set the pay scale is this: Do we reward according to our economic needs and the laws of supply and demand, or do we do what people (wrongly) regard as fair? Large organizations almost always go down the second route. Indeed, one of the reasons that outsourcing is so popular is that it offers a neat way out of the dilemma. If the cleaners and clerks and maintenance workers are outside the organization, they only have to be paid their market rate, however high the compensation of the knowledge workers inside.

Are We Really Hardwired?

There are two interesting contemporary scientific challenges to the "hardwiring" theory. One is the increasing evidence that learned behavior can win out against instinct, that the dominance of our genes is being undermined. The other challenge is from the emergent science of neuroplasticity, which suggests that, far from being hard-wired, the brain can be rewired.

The Theory of Cultural Evolution in Animals

We came across the first of these challenges in Chapter 2. Biologists such as Richard Dawkins and E. O. Wilson have suggested that in human society learned behavior ("culture") can operate independently of genes. Now other biologists are going much further, arguing that many other animals, including some very unsophisticated organisms, may exhibit "cultural evolution," which often runs directly counter to genetic preferences.

A Canadian marine biologist, Hal Whitehead, suggests that sperm whales learn songs from their mothers.[13] As we saw in Chapter 2, biologist Lee Alan Dugatkin has shown that female guppies tend to mate with the male guppies that have already been selected as mates by other females. The females will even switch from preferred mates in order to copy other females. Dugatkin shows that learned behavior has invaded the province of genes in marine bugs and many types of birds.[14] His conclusion is:

> Cultural norms may take on a life of their own and "run away" in very unexpected directions—directions that were never even in the picture for our primitive ancestors roaming the Savannah of Africa.

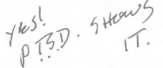

Neuroplasticity

Of even greater interest is *neuroplasticity,* which claims that the brain can rewire itself.

Children have an innate ability to learn language. But which language they learn, claims Dr. Jeffrey Schwartz,[15] determines how the brain stores sound. Now neuroscientists understand why: the particular sounds made by the language in question vary (Japanese sounds are very different from English ones), and each language forces a different rewiring of the part of the brain that processes language.

Brain scans also show that obsessive-compulsive disorders can be moderated or cured when patients deliberately think about other things. The brain circuits can actually be rewired through conscious effort. The brain is therefore plastic. Jeffrey Schwartz also claims: *"There is a mind independent of the brain . . . if the mind can rewire the brain, then in an important sense the mind is master of the brain."*[16]

How do the theories of cultural evolution and neuroplasticity affect what we can take away from evolutionary psychology? And may they have their own lessons for business?

Transcending Genetic Dispositions

From a business perspective, I find these three disciplines complementary. The explanations for human behavior provided by evolutionary psychology resonate with my business experience, especially my observations of people within corporations. This may be entirely a coincidence, but more likely, I think, it is because evolutionary psychology is at least partly right. There probably is a genetic predisposition toward behavior that made more sense on the savannah than it does today.

Nevertheless, this view is not incompatible with cultural evolution. Humans can *learn and transmit learning.* This means that genes are important in determining our behavior, but not necessarily decisive. If we have not yet learned to control and correct for all of our dysfunctional genetic inclinations, this does not mean that we cannot in the future, just as we have learned to welcome strangers on first sight. If we understand what we are up against, in terms of genetic bias, we are actually much more likely to be successful in correcting this bias.

Finally, the conflict between hardwiring and rewiring may be more apparent than real. Why can't we be both hardwired and capable of rewiring at least part of this hardwiring? Clearly, the brain is not completely plastic—but why should it be totally hardwired? And even if we really are totally hardwired, it may be functional to believe the opposite. We can change our behavior even if we cannot change our genes or our brains. I am confident that it could be empirically proved that fatalistic businesspeople are less successful than those who believe in free will.

I predict that executives will hear a lot more about cultural evolution and neuroplasticity. Part of the argument of this book is that we are moving beyond mechanical, cause-and-effect models—which are, and will remain, valuable—to embrace in addition more fluid, biological models. But beyond the biological models, there probably lie neurological models, which are even more free-form and sensitive to creative manipulation.

How to Manage and Mutate Stone Age Man

My conclusion, therefore, is that we *can* manage and mutate Stone Age man, and that it is well worth the effort to do so. If we accept the insights from evolutionary psychology, but also the possibility of change, what should we do differently? Some suggestions:

- We should recognize ourselves and our colleagues as what we are: twenty-first-century impostors driven by neolithic genes. The genes are sometimes helpful to business, as when they facilitate cooperation, but are generally a nuisance; they obstruct commercial progress and the good of our firms and our careers.
- We should start with ourselves. We have met the Flintstones and they are us. We should make continual and vigorous attempts to correct for our dysfunctional tendencies, like the undue avoidance of risk, the rejection of criticism, and the tendency to jump to conclusions about people on the basis of first impressions.
- If we wish to influence other people, we cannot appeal only to their reason. We must be skilled at baser appeals to their emotions. If we wish to manage people, we must manipulate their primitive propensities.

There are a number of structural remedies that help simulate the Stone Age clan, based on the general proposition that, all other things being equal, large, complex, and disparate organizations will never work as well economically as smaller, simpler, and more homogeneous ones.

- First, we should accept that the natural capacity of a cohesive unit is up to about one hundred fifty people—the size of the largest hunter-gatherer clans. When a unit holds fewer than one hundred fifty people, everyone can know everyone on first-name terms. Microsoft has broken down its monolithic empire into a proliferation of small units, each having typically only five to ten people. We tend to forget that, despite all the advantages of large firms with global reach, 60 percent of all employees worldwide work in small to mid-size businesses, often owned or run by a family.
- Second, firms above the ideal clan size tend to divide into separate functional, regional, or product "clans," which frequently squabble with each other. The near-universal experience of managers is that it is more difficult to do business with sister clans in the same organization than with strangers freely chosen by each clan.
- Third, organizational size, complexity, and heterogeneity lead to inefficiency *because of the expectations and behavior of the people involved.*

Since a large organization contains more people than a small one, and it is generally more difficult to detect or measure the real economic contribution of each person. This technical difficulty is exacerbated because of the socialistic tendency of organizations to meet "fair" expectations of employees based on a claim for a share of the pie simply because of clan membership, regardless of contribution.

The more complex an organization—the more things it does, the more customers and suppliers and products it has—the more difficult it becomes to measure and reward true individual contributions. A complex organization of a thousand people will have far more difficulty than a simple one with the same number.

Then consider heterogeneity, which is not the same as complexity. Complexity relates to what the organization does, heterogeneity to what the organization is. A heterogeneous organization is one comprising many different types of people, with different backgrounds, disciplines, degrees of skill level. For example, an organization with ten main disciplines such as engineering, computing, marketing, and so on, but comprising exclusively graduates, may be more homogeneous than another organization with only three disciplines but three different sets of educational and class backgrounds, nationalities, and styles. Evolutionary psychology suggests that people don't easily like or trust those from different camps.

McDonald's is an homogeneous organization. So is Mars. So is Hershey. So is Coca-Cola. In all these cases, there is one clear style, one culture, one common set of accepted behaviors, and, whatever their origins, one cohesive cadre of managers. By contrast, PepsiCo, Nestlé, Cadbury-Schweppes, and Westinghouse before its demise, represent much more heterogeneous organizations. Different product lines, cultures, and management styles coexist; differences are not suppressed, they are tolerated or even encouraged.

Incidentally, it is interesting that small national size carries no economic disadvantage, perhaps because scale effects are less important than simplicity and common identity. Of the ten wealthiest (per capita) nations, apart from the United States, the largest is Belgium, which has only ten million people. Of the ten countries with more than one hundred million people, only the United States and Japan are prosperous.[17]

Remember the lesson from Chapter 1, that diversity works, and that from Chapter 2, that the most successful organizations have a varied gene pool. How do we synthesize these insights with those from evolutionary psychology? I think we have to conclude, whether we are thinking of organizations or of societies, that heterogeneity is enormously valuable, but that it needs to be *managed.* Our genes are not cooperative or functional in this respect, so we need to interpose management mechanisms, culture, and vigilance to keep reminding ourselves of the value of variety. There is a second point too. Heterogeneity goes against our genes, yet is valuable. But the size and complexity of many organizations also go against our genes, and have no compensating benefits. The best solution is to have small, simple, and heterogeneous organizations.

So yes, we can manage and mutate Stone Age man. We manage by manipulating and correcting for our primitive instincts. We mutate by changing the business context, to capitalize on the good parts of our genetic heritage and to minimize the damage from the harmful parts. Only by recognizing what we are up against can we raise our managerial game.

How to Use the Natural Laws

- ***Manage and mutate Stone Age man,*** starting with yourself. Listen to criticism. You have no need to defend yourself.

  Allow second and third impressions to overrule first impressions.

  Take more risks. If the upside—value times probability—exceeds the downside, do it. If in doubt, do it.

  The one exception is not to take risks when things are going badly. Don't panic. Just cut your losses and get out.

  Don't be a prisoner to your emotions. Don't take decisions in the heat of the moment. Take time to calculate what is best for you.

  Don't thump your chest. Don't draw attention to your perspicacity or achievements. Don't tell people that you were right.

  When you are successful, beware. Don't believe that you are infallible. Remember how important luck is. Expect reverses and take them in your stride.

- ***Capitalize on the genetic predispositions of others.*** Act confidently, even when you are not confident. But don't believe your own propaganda.

  If you have an insight and want to lead, even among equals or superiors, go ahead and lead. Most people like to be led. The informal hierarchy is more powerful than the formal one.

Be careful to present yourself so that others' first impressions correspond to what you want. If you want them to think you dynamic, move fast. If you want to appear scholarly and reflective, wear tweed coats and glasses. Wear your façade with pride.

Be friendly and warm, especially when first meeting someone. Try to empathize.

Share information. Build trust. Don't criticize other people to third parties.

Try to avoid direct criticism of someone. Always praise first, to make them receptive. Criticize actions, not the person.

Only openly disagree with those below you in the pecking order. Otherwise, use the venerable line, "I agree with you, but . . ."

Build personal alliances throughout the organization, especially in unlikely places. If you are an engineer, hang around marketing until they accept you as one of them.

Realize that reputation is sometimes more important than performance. Reputation is three parts identification-empathy and one part competence.

- ***Manage Stone Age folk appropriately—expect and correct for irrationality.*** Be aware that the hierarchy may induce conformity and blindness to reality. Use formal hierarchy sparingly, and encourage dissent. Don't promote authoritarian characters to positions where awareness of the outside world is important.

  When hierarchy is subverted by an unofficial pecking order, don't try to resist.

  Don't seek to eliminate all forms of hierarchy. Don't expect delayering and single-status workplaces to usher in a new age of egalitarianism and democracy, or "empowerment" to generate initiative. Allow the natural rhythm of leadership and followership to operate. Allow people to work together naturally, selecting their own ad hoc alliances and teams.

  Be profligate and universal with status awards. Status is like flattery: no one is too smart or savvy to avoid its charm. Give special responsibilities, such as leader of project team X. Identify and celebrate unusual achievements, such as "beyond the call of duty" service to customers.

Encourage the natural tendency towards internal cohesiveness. Talk about colleagues and not employees. Encourage colleagues to say "we" not "I," "us" not "you."

Anticipate hostility towards out-groups. Focus it on competitors rather than other departments or functions within the firm. Sometimes hostility is focused on another out-group, the customers, with obvious consequences. Reserve your most severe sanctions for discouragement of this behavior. Encourage colleagues to think about customers as an extended part of the clan, as part of the club, along the lines of quality engineer W. Edwards Deming's dictum: "The customer is the most important part of the production line."[18] Encourage all employees to see as much of customers as possible, because familiarity breeds affection.

Counter the out-group feelings between different parts of the organization by forming cross-group project teams to achieve worthwhile ends. Make the teams as heterogeneous as possible.

Rotate people's jobs internally, with the explicit aim of putting different types of people into each clan (e.g., marketing people into manufacturing).

When hiring, ensure that everyone guards against first impressions and the clone mentality. Don't allow anyone to give their impressions of candidates to someone who has not yet interviewed them. Use objective testing and outside assessment.

Question any internal consensus. It's probably wrong.

Expect but discourage macho behavior: breast-beating, one-upmanship, self-aggrandizement, empire building, malicious gossip, personalized competition. The best way to counter macho behavior is to hire and promote as many women as possible and to ensure that female values effectively counter male excesses.

Don't expect people to take risks, welcome change, or be creative. If risk taking is essential, frame the situation as an emergency. Make it life threatening (or at least job threatening). Be up-front and even exaggerate any bad news: "Competitor X, if left unchecked, will have taken half our business within two years." "If return on capital doesn't double, we'll have to downsize." "This new technology could kill us." "Customer Y accounts for 60 percent of our profits but is very unhappy and ready to take its business away." "If we don't internationalize, we'll be taken over." Choose whatever is credible, really worrying, and at least half true!

Make it clear that failure through taking risks is more acceptable than refusal to take risks.

If you want creativity, make the environment nonthreatening and informal. (Children are creative, but only so long as they feel totally protected.)

- ***Change structures in order to counter primitive genes.*** Reduce your firm's size and complexity.

  If different parts of the firm have different ways of working and core competencies, split it into two or more new firms.

  Ensure that each organizational unit within the firm has no more than one hundred fifty members.

  Make the organization structure as simple as possible. Realize that matrix organizations come up against primitive man, and the latter wins. People gravitate towards one main sense of identity and loyalty. Therefore, use matrix forms sparingly and realize that there will always be one main affiliation and one less important dotted-line one.

  When risk taking is important, form a separate unit that has to take risks. Make it clear that membership of the unit is temporary and that there is a way back to the parent whether the fledgling business succeeds or fails.

- ***Use the specter of competition to rally your troops—but avoid fighting.*** Realize that business is not war.

  Collaborate with competitors as far as possible. Avoid direct conflict or damage.

  Don't put your competitor's back against the wall. He may panic, which may or may not help the competitor, but will certainly damage your firm.

  Remember that the only useful way of "beating" competitors is by having your own loyal fan club of profitable customers, who prefer what you do to anything any other competitor does.

5 Resolving the Prisoner's Dilemma

Game Theory

If men were actuated by self-interest, which they are not—except in the case of a few saints—the whole human race would co-operate. There would be no more wars, no more armies, no more bombs.

BERTRAND RUSSELL

We turn now to our most uplifting subject: the search for cooperation, especially human cooperation. Here we supplement biology with *game theory*, a branch of mathematics with links to many other scientific disciplines, including biology itself. The main lesson is how to cooperate effectively in pursuit of entirely selfish ends.

Game theory started when John von Neumann, a Hungarian genius who was also one of the architects of the first computer, published his mathematical *Theory of Parlor Games* in 1928. A branch of mathematics and statistics, game theory has since been applied to economics, biology, epidemiology, philosophy, physics, politics, the social sciences, military strategy, and business strategy.

Game theory deals with games where your chances at winning depend on what your opponent does, and vice versa; it attempts to simplify the world and produce the best mathematically derived outcome for any particular situation. In 1944, von Neumann and economist Oskar Morgenstern published *The Theory of Games and Economic Behavior.* They invented the concept of the non-zero-sum game, where it pays to collaborate and form coalitions.

The Prisoner's Dilemma

The most famous "game" in game theory, one that had been understood, in nonmathematical terms, for centuries, is the *Prisoner's Dilemma.* There are many, many variants of this game, but the basic idea remains the same.

Imagine two criminals caught and locked up in separate rooms. A robbery and murder have been committed, but the police have dubious evidence. If one of the criminals confesses before the other, the authorities will offer a deal: immunity from prosecution, but execution for the other criminal. If neither rats on the other, they can both expect five years in prison for the robbery. The rational thing for each individual to do is to rat, or fail to cooperate, as soon as possible. Cooperation between the parties is irrational for the individual prisoner, although if they both cooperated neither would be executed.

Self-interest Rules

The Prisoner's Dilemma can be expressed mathematically, with rewards rather than punishments. Assume that Brian and Lee are playing and that you are Brian. You are both invited to write down, simultaneously, either the number 1 or the number 2. If you write 1 and so does Lee, you both get five dollars. If you write 2 and Lee writes 1, you get twenty dollars and Lee gets nothing. If you write 1 and Lee writes 2, the opposite occurs—you get nothing and Lee gets twenty dollars. Finally, if you both write 2, you each get one dollar.

What do you do? You'll probably write down 2, reasoning as follows: If Lee writes 1 and you write 1, then you will win five dollars, but if you write 2, and Lee writes 1, you'll win twenty dollars, so 2 is better in this case. What happens if Lee writes 2? If you write 1, you'll get nothing, but if you write 2, at least you'll get one dollar. So whether Lee writes 1 or 2, you'll be better off if you write 2.

But the dilemma is that Lee is thinking the same way, since the payoffs are entirely symmetrical. If he follows the rules of self-interest, he'll also write 2. So you end up with one dollar. Yet if you had cooperated, you could each have had five dollars.

The conclusion of the Prisoner's Dilemma is that although mutual cooperation may be in everyone's aggregate interest, self-interest will tend to predominate, to society's disadvantage. The Prisoner's Dilemma was formalized as a game in 1950 by the RAND Corporation in California. It was soon realized that the world was full of Prisoner's Dilemmas. Trees in tropical rainforests spend all their energy growing toward the sky rather than reproducing. If the trees could agree not to grow more than ten feet tall, each tree would still enjoy the same sunlight and they could divert the surplus effort into tree sex. But they don't.

The Prisoner's Dilemma conclusion, up to the late 1970s, was deeply depressing. The economics of the past two hundred years had been built on self-interest. Yet now it appeared that self-interest was suboptimal. The dilemma was that it was inevitable. This appeared, too, to be confirmed by a lesson from evolution: the "Red Queen effect," which has also been called the "evolutionary arms race."

The Red Queen Effect

In Lewis Carroll's *Through the Looking Glass,* the Red Queen has to run as fast as she can just to stay in the same place. This is similar to running up an escalator that's going down. It's also how evolution works in animals.

Lions chase antelopes. Lynxes chase rabbits. Over time, the antelopes and the rabbits get faster. Why? Because the antelopes and rabbits that are faster than their peers survive longer, and pass their genes on to the next generation. This is great for antelopes and rabbits, but it doesn't improve their position vis-à-vis predators. The same improvement in speed happens via natural selection for the lions and lynxes. So the ninety-ninth generation of rabbits flee faster from the ninety-ninth generation of lynxes, yet are in no less danger than their ancestors.

Richard Dawkins calls this the "evolutionary arms race." There is constant escalation and improvement in the arms on both sides of the predator-prey divide, but no change in relative position.

Unfair to antelopes and rabbits? Maybe. That is the price of progress via natural selection.

The evolutionary arms race applies to business too. Executives today work much harder and much longer hours than they used to. There is no net individual advantage in this.

Executives and firms have to keep getting better just to stay where they are. If an organization bucks this trend—managing to hold market share despite not improving what it offers customers—this must mean that it's not in a competitive marketplace.

If you went through the business plans of the five largest competitors in any market, it's almost certain that all five would be planning to gain market share. Each company is going to be better than it used to be, so it should get more business. This seems such a reasonable assumption, yet it is plainly impossible for everyone to gain share. The business plans fail to factor in the Red Queen effect. No one else is going to stand still. Your market share escalator is programmed to go down, and doing things better may only keep you where you are.

But is there really no escape from the evolutionary arms race? For animals other than humans, no. But for humans, and for business, it may be different.

The Prisoner's Dilemma Revisited

The evolutionary arms race occurs for precisely the same reason that the Prisoner's Dilemma can lead each individual to act against the collective interest: the inability to cooperate. If lynxes could cooperate with rabbits, they could call a moratorium on getting faster and devote their evolutionary efforts to some more beneficial objective. But of course lynxes can't collaborate with rabbits to defeat the current version of evolution.

And yet, animals do collaborate for some purposes. In the 1970s, economist and geneticist John Maynard Smith turned to game theory to explain why animals typically don't fight to the death. His innovation was to play the Prisoner's Dilemma many times.

By running a version of the Prisoner's Dilemma with hawks playing doves, and replaying the game many times, he showed that the best results were obtained by a strategy he called "Retaliator," where a dove turns into a hawk when dealing with hawks.

Initially, Maynard Smith was ignored. Then game theorists started using computers to play Prisoner's Dilemma games over and over. In the late 1970s, tournaments were organized with competing computer programs that played the game two hundred times. To general surprise, the "nicer" or more cooperative programs tended to win. The strategy that came out on top was "Tit-for-tat," devised by Canadian political scientist Anatol Rappoport. Tit-for-tat was similar to Retaliator; it started by cooperating and then mimicked the last move of the other player. The organizer of the tournaments explained the success of Tit-for-tat:

> What accounts for Tit-for-tat's robust success is its combination of being nice, forgiving and clear. Its niceness prevents it from getting into unnecessary trouble. Its retaliation discourages the other side from persisting whenever defection is tried. Its forgiveness helps restore mutual co-operation. And its clarity makes it intelligible to the other player, thereby eliciting long-term co-operation.[1]

Long-term advantage often requires cooperating players to take turns in collecting the payoff: I let you win the biggest prize this time, perhaps taking nothing myself, if you let me take the biggest prize next time. Cooperation is about comprehending how to make the pie bigger, on the understanding that when we have to divide it, we will behave reasonably, within the context of a long-term relationship.

Ridley's Theory of Social Coagulation

In 1996 came one of the most important books of the decade: Matt Ridley's *The Origins of Virtue*,[2] a thesis on cooperation and virtue which draws lessons from biology and economics. It also has profound implications for business.

Ridley gives a unique twist to the ideas of the selfish gene and evolutionary biology. He argues that society is a product of our genes and our evolution. Humans are unique because we are organized into large groups with complex interrelationships between individuals—and because we cooperate in a qualitatively different way from all other animals. This is the highest and most successful form of evolution. He says: *"The essential virtuousness of human beings is proved not by parallels in the animal kingdom, but by the very lack of convincing parallels."*[3]

The advantage of society rests in division of labor and socialization, which modern humans have taken to a happy extreme.

Division of Labor

If you've studied any economics, you'll probably recall Adam Smith's example of the pin factory where ten people, through specialization, were able to produce forty-eight thousand pins a day. Smith was a Scottish political philosopher, and his 1776 book *The Wealth of Nations* invented the concept of division of labor: *"The greatest improvement in the productive powers of labour, and the greater part of the skill, dexterity, and judgment with which it is any where directed, or applied, seem to have been the effects of the division of labour."*

Smith posits three key advantages of specialization:

- Practice leads to higher productivity.
- Specialization saves time switching from one task to another (which is, incidentally, the main insight behind business process reengineering, a major source of productivity improvement in the 1990s).

- Specialization makes it worthwhile to invest in tailored machinery to boost productivity, thus enabling "one man to do the work of many."

Smith demonstrates—and here comes the link with increasing degrees of cooperation—that:

- division of labor is limited by the size of the market, and can therefore increase when market size increases; and
- division of labor increases with better transport and communications.

It turns out that division of labor, increasing specialization, and "trade" are themes noted by biologists and anthropologists in explaining how complex organisms evolve and thrive. Increased cooperation is both a cause and a result of such success.

Biological research has revealed that the bigger the cells in small organisms are, the more likely they are to divide the labor, with some cells specializing in reproduction. The social insects—like ants, termites, and bees—have been hugely successful because their societies contain specialized roles that require cooperation.

Human societies organized into bigger groups have greater numbers of more differentiated jobs. The isolated and now extinct Tasmanians had only two castes and lived in groups of fifteen or fewer; but the Maoris, who lived in groups of up to two thousand, recognized sixty different professional roles.

Ricardo's Law of Comparative Advantage

The links between cooperation, division of labor, and trade were first made explicit in 1817 by David Ricardo, a very rich investor, economist, and radical British politician. His counterintuitive law of comparative advantage applied division of labor to groups and countries.

Until Ricardo, it seemed obvious that countries could only trade if one was better than the other at producing something. Ricardo said that in fact there was a basis for trade whenever the relative ratios of productivity were different, whatever the absolute levels—which implied that there was virtually no limit on possible constructive trade. If country X is better than country Y at producing two products, there could still be trade between them that would enrich both countries. If country X is twice as productive in steel and four times as productive in leather goods, then country X should specialize in leather goods and country Y should specialize in steel, where it has comparative advantage, despite being inferior in absolute terms.

Specialized business and trade—which are essentially cooperative intergroup activities—lie at the heart of human advances. As Matt Ridley explains so well:

> 200,000 years ago, stone age tools were travelling long distances from their quarries . . . Where the Neanderthals all lived in much the same fashion, their replacements began to show great local variations in their stone technologies and styles of art . . .
>
> [The] invention [of trade] represents one of the very few moments in evolution when *Homo sapiens* stumbled on some competitive ecological advantage over other species that was truly unique. There is simply no other animal that exploits the law of comparative advantage between groups. Within groups . . . the division of labour is beautifully exploited by the ants, the mole rats, the Huia birds. But not between groups.
>
> David Ricardo explained a trick that our ancestors had invented many, many years before. The law of comparative advantage is one of the ecological aces that our species holds.[4]

The importance of trade and cooperation can be graphically illustrated by contrasting the native Tasmanians to the native aboriginal Australians. When Europeans landed on Tasmania in 1642, they ended ten thousand years of isolation and found the most primitive human society in the world. Native Tasmanians couldn't light a fire from scratch. They didn't have bone tools or multipiece stone tools or axes with handles or boomerangs. They didn't know how to fish or make warm clothing. The Aboriginal Australians could do all these things; Tasmania's isolation had kept its population poor and technologically destitute.[5]

Isolated groups suffer because most groups get their ideas and innovations from outside via trade in ideas and goods. Human society progresses via increased trade, specialization, and intergroup cooperation.

Beyond Baboonery

Ridley observes that two junior male baboons will join forces to beat off the consort of a female baboon. Then they chase after the female, and the one who catches her will mate. Cooperation is used to achieve selfish ends. This is the basis of our cooperative instincts.

Ridley takes up the theme expressed by Richard Dawkins in his concept of memes:

> Because of the human practice of passing on traditions, customs, knowledge and beliefs . . . there is a whole new kind of evolution going on in human beings—a competition not between genetically different individuals or groups, but between culturally different individuals or groups. One person may thrive . . . not because he has better genes, but because he knows . . . something of practical value.[6]

Selection between groups happens, and the cooperators grow at the expense of the noncooperators. The history of humanity is one of ever-increasing and ever more complex interrelationships. Society is not an artificial construct or a tyranny, but the highest form of evolution. What drives progress is increased specialization, and increased trade.

I believe that technology is a semi-independent variable too, part of the great trinity that drives progress. Technology itself is a form of culture. It is impossible to explain the explosion of productivity since 1750 purely on the basis of increased specialization and trade—for capitalism to conquer, society required new miracles of technology.[7]

Business Collaboration as a Means to Defeat the Evolutionary Arms Race

Ridley is placing trade, and therefore necessarily business, at the center of the process whereby humans evolve into virtuous collaborators. This is evolution via memes—by cultural transmission—rather than by natural selection. Science is the process whereby we learn about our environment and transmit that knowledge. Business is the process whereby economic information is replicated and used to improve the material conditions of life. The process of constructive human evolution, therefore, requires progressive acceleration and intensification of the transmittal of scientific and business advances. Individuals and society become progressively more complex and differentiated, increasing the extent of interdependence and trade between individuals and groups of individuals.

Yet, as we saw in Chapter 2, the process really starts at an earlier stage, with the formation and replication of business genes—units of economic information. These drive the process of economic development. Like biological genes, business genes derive their power and ability to replicate themselves from combining with many of their fellows and finding vehicles that will protect and incorporate them, including animate vehicles such as individuals, teams, and corporations. Cooperation is at the heart of this process.

Indeed, cooperation and competition are essential complements to business genes, individuals, and corporations alike. Without cooperation between business genes, between individuals, and between individuals and business genes, there could be no corporations; and without individuals and corporations, there could be no competition. Cooperation between individuals and groups is *how* we compete with other individuals and groups. Over time, cooperation is becoming relatively more important. A sole trader—a single-person business, such as an independent consultant or an actor—still needs to cooperate, with intermediaries or agents, for example. When the typical business unit is larger than one—when the corporation rather than the individual is the modal production unit, a comparatively recent event in human history—cooperation becomes not just an incidental requirement, but is essential for success.

Cooperation is not just an internal process. Increasingly, it occurs externally, beyond the boundaries of the organization and beyond geographic boundaries too.

Corporations and Cooperation

The modern corporation is unique in economic forms in that it comprises internal (as well as external) cooperation. The essence of a corporation is the free consent of individuals to cooperate to achieve mutual economic ends. A corporation is not a slave plantation or an army. The corporation does not own the employees. It is an ever-shifting network of cooperators using a set of economic resources (money, machines, buildings) and a set of common knowledge and technology to provide customers with what they want in exchange for money, which is then shared out between the internal and external cooperators (the employees and suppliers, including suppliers of capital). What makes the corporation work is a web of free cooperation operating at many levels.

The relative success of corporations is not just a function of how well they compete with (or avoid) each other, but also of how well they craft or contrive the multilevel process of cooperation.

Because cooperation is based on instinct and emotion rather than rationality, there is another currency that is important in eliciting cooperation, which supplements the currencies of cash and reason. The currency of cooperation is commitment, trust, and love.

There are two kinds of successful corporations: the excellent competitors and the excellent cooperators. It is easy to recognize which companies are in which camp.

The excellent competitors include (in their heyday) ITT under Harold Geneen, GE before Jack Welch, IBM (before the fall), Hanson (before its demerger), Ford, most oil companies, Glaxo Wellcome, Monsanto, and any companies that are run efficiently and at low cost.

The excellent cooperators include companies that inspire significant affection in their customers, employees, and suppliers: The

Body Shop, CNN, Federal Express, Hewlett-Packard, Johnson & Johnson, Levi Strauss, Matsushita, Viking Direct, and Virgin. Many family-owned or family-run companies fall into this category. The personality of the founder(s) often infuses the spirit of firms that know how to cooperate.

Some statistical support for the importance of cooperation is provided by a study undertaken by the Business Round Table and quoted by Robert Waterman.[8] A thirty-year study of "socially responsible" companies—presumably excellent cooperators—showed that they outperformed the Dow Jones index by seven times.

The Theory of Co-opetition

In 1996, Barry Nalebuff of Yale School of Management and Adam Brandenburger of Harvard Business School put forward the *theory of co-opetition,*[9] which aims to combine competition and cooperation:

- Cooperation is how we create value; how we create the pie.
- Competition is how we capture value; how we grab our slice of the pie.

Drawing on game theory, Nalebuff and Brandenburger say that business is a game where in order to create value the company needs to relate to other players. To the conventional categories of customers, suppliers, and competitors, they add the "complementor," the previously overlooked counterpart to the competitor.

Microsoft and Intel are complementors. Microsoft's sophisticated software packages require ever more powerful chips from Intel. The chips in turn make the software feasible and economic. Sometimes direct competitors are complementors, if, for example, they draw in more customer traffic to a shopping mall. As we'll see later, all networks, like telecommunication systems, transport systems, or the Internet, benefit greatly from increased traffic. It follows that the actions of direct competitors, if they enlarge the size of the market, actually benefit all the other competitors.

Nalebuff and Brandenburger provide a mnemonic, PARTS, to

help apply game theory to business. PARTS stands for Players, Added value, Rules, Tactics, and Scope.

Players. Identify the players and categorize them into customers, suppliers, competitors, and complementors. A competitor is a complementor if your customers value your product more when they also have that other player's product. If they value your product less when they have the other player's product, then it is a competitor. The same concept applies to your suppliers, if they are very important to you. If the supplier is more likely to supply you if the other player is around, it's a complementor. But if you are both fighting over the supplier's scarce supplies, you're competitors.

Added value. Add up the total value supplied by all the players. Now repeat that, but for all the players except yourself. The difference is your unique value—and it's often quite small.

Your strategy, and in particular whether you encourage or rebuff cooperators, can determine how much value there is in the system. Nalebuff and Brandenburger do not say that it is always better to cooperate. As an example, they offer the telling contrast between Nintendo's competitive strategy in video games and IBM's competitive strategy in the PC market.

Nintendo's strategy was to ensure that it captured the lion's share of the value in the video games network. It limited the number of games its developers produced to five new games a year, so that quality ruled rather than quantity. It carefully controlled supply to the major retailers, so that there was always pent-up demand and the retailers wanted the games more than Nintendo needed the retail space. It restricted the size of its market, baking a slightly smaller pie than possible, but it made sure that the pie was highly profitable and that it took most of it. Five years after entering the U.S. market, Nintendo's market value was higher than that of Nissan and Sony combined.

By contrast, IBM invited Intel and Microsoft to help develop its PC. Open architecture and cooperation led to speedy development and a large market. But when other companies copied the IBM PC, it was Intel and Microsoft that cashed in. IBM should have made Intel and Microsoft pay to play, or insisted on cross-shareholdings. IBM brought most to the party, and took away least.

Rules. Rules are an important part of the game and can often be subtly shifted in your favor. But rules can always be rewritten by a creative player who has real value to add. Take the case of advertising agency Cordiant, Maurice Saatchi, and British Airways (BA). BA was a big client of Cordiant. Maurice Saatchi had been a founder of the company but was ousted. He took with him the key account executives from the BA account. Cordiant was confident that it could keep BA's business because the account executives had noncompete clauses in their contracts: they couldn't compete for business against their former employer. So what did Maurice Saatchi do? He went to BA equipped with cutout pictures of their former executives. What a pity, he said, that these guys can't serve you, explaining their noncompete clauses. So BA went to Cordiant and asked it to lift the noncompete clauses. Cordiant complied, reckoning that it would lose the account anyway and not wishing to forfeit possible future goodwill. End of noncompete clauses in one fell swoop. Yet for decades previously such clauses had operated effectively in many different professional service businesses.

Tactics. Business, claim Nalebuff and Brandenburger, is often conducted in a fog, where reality is difficult to see clearly. Game theory can tell you whether and how to lift the fog. When a new product really is superior, they suggest you shout it out to the world. When Gillette launched the Sensor razor, it was so convinced that it had a superior product that it spent $100 million on advertising it to lift the fog. Consumers, faced with such confidence, felt that there must be something worth trying, and Gillette's global sales rose by 70 percent.

But sometimes fog is useful to companies and enables them to keep a larger share of the pie. A good example is the impenetrably complex fare schedules used by airlines. A misguided attempt by American Airlines to clear the fog occurred in 1992, when it introduced "value pricing" and simplified fares down to four categories. Other airlines retaliated by simplifying their fare structures too, and price realizations crashed. Airlines in the United States managed to lose $5 billion that year.

Scope. Look beyond the boundaries of the game. No business game is an island. Players in one game also play in others. Anticipate and prevent, or at least delay, such invasions. In 1980, a niche toiletries company, Minnetonka, launched Softsoap, an up-market liquid-based soap. It was a great product, but unpatentable. How could the large toiletries players be prevented from moving in on their product? One way was to tie up for a full year the entire production of the only two makers of the product's pump dispensers. By the time the majors entered, Softsoap was identified with its category. The brand was eventually sold to Colgate-Palmolive for $61 million.

The sum of the PARTS is simply analyzing the relationships between all the players in the system. Who needs whom? Who can benefit from the relationships? Who are the actual or potential complementors? Where could cooperation lead to a bigger pie? Even where competition would deliver more value to the corporation than cooperation, adversarial tactics may subtract more value than they add.

The Cathedral *vs.* the Bazaar

What architecture of corporations—what structure of corporations in society—is likely to facilitate the greatest trade, specialization, innovation, exchange of information, and wealth creation?

Is it better to have a series of large, specialized corporations, each built like a cathedral, with intricate internal symmetry, a sense of their own distinctness and holiness, and a dominating presence; or to have a larger number of smaller enterprises, that exist next to each other, jostling for position and custom, open to each other's secrets and freely exchanging information, like bookmakers in a betting ring, or traders in a bazaar?

Equally, is it better to have a centralized policy covering a wide continent like Europe, North America, or Asia; or to have a series of small, independent states?

The cathedral versus bazaar question arises from a recent debate on the better method for debugging software. Eric S. Raymond contrasts the two styles:

> I believed that the most important software needed to be built like cathedrals, carefully crafted by individual wizards or small bands working in splendid isolation . . .
>
> Linus Torvalds' style of development [as practiced in his

> software engineering firm Linux]—release early and often, delegate everything you can, be open to the point of promiscuity—came as a surprise. No quiet, reverent cathedral-building here—the Linux community seemed to resemble a great babbling bazaar of differing agendas and approaches (aptly symbolized by the Linux archive sites, who'd take submissions from anyone) out of which a coherent and stable system could seemingly emerge only by a succession of miracles.[10]

Linus Torvalds believes that bugs are best fixed by being identified and later corrected, by as large a number of people as possible, the identifiers and the fixers typically not being the same people. Another way of expressing it is: "Debugging is parallelizable." In software debugging, the bazaar is often better than the cathedral, because an unseen army of collaborators comes to the rescue of the corporation, and many different corrections and improvements can proceed in parallel.

The Cathedral *and* the Bazaar

Linus's approach and the processes around it typify the Internet culture, where nobody is in charge and information is freely available. I'll comment on its implications for networks and economics in Chapter 11. Both cathedrals and bazaars are useful, competing methods of human cooperation and exchange. Competition between different groups, some organized more like the bazaar, others more like the cathedral, drives progress. Sometimes it is useful for a company to have large-scale and more proprietary exclusivity; sometimes smaller scale and greater openness is preferable. As for which works better, the answer appears to be an intermediate degree of concentration or fragmentation.

Diamond's Principle of Intermediate Fragmentation

Jared Diamond, professor of physiology at UCLA Medical School, has proposed that business and society benefit from intermediate fragmentation:

> You don't want excessive unity and you don't want excessive fragmentation; instead, you want your human society or business to be broken up into a number of groups which compete with each other but which also maintain relatively free communication with each other.[11]

To prove his point, Diamond contrasts the centralization of decision making in Renaissance China with the possibilities inherent in the more fragmented Europe. In 1400, China had the world's largest fleet, comprising hundreds of ships and total crews of twenty thousand men. Then, in 1432, a new emperor sided with the anti-navy faction and decided to dismantle the shipyards and stop sending out the ships. And, because the emperor was the sole ruler of this huge nation, that was the end of China's exploration of further horizons. Sixty years later, Columbus wanted a fleet to sail across the Atlantic Ocean. Being Italian, he tried to raise support in Italy. Everyone in Italy thought it a stupid idea. So Columbus tried again in France, with the same result. He traipsed from country to country until finally, on the seventh attempt, the King and Queen of Spain conceded him three small ships. Europe's fragmentation made Columbus's voyage possible—and the rest is history.

But Diamond observes that extreme fragmentation, as it exists in India, favors innovation little better than extreme centralization. And he points out that many industries have a minimum efficient scale, so that an extremely fragmented and geographically protected industry, like brewing in Germany, cannot be as efficient as a more concentrated and competitive one, like America's beer industry. There are one thousand small local beer companies in Germany, which are high cost but protected from competition with each other because each German brewery has virtually a local monopoly, and protected from imports because of the German beer purity law. The average brewery in the United States produces thirty-one times more beer than the average German brewery, and the German industry has productivity only 43 percent that of the United States. As Adam Smith observed, too small a market constrains specialization. A highly localized market is likely to be less efficient than a continental or global one.

Hence the virtues of intermediate fragmentation, where competition and collaboration coexist. The ideal model, according to Diamond, is Silicon Valley, which

> consists of lots of companies that are fiercely competitive with each other, but nevertheless there's a lot of collaboration, and despite the competition there is a free flow of ideas and a free flow of information between these companies.[12]

Sun Microsystems is a great example—drawing on Silicon Valley's terrific technical infrastructure and then helping other Silicon Valley companies.

Sun pioneered the UNIX operating system that would work on any computer. Sun's founders were all twenty-something graduates who designed the hardware and software for workstations. They made almost nothing from scratch, buying standard components from many different local firms. Sun's key strength was in product design, and its sourcing strategy made it possible to introduce complex new products quickly and continually.

Customers loved Sun's open system and the company grew rapidly—but it kept using business partners rather than building its own operations. It used the sales and service organizations of several hundred partners, while not losing control of its customers.

A similar approach with even more spectacular results was followed by Cisco. In 1998, it was the fastest growing firm in world history, reaching a market value of $100 billion within twelve years (Microsoft took twenty years to do the same). Ten thousand dollars of Cisco stock when it went public in 1990 was worth $6.5 million by 1999. Cisco is the company that has the best claim to "make the Internet," since it sells routers, which are devices for sending data between separate computers. The routers, switches, and other data-networking products, plus relevant software and services, are said to be the "plumbing" of the Internet. Amongst Silicon Valley firms, it is unusual in that its sales are mainly tangible products that take up space.

But although it sells physical products, with an amazing 30 percent net margin, Cisco makes very little. It sources from thirty-four plants globally, and thirty-two are owned by other firms. Executive Vice President Don Listwin comments, "You've heard of just-in-time manufacturing. Well, this is not-at-all manufacturing." Cisco outsources almost everything it can, entering close partnerships with hundreds of firms. Another Cisco executive VP, Gary Daichendt, says, "over 80 percent of our business is fulfilled through our partners." Michael Rich, who is the CEO of a Silicon Valley partner, NetSpeak, pays tribute to the Cisco partnership system: "What they do is create an environment that lets smaller companies like NetSpeak innovate . . . We're able to do that as an added-value sale on top of a Cisco network . . . We strongly support Cisco's strategy for an ecosystem . . . it will make them the Microsoft of networking."

A 1999 study by PriceWaterhouseCoopers showed that firms involved in alliances with other firms had 20 percent higher growth than similar firms without alliances. Andersen Consulting says that the average large corporation went from zero alliances in 1989 to more than thirty in 1999, and predicted that alliances will represent at least $25 trillion by 2004.

Selfish Genes Urge Humans to Behave Selflessly

As made evident in the Prisoner's Dilemma, long-term rewards are reaped through cooperation, not short-term self-interest. Only by behaving in a consistently trustworthy manner—ignoring the opportunities to gain short-term advantage—can individuals be considered trustworthy, therefore opening doors to valuable business opportunities.

Cooperation is motivated by selfish genes, but requires selfless behavior—therein lies the paradox. As Ridley says:

> The virtuous are virtuous for no other reason than . . . to join forces with others who are virtuous, to mutual benefit. And once co-operators segregate themselves from the rest of society a wholly new force of evolution can come into play: one that pits groups against each other, rather than individuals.[13]

For the businessperson, business life, like the Prisoner's Dilemma game, is best seen as the gradual unfolding of a series of opportunities to cooperate. No transaction is an independent event. Success depends on your skill at cooperating, the number and quality of people who will cooperate with you, and the reputation you build. The development of a career in business is not so much about building technical skills as it is about building valuable contacts, people who want to do business with you.

How to Use the Natural Laws

- ***Cooperate with the best cooperators.*** Build relationships with the cooperators who possess the blend of business and cooperative attributes that can take your career and business to the highest peaks. Remember that the objective of a career is to build an ever-increasing network of skilled cooperators.

- ***Build a reputation as someone who creates wealth for others and who is totally trustworthy.*** Keep your word, without calculation of short-term gain.

- ***Always cooperate first.*** Trust others until they prove themselves unworthy of your trust. Only withdraw cooperation from noncooperators. Punish the latter, but then rebuild mutual self-interest with clear signals: I will cooperate if you will, but *only* if you will. Demonstrate the disadvantages to others in their failure to cooperate.

- ***Be willing to take turns in extracting advantage.*** Understand that reciprocity is a long-term concept, not one requiring mutual advantage in each individual transaction.

- ***Cooperate daily.*** Teach yourself that cooperation, like brainstorming and networking, is cumulative and self-reinforcing. Seize all available opportunities to cooperate with useful allies, because cooperation builds skill at cooperation, besides building your good reputation and your reciprocal obligations. Become an evangelist of cooperation. Remember: cooperation is the highest form of self-interest.

Part One Concluding Note

In Chapter 1, we saw that evolution occurs at many levels, but always through the same process of inheritance, experimentation, variation, selection of variants best adapted to the conditions of life, and ruthless culling of inferior variants. Although it takes a very long time, evolution achieves astonishing results. Evolution proceeds through the creation of new variants and new species, which split off from existing forms of life, and through the extinction of less adapted species.

Driving the whole process are genes with similar chemical structures but varying genetic messages. As we saw in Chapter 2, genes are replicators who collaborate with each other to find vehicles—animals and plants—that can help the genes survive and reproduce. We also saw that our species is unique in having devised "memes," cultural transmission in the form of languages, art, architecture, science, traditions, and ways of doing things, including business enterprise. Memes may offer a way of controlling our genes and creating a new type of evolution.

We also examined the theory of business genes. The most fundamental unit of value in business, similar to DNA, is a unit of useful economic information. This is a meme, but to distinguish it from nonbusiness memes we called it a "business gene." Business genes include basic technologies, ideas, products, skills, and individual executives and entrepreneurs. To achieve their purposes, they combine with many other business genes and find vehicles for their replication: more developed technologies, corporations large and small, markets, channels of distribution, and knowledge vehicles such as books, institutes, and university departments. As in the human process, business progress flows from experimentation, new combinations of business genes, the creation of new business genes, and a struggle for life between the business genes. Corporations are throwaway vehicles for the replication of ever better business genes.

Chapter 3 looked at the experiments of Soviet scientist G. F. Gause on small organisms. His "test-tube wars" demonstrated that with limited resources, organisms of the same species will compete to the death, but organisms of slightly different species will cooperate to survive. Gause also showed that if one species can invade another's territory without the invaded species being able to reciprocate, the former will become dominant. He further demonstrated that there was a difference between coexistence, where each species can invade the other, and bi-stability, where neither species can invade the other.

We concluded that business genes and corporations should differentiate themselves to survive. They should also find positions where they cannot be invaded by competitors, preferably positions where they can become dominant by invading a species that cannot retaliate.

We also considered the idea of ecological niches, unique ways of making a living in a specific place in the economy of nature. This reinforced the idea of specialization and differentiation being essential to prosperity.

In Chapter 4, we took a tour into evolutionary psychology and speculated that there is a profound mismatch between the inclinations of our genes and the imperatives of modern business life. Our genes are still geared up for life in the Stone Age, before the invention of agriculture and commerce. Life on the savannah was hard and frequently threatened. Stone Age man survived by giving emotion precedence over reason, making quick judgments on first impressions, and banding together in small clans up to a maximum of one hundred fifty people; by being friendly, specializing, and cooperating within the clan, and by breast-beating; by conforming and herding, being willing to fight other clans, avoiding risk whenever there was not a direct threat to life, and panicking when there was.

While some of these traits—such as a propensity to demonstrate friendliness and work constructively in teams—are useful for modern business, most of them are not. Evolutionary psychology helps to explain the pathology of many large organizations, where there is often a tension between the formal organization and the informal, the proliferation of informal pecking orders, an unhealthy preference for hierarchy, and an unwillingness to take responsibility; the rejection of negative feedback, a socialistic attitude to rewards, bickering between different departments, hostility to outsiders within and beyond the corporation, herding and conformism within it; the suppression of conflict and heresy, the tendency to be unrealistically optimistic, the fear of risk, and hysteria when things go wrong.

We posited two remedies for the mismatch between neolithic genes and modern corporate life. One is to adapt our behavior: to correct for our natural biases, to cool our emotions, to accept criticism, conflict, and contrary views. We should reason to make realistic projections and collaborate with out-groups as intensely as with the in-group. We must learn to take more risk than we want, avoid seeking status or sucking up to it, and behave rationally under pressure. Our other option is to adapt corporate life to our genes, and eschew organizations of more than one hundred fifty people.

Finally, Chapter 5 examined the evolution of human cooperation. Humans have learned to cooperate and live in large, interrelated groups, societies of ever greater differentiation and complexity, linked by business relationships and trade. At the root of this process are business genes—customs, ideas, information, technology, and skills that can be passed on from one human to another.

We saw that competition and cooperation were two sides of the same coin, comprising the links between business genes and their vehicles. Wealth can be created by mediating the selfishness of each business gene and individual, and using that selfishness to create collective advantage, more wealth, and progress. We also saw that cooperation is the more basic process, pre-dating competition and requiring more conscious volition. Progress requires ever greater degrees of cooperation among people willing to take a long-term view of the value of collaboration: cooperators who look beyond individual transactions to an ongoing stream of transactions facilitated by trust and relationships.

In Part Two, we leave biology and turn to physics in an attempt to understand another dimension of the natural laws around us: the properties and interactions of matter and energy.

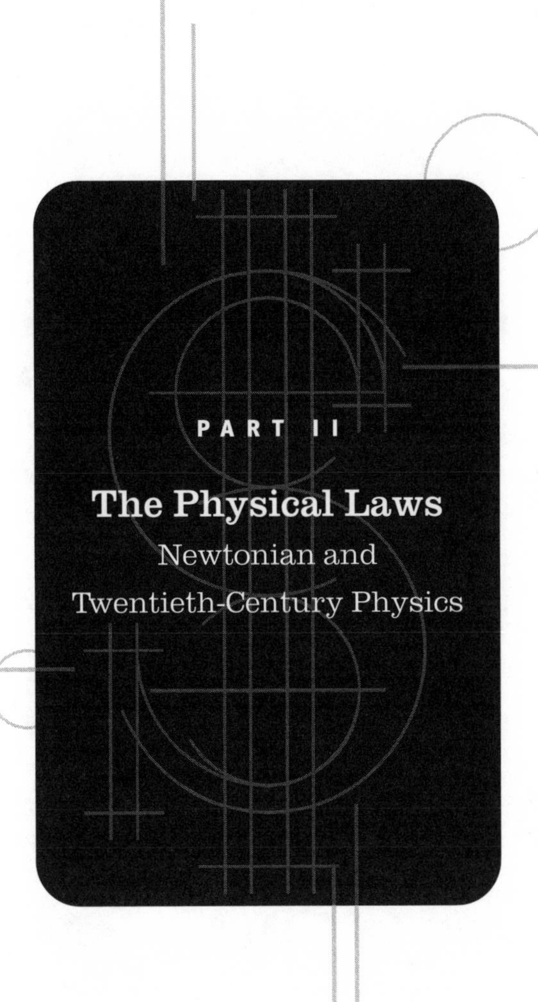

PART II

The Physical Laws

Newtonian and Twentieth-Century Physics

Newton's Impact

Newton's Laws of Motion and Gravity

Nature and Nature's laws
lay hid in night
God said, "Let Newton be,"
and all was light.
ALEXANDER POPE

Sir Isaac Newton (1643–1727)[1] proved that there are some basic, universal laws, identifiable by precise mathematical relationships, that govern all physical movements on the planet. Thanks to our understanding of Newton's three *Laws of Motion* and his *Law of Universal Gravitation,* we can predict what will happen if we put a ship on the sea or roll a penny down a slide, and this knowledge has allowed us to build bridges, fly planes, and send men and women into space.

Newton's *Philosophiae Naturalis Principia Mathematica* was published (in Latin) in 1687. In it he posited three laws of motion:

LAW I *Every body continues in a state of rest, or of uniform motion in a straight line, unless it is compelled to change that state by a force impressed upon it.*

LAW II *The change in motion is proportional to the motive force impressed: and is made in the direction of the straight line in which that force is impressed.*

LAW III *To every action there is always an opposite and equal reaction; or the mutual actions of two bodies are always equal, and directed to contrary parts.*

Newton's first law restates Galileo's law of inertia, that bodies remain at rest or in constant motion, except when moved by an outside disturbance.

The second law is that force (F) is directly proportional to the change in momentum that it generates. Twice as much force will cause twice as much change in an object's momentum. Newton provided an original definition of momentum—mass times velocity—where mass (m) is the "quantity of matter" in an object. Change in velocity is the same as acceleration (a). Hence Newton derives his famous formula: $F = ma$ (force equals mass times acceleration).

The third law of motion is Newton's most original. If similar objects collide, they bounce off each other with equal force. If an object's motion is disturbed (if its momentum changes), then the motion of another object must also be disturbed so that the "aggregate" momentum is unchanged. The second disturbance must be precisely equal to the first, but in an opposite direction.

From these three laws, and Galileo's law of uniform acceleration, Newton arrived at the concept of gravity. An object falls and its momentum increases as it approaches the ground. Newton's three laws say that some force must be responsible for acceleration, and this force must be constant if (as Galileo showed) acceleration is constant. Newton called this force "gravity." He concluded that the force of gravity on an object is constant and directly proportional to the mass of the object. Hence Newton's law of gravity (also known as his "inverse square rule") that *between any two bodies, the gravitational force is proportional to the product of their masses, and inversely proportional to the square of the distance between them.*

Incredibly, the same force that makes an apple fall from the tree is the same that holds the planets of our solar system in place. Newton's laws of gravity—together with the data and laws provided by astronomer Johannes Kepler—finally established that the earth revolves around the sun and not the other way around. Newton showed that the planets' movements around the sun fitted the equations of gravity, but required (for the calculations to work) slightly elliptical orbits around the sun. Planets try to "go straight," but gravity forces them into a curve. The orbits can be calculated if we know the mass of the planets and the distance (and hence the inverse square of the distance) between them.

Once the force of gravity is appreciated, the heavens no longer appear to move randomly or in a complex pattern, but like clockwork. Gravity bends the movement of planets and moons, and the extent of gravity is directly related to how close an object is to the sun or other force of gravity, and the relative mass of the object and the sun.

Newton synthesized centuries-worth of scientific insight, and in many ways he became a symbol for the new scientific perspective. In praising him extravagantly, contemporaries and later writers were really celebrating a new sense of intellectual coherence and liberty, in which Newton played a leading and well-supported role. Newton's economical theses on motion and gravity showed how a few simple rules, worked out from first principles and validated by mathematical proofs, could have universal application. We were suddenly allowed to believe that the world was predictable and controllable by scientists and engineers. This was deeply reassuring and inspiring, and remains so today even though we now know that Newtonian physics is incomplete and very slightly inaccurate.

It is common these days to point out that the "Newtonian," mechanical, and rational view of the world has huge and distorting gaps, and I'll address these later. But Newtonian tools and concepts pervade our lives—especially our business interactions. For example, the simple ideas of profitability and the power of comparing a few simple and universal numbers—return on sales, return on capital, and the internal rate of return on a project or investment. Would we be wealthier with or without the idea of budgets and the practice of reviewing them? Is it sensible, or just old-fashioned, to look for the few causes determining success or failure, to identify common characteristics, and to test our theories with numbers? And would we really be better off without the machine metaphor and the mechanical view of life, the universe, and everything?

Perhaps the reason that business writers find it more attractive to tear apart the rational, machine-based, analytical approach to business rather than to celebrate it is that there is little to add to the rational school. A long line of management thinkers, from Frederick Taylor to the Harvard Business School writers, culminating in the "microeconomic" analysis of business positions by Michael Porter, has mined this seam so well that there is apparently little more to say. Taylor's *The Principles of Scientific Management* came out in 1913, and Porter's ground-breaking *Competitive Strategy* in 1980. Between these two dates, virtually everything of a Newtonian and rationalist nature that could be said about business relationships and what determines profitability was said, and said well.

The golden age of Newtonian business analysis may be over, but in my view one key insight has been insufficiently appreciated, and another overlooked altogether.

Action and Reaction

Newton said that action and reaction are equal and opposite. Loosely interpreted, this means that any powerful development, whether a school of thought, a new technology, or a new market, will bring in its wake an equally significant opposite development. We can see this clearly in the realm of ideas or proposals for organizing society: capitalism produces socialism, the experience of trying to make socialism work produces a neocapitalist revival, and the primacy of global free markets will doubtless produce another powerful backlash. I've drawn the same parallel to business ideas: because the rationalist, Newtonian school of business thinking has been so powerful, it has conjured into existence an opposite, systems-based school. Ideas and actions break inertia, and, once inertia is broken, a strong reaction inevitably follows.

Applied to business and markets, this simple insight is an almost infallible guide to what is around the corner. Never mind the important new market, think about the one after that, its opposite. Thus Henry Ford standardized and mass produced the modern car, but then the market craved variety, so General Motors produced a range of different models, each one tailored to fit individual customers' needs or images. Once there is a mass market in anything, be it a product or a service, there is a demand for the opposite: niche markets tailored to particular customer groups.

The beauty of the dynamic is that it works both ways. Once there are expensive luxury products, there is a demand for a stripped-down economy version. As soon as luxury hotels, planes, and boats become the norm, then mass tourism will emerge. Then, once package tours are prevalent the market for something superior and intimate will reemerge on a large scale. Once, a common complaint among businesses was that constant traveling was an expensive nuisance, so videoconferencing and the Internet were substituted. Now people are rediscovering the virtues of face-to-face communication.

New technology and markets often fail to have the drastic impact on their predecessors that is confidently predicted. Personal computers breed prolifically, and gurus pontificate on the "paperless office," yet paper and photocopying persist. The phone, the fax, the Internet, and videoconferencing do not stop meetings or travel or book reading.

The Gravity of Competition

There is one direct parallel between Newton's laws of motion and the nature of business that has been overlooked: the one between gravity and competition. I believe I can establish that this has definite metaphorical and conceptual value. It may even be possible, in the fairly near future, to use Newton's principles to establish a quantitative (inverse) correlation between your exposure to the largest competitor in your arena and the return on capital earned by your business. Let me first explain the concept, using the metaphor of gravity.

Competition is the economic equivalent of gravity. Just as gravity depresses objects and stops stars from moving in a straight line, so competition depresses returns on capital. "Margin gravity" depresses managers and investors. The extent of margin gravity is proportional to the proximity and power of competitors. Weak gravity indicates distant or tangential competitors. Strong gravity implies close, in-your-face challengers.

Black Holes

A "black hole" is formed when a huge, heavy star burns up all its fuel and collapses so far into itself that nothing can escape from it. No light, nor any other kind of signal, can emerge. Black holes are only created by a very heavy star, one about three to six times heavier than the sun, according to Einstein's theory of general relativity. When such an enormous star dies, a black hole collapses all the space around it. The resultant mega-gravity curves the adjacent space to a fantastic degree. The gravitational pull approaches infinity.

The metaphorical business "black hole" exists when competition is so intense and head to head that margin gravity approaches infinity. No profits or positive cash flow can escape from such a black hole. Industries with black holes include textiles, steel, airlines, memory chips and other basic semiconductors, and CD-ROMs.

Competition-free Zones

There are places that are free, or virtually free, from margin gravity: spaces where competition does not operate, where margins are limited not by competition, but by what customers can afford and by the distant hiss of competition from all other products and services clamoring for the customer's wallet. These noncompetitive spaces, where gravity doesn't work, are the most desirable places in the economic universe because margins can be extremely high and returns on capital astronomical.

Corporate Gravity

What can stop your firm from moving forward in a straight line and achieving its business plan are competitors. The force of competition is a function of two things: the relative size (or, more precisely, mass) of your most important competitor, and your distance from that company. This means that a small and underresourced but very adjacent competitor may cause you more trouble than a huge, rich, and successful corporation that is not fully committed to your markets.

What Is Size?

"Size" (or mass) refers to the resources that a competitor can devote to a market. It implies profitability, skill, and fitness to serve customers rather than size in revenues. Size can also refer to the strength of a balance sheet, ability to get new capital, a firm's price/earnings ratio, and the strength of its reputation, brands, and relationships. Though we can't measure these aspects of "size" quantitatively, a good proxy may be a concept that has been used in business since it was invented around 1970 by the Boston Consulting Group: Relative market share (RMS), your revenues in the business segment divided by the revenues of your largest competitor. If this number is over 1.0, it implies that you are the segment leader; if less than 1.0, that you are smaller than the leader; if exactly 1.0, that you are coleader with one or more rivals of the same size.

What Is Distance?

"Distance" is the extent to which the competitor is close to your own customers. A distant competitor is one whose focus is elsewhere. A close competitor is one that has the same target market and the same approach toward reaching customers as you do.

Distance can usefully be envisioned as a series of ever larger squares, with the corners being:

- Customer type
- Product type
- Geography
- Type of value-added provided (e.g., research and development, production, distribution, marketing, sales), either an integrated operation or a specialist by stage of value added.

If you and a competitor are serving the same type of customer with the same type of product in the same geographic area, and providing exactly the same type of value added, there is virtually no distance between you and the other company. You are on top of each other. The converse also applies: the distance is huge if the customers, products, geographic markets, and type of value added are all different. A crude scoring system to calculate distance is to score any business segment on these four dimensions as follows:

1 = identical or very similar

2 = adjacent, close, similar but with a few differences

3 = neither very close nor very distant, considerable overlap

4 = not very similar or close but some overlap

5 = distant, dissimilar, fundamentally not the same

For example, Coca-Cola and Pepsi-Cola would score 1. Dr. Pepper and Pepsi-Cola would score 2. A snack product like Pringles and Coca-Cola would score 3, because they are not direct competitors but may well compete with each other as impulse purchases. A slow bus service and a taxicab might score a 4, since they would be occasional substitutes for each other. The bus service would not compete at all with an international flight, and so would score a 5.

You can then calculate distance on a scale of 1 to 625 by multiplying the four numbers (the scores on the four dimensions). For example, competing with the same customer type and product in an adjacent geographic area but with a very different value-added focus would produce a score of $1 \times 1 \times 2 \times 5 = 10$. A score of 8 or below indicates dangerous proximity, and anything below 20 indicates close competition.

After making the calculation, your nearest competitor may not be the one you first thought of. In this case, you'll need to calculate the "size" of the competitor you now think is closest. Remember also that the calculations shouldn't be made at the overall corporate level, but within each separate business segment, accounting for the differences in competitors, customers, profitability, or strategy.

Measuring Corporate Gravity

Newtonian theory states that the closer you are to a large object, the stronger is gravity's pull. The effect of gravity on a moving object can be precisely measured if you know the mass of the object and its distance.

In the corporate world, the gravity of competition is strong if you are close to a "larger" competitor. But what is the gravity itself? It is not, demonstrably, the ability to serve customers well. This is unaffected by close, head-to-head competition. Indeed, from the customers' viewpoint, close competition is usually beneficial. Instead, the "gravity" is the margin that can be earned by each corporation. What depresses margins is the gravity of competition.

To enjoy high margins, you must be a long way away from competent competitors. To avoid margin gravity, you must avoid close competitors, whether large or small, *regardless of whether you are larger than they are.* If you are larger than they are, you will hurt them more than they will hurt you, but you will still be hurt. Margin gravity gets increasingly serious as a function of the "size" (competence and resources) and "distance" (similarity of target market and method of serving it) of competitors.

Margin Gravity Is Not Linear

In Newtonian astronomy, what matters in calculating orbits is the mass of the objects and the inverse square of the distance between them. It is a logarithmic rather than a linear relationship. The same is likely to apply to the gravity of competition. We may be fairly confident that, if we can increase the distance between our firm and its most important competitor, or if we can increase our relative size, the impact on profits will be more than linear. This makes sense intuitively, because margin gravity should decrease more than proportionately to an increase in distance or a decrease in the relative size of the competitor. But is there any quantitative, empirical support for this hypothesis?

It so happens that there is. In the 1980s, the consulting firm of which I was a cofounder measured the relationship between return on capital employed (ROCE) and relative market share (RMS) for its clients in many thousands of business segments in many different countries. We found that there was a strong correlation between high relative market share and high profitability. We also found—and this is the key point for margin gravity—that *the relationship was more than linear.* A 10 percent improvement in relative market share produced a greater than 10 percent increase in profitability. It followed that the greatest benefit in profit terms usually came from increasing market share in those markets where the client was already very strong. This is very similar to the concept of "increasing returns to scale" promulgated by economist Brian Arthur at about the same time.[2] If profitability increases more than proportionately as market share increases, it should also increase more than proportionately as the distance from competitors increases.

Similarly, when you move further away from competitors, returns should increase more than proportionately to the distance moved.

How Do You Increase Your Size Relative to Your Main Competitors?

One obvious answer is to increase your relative market share. Your sales have to increase faster than the competitor's, either by finding new customers or selling more to existing ones at a rate faster than your rival. You could also increase your relative rate of retaining the customers you already have.

But, as we've seen, there is more to "size" than the simple definition of relative market share. "Size" also means increasing your ability to serve customers, your reputation, and your financial resources. These are what underpin the sales: commitment to the market, understanding of it, and ability to court popularity among customers through better products or service, faster delivery, superior marketing, or lower prices.

Take a simple market like home-delivery pizza. Before Domino's Pizza became the dominant supplier of take-home pizza, the market was fragmented into a very large number of small players. Then Domino's did something different. They invented the promise of "guaranteed home delivery within thirty minutes," something that no one had been able to offer before. It was made possible by use of a special envelope to keep the pizza hot, plus a network of motivated delivery personnel. Now the Domino's network is distinguished by being denser and bigger than that of all its competitors.

The same thing happened with the courier market. Business student Fred Smith earned a C from his professor for his paper proposing guaranteed overnight delivery of documents. Impossible, snorted the prof. But Fred Smith founded FedEx and proved that overnight delivery was feasible. He did something different from his competitors and then defended it; even today, he says, "The main difference between us and our competitors is that we have more capacity to track, trace, and control items in the system."

How Do You Increase Your Distance from Your Main Competitor?

In principle, it's simple. Increase the differences in your stages of value added and in the customer types, product types, and geographic regions that you serve.

The only caveat is that moving away from one competitor may bring you closer to another. If you are much larger than the new nearest competitor (or, more precisely, if your relative market share versus the new competitor is higher than it was against the previous closest competitor), this may not matter. But if the new main closest rival is larger in the relevant segment than the old one, you will have taken a step backwards. Therefore you need to juggle the possibilities until you can find a way of both increasing your distance from the nearest competitor and increasing your relative size versus that company.

Escaping Corporate Gravity

There are clear and important lessons to be learned from the concept of corporate gravity:

- The best way to avoid being thrown off course is to avoid competitors.
- Competitors exert downward pressure on margins—that is, margin gravity—according to their relative "size" and "distance."
- Resources should be concentrated in segments that exist or can be created where competitors are as far away and as insignificant as possible.
- "Competition-free zones" are not subject to significant margin gravity. The only thing that distinguishes them from normal business segments is the absence of relevant competition. The customers may be the same as in other business segments. The technology may be the same. The suppliers may be the same. The executives may be of the same ilk. But in competition-free zones, the laws of economics and cosmology are light years apart from the laws in normal business. The value of these zones is truly astronomical. Everyone's goal in business should be to create and maintain competition-free zones.
- In competition-free zones, the constraint on margin is not direct competition. It may not even be the wish to deter potential competition, or avoid the wrath of regulators. The

real economic constraint is simply the size of the market and its price sensitivity. Margins should find the level at which the value of the future stream of earnings is optimized. This may be difficult or impossible to calculate, but returns may be extremely high. The size of the future market may be maximized by having *higher* rather than lower margins, if a chunky portion of the margin is then reinvested in improving the product and service and in marketing it more effectively.

- In normal competitive markets, don't expect any action or innovation to be ignored by the competition. Work out in advance your reaction to your competitor's reaction—and to subsequent reactions.
- Improvements that anyone can copy—or that even only one competitor can copy—will benefit customers, but not your firm or its investors.
- All energy should be devoted to improvements and innovations that increase your distance from significant competitors. This should not be thought of in the conventional terms of having a competitive lead.
- A lead is something that connects two parties. You shouldn't be seeking a lead. You should be seeking to escape from the gravitational pull of competitors. An ever-growing distance from competitors is easier to achieve than an ever-growing lead over them, and also much more valuable. To gain a lead, you do things better. To put distance between you and them, you go in a different direction—preferably the *opposite* direction to theirs.

How to Use the Natural Laws

- ***Escape from the gravity of competition.*** Systematically increase the distance between yourself and competitors, focusing on your type of value added, product type, customer type, and geographic markets served. Work out how you can do things differently from your closest large competitor in order to increase the distance between you.

- ***Where you are already the leader, increase your relative size and the degree of difference between yourself and all significant rivals.***
- ***Focus all your energies, cash, and people on business segments where you are already large and a long way distant from any competitor,*** or where you can reach this state.

7 Farewell, Clockwork Universe

Relativity

> *No one can recall without a thrill his first encounter with Einstein's Carollian world where space-time is curved, a fourth dimension, and honest witnesses blithely disagree on the most elementary questions of what happened when and where.*
>
> STEPHEN HAWKING

The great clockwork universe of Isaac Newton—the rational, mechanical world where causes and effects can be calculated and where our experiences are based on solid reality—is the world we think we inhabit. Yet the twentieth century introduced a new form of physics demonstrating that, at least in the world of very small and "fundamental" matter, the world is a great deal more unpredictable and complex than Newton ever knew.

Newton and his successors living before the twentieth century believed in absolute space and time, and in our ability to measure and control all aspects of the machine called the universe. It was a beautiful dream: science leading us toward the complete control of everything, including, Freud added, ourselves. Yet the dream was shattered, first by Albert Einstein's insights into relativity, and second, and even more disturbingly, by

Niels Bohr and the other great discoverers of quantum physics. In this new world, nothing is fundamentally real, measurable, or controllable. Nothing is what it seems.

We businesspeople still live in the Newtonian world. It works for us. If we didn't believe that our actions could lead to positive results, if we stopped measuring cause and effect, threw away our budgets and financial statements, or stopped quantifying the effects on profits of competition and customer retention, we'd likely be highly unsuccessful at what we do.

I'm not going to ask you to throw away the habits of a lifetime, your Newtonian, mechanical business models. They have great value. In the last chapter I asked you to hone those models, to understand the impact of competition on profits in a much more rigorous, Newtonian way. But we're about to see that this is only part of the picture. There are things that we cannot control or even understand through Newtonian thinking. For example, we think of "organizations" in a classic Newtonian way, and we deceive ourselves into thinking that we can easily control and "organize" them. Relativity and quantum physics add a whole set of new, fresh, and liberating insights into life and business.

Read on—and you'll find that the world you thought you knew is not the world that you *really* inhabit.

Einstein's Special and General Theories of Relativity

Albert Einstein (1879–1955) was the first scientist to establish that there were fundamental truths about the physical universe that had eluded Isaac Newton. Einstein's theories of relativity provided a new basis for understanding space, mass, and energy. The special theory came first, in 1905, showing how atomic and subatomic particles work. The general theory, published in 1916, rested on Einstein's insight that acceleration is precisely the same as gravity, and made modern cosmology possible. Without Einstein's theories we would not have transistors, electron microscopes, photoelectric cells, computers, nuclear bombs, or nuclear power.

The Warping of Time and Space

Relativity, particularly the general theory, is very hard even for physicists to understand, so I am not going to try to describe it. Instead, I'll note some of the most important details of Einstein's thinking:[1]

- Light is a stream of particles whose energy can be calculated (the discovery of "Planck's constant" later proved this point). These measured particles of light came to be called "photons."

- The special theory of relativity contradicts our intuitive views of time and space. Einstein says that nothing can travel faster than the speed of light and that light's speed does not change in tandem with the velocity of the observer. Yet it follows that no two observers going at different speeds will agree precisely when an event occurs. Time and space, therefore, are not fixed, absolute quantities. It also follows from the special theory that *where* an observer is determines *when* he or she thinks something has happened. To say, "This happened at this time and this place," is never an absolute statement.

- The special theory can be applied, as Newtonian physical laws could not, to predict what happens at the subatomic level. As Einstein said, "the mass of a body is a measure of its energy-content." Hence his brilliant equation, $E = mc^2$, where mass (m) is expressed as an amount of energy (E) when multiplied by the square of the speed of light (c). (The special theory was very helpful in elaborating quantum theory, which arrived courtesy of Max Planck and Niels Bohr in the early years of the twentieth century).

- The general theory addresses gravity and corrects Newtonian physics. It extends the special theory to take in systems that are accelerating, like bodies in space. As a result of the general theory, therefore, we enjoy all the insights from twentieth-century cosmology, including the expanding universe and black holes.

- Einstein envisioned someone falling inside a plummeting elevator that had broken its cables: the person would free-fall inside the lift, just as astronauts in orbit around the earth feel weightless because they are "falling" toward it. Einstein posited that gravitational force and the force of something that is accelerating are indistinguishable. In other words, there is no way to tell the difference between gravity and acceleration, so there is no real difference between them. Gravity is not, as was previously imagined, the force by which all objects are attracted to each other. Rather, gravitation is the warping of space and time by physical mass. Space is curved, and the elliptical orbits of the planets can be calculated precisely using the general theory of relativity.
- It follows from the general theory that time is not independent of space. Time looks and acts like a fourth spatial dimension, and can be warped by gravity. Given that the speed of light is a constant, time and space become a united frame of reference. Einstein refers to events in a four-dimensional "space-time continuum."
- Einstein eventually questioned whether "space" and "time" were realities of nature rather than being psychological effects. If the shape of "space-time" depends on gravity—requiring material bodies—space and time would be meaningless without bodies. Einstein therefore stated:

> It was formerly believed that if all material things disappeared out of the universe, time and space would be left. According to the relativity theory, however, time and space disappear together with the things.

Time as Part of the Physical Universe

Einstein's greatest legacy is probably his elevation of space and time to tangible things on which we can experiment. Time, he says, is itself part of the physical universe: it is relative, not absolute. So instead of the three dimensions of space, we should think of the four dimensions of space-time, time being the fourth. Space and time can be changed depending on how fast you travel and how much gravity you experience. Space and time, energy and mass—these are linked together. When the sun shines, it is converting some of its mass into energy and light: it is a nuclear reactor. Einstein's insights led us to the development of nuclear power and nuclear bombs. His reaction to Hiroshima? "If I had known they were going to do this, I would have become a shoemaker."

Can Relativity Be Applied to Business?

Einstein's theories are difficult enough to apply within the context of science. Can they be applied to business? In a strict sense, the honest answer is no. But ask instead the question: Have Einstein's theories of relativity usefully influenced our modern world-view of life and truth? The answer, surely, is yes. So, as long as we acknowledge that there are no Einsteinian equations to support our arguments, and that we are not strictly applying relativity theories, I think that it is fair to suggest that there are two ideas, broadly derived from relativity, that are extremely instructive, namely:

- Time is not a separate dimension in business; rather, it is integral to competitive advantage.
- We need a "relative," not absolute, view of our world, including our business world.

Time: At the Heart of Competitive Advantage

Einstein incorporated time into the physical universe. Time, he said, was not "other," an objective external dimension against which everything else should be measured. Instead, time and space were linked together as dynamic things on which we can experiment. Physicists and astronomers today often talk about "space-time" as one concept.

A common phrase born in the nineteenth century is that "time is money." In other words, time is intimately bound up in the process of production and can substitute for, or be substituted for, monetary value. Today we might add that "time is product" and "time is service." The same product or service offered in less time (or more) is not the same product or service; it is different and better (or worse). A new product or generation of improved product that is offered to customers after a one-year gap, rather than the previous two years, accelerates the value delivery to customers.

A major challenge for any business is to integrate time into the product or service you are offering. The objective is to deliver the product or service faster than you used to and faster than your rivals. There are various techniques for doing this—we'll come to a few in a moment—but the biggest obstacle and opportunity is mental. We think about time as external, as another dimension, even as the enemy. We do not, but should, think about "product-time" or "service-time" as internal, part of something that we offer, a crucial dimension that is intrinsic to our way of doing business.

The first mental challenge, therefore, is: *think of time as a friend, a resource, a colleague, and as part of the value you offer customers.* This really is a challenge. We're used to thinking of time as a constraint or an unwelcome intruder. In the words of Andrew Marvell's great poem:

But at my back I always hear
Time's wingèd chariot hurrying near.[2]

This is the wrong attitude, yet we should realize how deeply it is woven into the fabric of our thought.

Time Is Abundant, Time Is Available

How can we change our mental map of time? Here are a couple of related thoughts that are profoundly and demonstrably true, and that invalidate our usual view of limited time. First, *there is no shortage of time;* rather, we are positively awash with it. I may need some time (which we enjoy in abundance!) to persuade you of this, so I will pass swiftly on to point two: *very little of what a firm (and by inference, an executive) does adds a great deal of value to customers.* Most of the value that is added comes in short bursts, oases of productivity, surrounded by a desert of low-value processes.

This second point has actually been proved quantitatively by a very large number of surveys, especially those associated in the late 1980s and the 1990s with the techniques of time-based competition and reengineering (also known as business process reengineering, or BPR). I don't want to go into detail because I'd rather you focus on the principle, on your mental map, on how you think about business. But Mark Blaxill and Tom Hout of the Boston Consulting Group sum up their evidence from a huge amount of client work as follows:

> Typically, less than 10 percent of the total time devoted to any work in an organization is truly value-added. The rest is wasted because of unnecessary steps or unbalanced operations.[3]

What generally happens is that the high-value work takes a small amount of time, but most of the time needed for a product or service to be produced is time spent waiting, usually for some other executive or part of the organization (and occasionally customers themselves) to respond or take action. Delays come from procedural constraints (that always can be eliminated), quality problems (ditto), and structural difficulties, (fixable by redirecting the flow of work; that is, by changing the structure). Very rarely are firms' structures designed to speed the product or service to the customer. When they are, there are nearly always large cost and quality improvement by-products.

So let's come back to the first point: time is plentiful. I know this sounds like nonsense. We're all stressed, we're all busy, we're all trying to "manage" our time better, to dole out such a scarce resource as parsimoniously as possible. Yet herein lies the problem, and the answer.

Think for a moment. *If only 10 percent of our time is really used to great effect, it follows that 90 percent isn't, and therefore this time is available for high-value activity.* If we take the numbers literally, we could double our high-value activity and still have 70 percent of our time left to waste. This goes both for individuals and for the corporations in which we work. So we shouldn't be worried about shortage of time; this is an illusion. We don't need to speed up. What we need to do is stop spending our time in low-quality, low-output ways.[4]

Integrating Time into Your Product and Service

Einstein's challenge is this: think of time, or the reduction of time, as part of what you offer customers. Think product-time. Think service-time. It's all part of the same thing. Never think "product" or "service" independent of "time." Time is a key dimension that must be embraced to achieve success.

See if you can live this concept for an hour, for a day. It really is a revolution in the way we think. If you're wasting your own time and that of the customer, there is a wide buffer zone of improvement available, not from speeding up what you do now, but from only doing things that are important to the customer and from organizing around the customer.

Just a few hints about how to achieve this:

- Measure the time it takes to do things for customers. The time from taking an order to fulfilling it is the most important "thing." But there are others. For example, evaluate the time it takes to introduce a new product or service; to provide after-sales service and respond to questions or complaints; to incorporate an important customer suggestion into a product or service; and so on.

- Find out the dimensions of time and time saving that are most important to customers. Then find a way of delivering on these aspects two to three times faster than you have done historically, and two to three times faster than your fastest rival.

- Identify separately the procedural, quality, and structural issues that are wasting time.

- Map out the process of delivering the product or service to the customer, and where the time is being used. Identify gaps that interrupt the flow and eliminate them.
- When you have improved your delivery time to customers by two to three times, focus your marketing and selling effort on selling more to your existing customers, for whom the benefit of faster delivery and greater responsiveness is greatest, and on finding new customers who will also value the time benefit significantly more than other customers.
- Measure customer retention—that is, the proportion of customers who repeat purchase from you. Ensure that you raise the customer retention percentage each year, especially the retention of your most valuable and profitable customers. Use your time advantage to further improve the customer retention.

A Relative World View

Back in 1905, while explaining what became known as the special theory of relativity, Einstein took the first step—later steps coming courtesy of quantum theory, to a much greater extent than Einstein liked—toward undermining our view that anything is absolute and fundamental. Einstein said that the speed of light was a constant. It follows that if two different observers are traveling at different speeds, they won't agree on the precise time that anything happened. Practically, the differences are very small indeed. But the mold of absolute measurement and absolute reality was broken, once and for all, by Einstein's insight.

You can see the difference between the seventeenth- to nineteenth-century view and the twentieth-century view almost everywhere: in science, in literature, in popular songs, in art. The old view was one of certainty, predictability, and absolute confidence. The heritage bequeathed by the twentieth century is uncertainty, unpredictability, and skepticism. I said that you can see this *almost* everywhere. The most important exception is business, where the world view hasn't really changed at all.

Gödel's Incompleteness Theorem

The relativist gestalt was powerfully reinforced in 1931 by Kurt Gödel's incompleteness theorem, one of the twentieth century's most sublime and devastating pieces of logic.

Gödel may quite possibly have been the most eccentric of top twentieth-century scientists, easily trumping his friend Einstein. After working in Vienna beginning in 1924, Gödel fled to Princeton in 1938. The attempt to secure him American citizenship barely survived his long and pedantic exposition of the many grave flaws in the U.S. Constitution. He eventually starved himself to death, convinced that his food was being poisoned.

Gödel's incompleteness theorem shattered the dreams of mathematicians by demonstrating that, even in a very simple system like arithmetic, statements could be written down that could neither be proved nor disproved within the rules of that system. Any consistent numerical system generates formulas—like "a number is equal to itself" or "zero is a number"—that cannot be proved, except by importing axioms from outside the system.

Gödel's proof was not confined to mathematics. Reality, he demonstrated, is a construct, not a given. One implication is that the very process of thinking adds to what we think about . . . so the process can never be completed. No finite language or system can capture all truth.

So Gödel's theorem really takes the implications of Einstein's theories of relativity one stage further: we can dismiss the possibility of absolute truth. (Incidentally, in 1949 Gödel solved Einstein's general relativity equations in such a way that the entire universe was rotating, and time travel entirely feasible. It is unlikely, however, that Gödel's solution is correct, since his universe was not expanding and ours almost certainly is.)

Relativity in Business

Relativity and the absence of absolute truth should be a central tenet in business. Just to mention some of the important relativities:

- The customer's perspective will always be different from the supplier's. Often the differences are large. During the two decades when I was a consultant, I never found that the client's view of what his customers wanted entirely matched the customers' view. The only antidote is to keep asking the customers what they want and how well you and your main competitors are performing in each desired dimension. And to listen to what the customers say. And then to act on it. This is 80 percent of what good business is about, and very few people do it well.
- Your firm's perspective on what customers want will always be different from the customer's perspective (this is the inverse of the first point) and—here is the rub—it will be wrong in proportion to the distance of the executive from the customer front line.

This is a problem, because decisions tend to be made well away from the customer front line, in the chief executive's suite or the board room. They are meant to benefit the customer, but given the distance and the differences in perspective, it is a safe bet that the decisions won't achieve the desired effect. There are two remedies.

One is to move the decisions closer to the customer, ideally to have the decisions made by the people who deal with customers daily, or even by the customers themselves. These don't include decisions on issues such as pricing, where the customer's interests conflict with the supplier's. I mean decisions on new products, on how production and service are organized, and on everything to do with customer value except pricing and margin decisions.

The other remedy is to ensure that the decision makers, especially the chief executive, are in daily contact with customers.

In my experience the first remedy, although radical, is more realistic than the second. Humorist Dave Barry makes the point tellingly:

> My theory is that the most hated group in any large company is the customers. They don't know about company procedures or anything about what you do, which drives you crazy! At the same time, your bosses, who are idiots who don't have to talk to customers, tell you day in and day out that the most important person in the world is the customer.[5]

- There is no absolute product quality; it is all perception. The customer's view about product quality is unlikely to be the same as yours. In fact, customers may not care very much about quality. Even if they do, other things may be confused with quality or imputed to quality. A terrific brand, brilliant advertising, stunning service, fast delivery, or plain and simple market leadership—all these may be confused with quality.

  Clearly, some quality differences are so marked as to be indisputable. A Cartier watch is better quality than a Swatch, a Mont Blanc pen is superior quality to a Bic ballpoint. But when products are more similar, perceptions of quality may be more important than objective differences. Are McDonald's burgers really better than those from Burger King? Is a Coke better than a Pepsi? Is an Agatha Christie murder story better than one from Patricia Highsmith?

  Remember that quality is a means to an end, not an end in itself. Quality is what the customer likes. But if your customers don't value quality, apply your effort towards something else that they want more.

- Your main competitor's perspective will not be the same as your own. Don't imagine that your rival will think like you or even interpret the same data the way that you do. Try to get inside his head. If this is impossible, just observe what he does and draw inferences about how his world view is different from yours.

The Medium Is the Message

A final, important "relativist" insight comes from Marshall McLuhan, English professor turned media guru. In his groundbreaking 1964 book, *Understanding Media: The Extensions of Man,* he writes:

> In a culture like ours, long accustomed to splitting and dividing things as means of control, it is sometimes a bit of a shock to be reminded that, in operational and practical fact, the medium is the message . . . the personal and social consequences of any medium—that is, of any extension of ourselves—result from the new scale that is introduced into our affairs by each extension of ourselves, or by any new technology.[6]

What McLuhan means is that media are not neutral: they have their own "message" and effects, quite independent of content, and often more important than the specific content. The development of the printing press and printed books, for example, had profound consequences. People no longer had to go to church to read the Bible nor rely on a priest to interpret it for them. They could read it themselves and develop their own interpretation. Therefore Protestantism and individualism are linked together because of a change in the "medium"—the advent of mass-produced, cheaper books. The medium, in this case, was more important than the message.

When television arrived it had an enormous social impact, quite independent of the content of broadcasting. The medium itself elevated visual impact, downgraded thought, and collapsed time and space by bringing centuries of history and news from around the world into everyone's living room. TV is a "cool" medium in that it cools down its content, taking the edge off bloody conflict and splicing it with hip Levi's commercials. TV is a one-way medium that gives enormous power to image makers and broadcasters, and arguably (to my mind, at least) reversed a century of progress in widening and deepening the intellectual powers of ordinary people. The content can be excellent and intellectual, but the passive nature of traditional television viewing and the inherent preference given to image and emotion over substance and reason corrode thought and creativity. The medium is the message.

The Internet as New Medium and New Message

What's great about media, however, is that they don't stand still. Cheap telecommunications, a large fax network, and, above all, the Internet are going to transform society at least as profoundly as television, but much more constructively. The Internet is a rich medium that connects individuals to other individuals, businesses to each other, and individuals to businesses.

Unlike TV, which was biased toward the "center" of society and was very much *de haut en bas,* the Internet shifts power to individuals and consumers, away from governments, image makers, élites, and big business. The Internet favors individual thought and action. It gives power to entrepreneurs and "insurgent" businesses, and takes power away from established corporations with physical assets and "legacy mindsets."[7]

Previous media revolutions had a significant impact on business—television promoted mass marketing and increased the need for consumer goods on a global scale—but they had even more impact on society as a whole. The Internet will have an important effect on society, but may well change business to an even greater extent. Here the medium really is the message. Most of us in business have already learned that it is a mistake to think about the Internet primarily as a channel of distribution; it has changed the nature of business and the specifics of competition in business in a much more radical way. Those who have grasped the enormity of the change will have an enormous advantage over those who have not.[8]

How to Use the Natural Laws

- ***Think service-time.*** Dramatically reduce the time you take to deliver products and services to your customers. Think not of products and time, but product-time; not of service and time, but service-time.

- ***Realize that customers' and competitors' perspectives will always be different from your own.*** Struggle to understand their viewpoints. Influence the customer's view by staying close to the customer front line, molding customer perception even as it is being formed. Immerse yourself in your market. Define it. Change it.

- ***Understand how the Internet can change the "message"***—the commercial reality—for your industry, your business, and your career. Find ways to deliver far more rich and individualized value to more customers at lower cost and greater speed. Manipulating the Internet to expand your reach is vital to the survival of your business.

8 The Triumph of Twentieth-Century Science

Quantum Mechanics

Quantum mechanics surpasses any other conceptual breakthrough in the breadth of its scientific ramifications, and in the jolt its counterintuitive consequences gave to our view of nature; the micro-world is fully as strange as the cosmos.

PROFESSOR SIR MARTIN REES, the U.K.'s Astronomer Royal

The opposite of a trivial truth is plainly false. The opposite of a great truth is also true.

NIELS BOHR

Quantum mechanics (also known as quantum physics or quantum theory) is the jewel in the crown of twentieth-century science, the most majestic triumph of insight and intellect. Quantum theory shows how the universe, at its most fundamental level, *really* works—and its revelations can be somewhat unnerving to those more comfortable envisioning a predictable universe as described by Newton. Even Einstein found quantum theory so strange and subversive that he refused to accept it all, comparing it to "the system of delusions of an exceedingly intelligent paranoiac"; hence his famous observation that "God does not play dice with the universe."[1]

So what is quantum physics, and how was it discovered?

Niels Bohr and the Quantum Leap

The great Danish physicist Niels Bohr (1885–1962) first realized, around 1912–13, that Newtonian mechanics could not explain how atoms behave. Ernest Rutherford (1871–1937) had already developed a model of the atom as a miniature solar system with a tiny nucleus of protons and neutrons orbited by even smaller electrons, and it was already known that atoms were unstable. Bohr guessed that electrons changed orbit when they radiated light; he therefore identified the emission of a "quantum" with the "jump" of an electron from one orbit to another.

According to Bohr's model, electrons "excited" by a bombardment of energy may leap from one orbit to another inner or outer orbit, instantly passing from one position to another, nonadjacent position, without physically traveling the distance between the two points.

This led to the hypothesis that when an atom has a choice of states to leap into, it decides entirely at random. A quantum leap (or jump, the term physicists prefer) is the *smallest* change that can be made, and it happens unpredictably.

Over the next two decades, mathematical modeling of the atom led to new and counterintuitive insights. Two of the most important of these are *Heisenberg's uncertainty principle,* and *Bohr's principle of complementarity.*

Heisenberg's Uncertainty Principle

In 1927, Werner Heisenberg proved that uncertainty is inherent in the equations of quantum mechanics. He showed that if we try to measure *both* the position and the momentum of an electron, we will fail, because the more accurately we know where the object is, the less certain we can be of its momentum, and vice versa. The uncertainty principle therefore states that it is not possible to calculate accurately both the position and the momentum of a subatomic particle. Though we can measure the atom, our results will inevitably be inaccurate, not because of any defect in our measuring techniques, but because we still don't completely understand the logic—if there indeed is any—behind how tiny matter behaves.

Heisenberg therefore declared as "useless and meaningless" the assumption that there existed such a thing as a "real world" subject to the rules of cause and effect.

The Principle of Complementarity

In 1927, Bohr declared that light is both wave-like and particle-like, simultaneously. This is possible because our perception of the shape of light depends entirely on the tools we use to view it. If we observe a photon with a particle detector, we see a particle. Observing the photon with a wave detector, we see a wave. Neither, Bohr insisted, is more real or accurate. We can only see a wave or a particle at any one time, yet both descriptions are necessary to fully define the physical presence of light. The two methods complement each other.

"Both/and," in this case, is therefore a more valuable, more precise perspective than "either/or."

Erwin Schrödinger (1887–1961) was a brilliant Austrian physicist who, like Einstein, failed to discover the underlying cause of atomic and subatomic behavior. Experiments have proved beyond any doubt that quantum mechanics is correct in saying that photon particles behave randomly and yet in a related manner. One photon has an instantaneous effect on another proton, even when logically it can't. The fundamental particles that make up the world seem to be inseparably connected to each other, part of some indivisible whole; the particles "know" what the others are doing.

How Relevant Is Quantum Theory to the Nonmicroworld?

As difficult as it is to grasp, our lives would be radically different without quantum theory. It can predict experimental results to many decimal places. It has given us the power to create the transistor, the microchip, nuclear energy, and lasers. Modern cosmology would be impossible without quantum theory. The question we must now pose is: how relevant is this physical theory to anything else, and specifically to business?

For the most part, I'm unconvinced by some claims that there is a new "quantum" theory of society and business that replaces the allegedly dominant "Newtonian" theories. But there are two positive points where I think it *is* valid and instructive to use quantum theory as a metaphor for business purposes.

Escaping the Tyranny of Either/Or

Both Heisenberg's uncertainty principle and Bohr's principle of complementarity are direct exponents of something that was, in the 1920s, new to science: a both/and rather than an either/or approach. The methodology was a response to the fickle nature of quantum reality. Whereas it would be impossible to say, for example, that a cat was both in the living room and in the bedroom simultaneously, it *is* possible, according to Heisenberg, to say that a particle could be in two places at once because given the existence of quantum leaps and discontinuities within atoms, our perception of their position and momentum will never be accurate. And, Bohr adds, light can be a series of waves and a stream of particles at the same time. Both descriptions, Bohr says, are complementary and necessary to help us understand light's true nature.

The acceptance of dual reality as an alternative to a perspective where all reality is mutually exclusive is, I believe, a valid and relatively novel way of thinking. And it is particularly well suited for the successful conduct of modern business itself. Name almost any issue that used to be regarded as "either/or," and it can be shown that often a trade-off can be avoided and a "both/and" solution created. For example, if we are sufficiently creative or lucky, we can keep the stock market happy *and* be socially responsible. We can aim for high profits *and* deliver top value to customers. We can have high quality *and* low costs (quality may even have "negative costs"). Whenever a trade-off is proposed, we should assume that there is a way around it—and, with a little creative thinking, there usually will be.

Three companies that have worked closely together to promote each others' interests are Disney, McDonald's, and Coca-Cola. They engage wherever possible in joint marketing and promotion of products and characters from all three companies. The bond is loose and emotional rather than legal: for example, McDonald's and Disney executives were very much in evidence at the funeral in 1997 of Roberto Goizuetta, the legendary leader of Coca-Cola.

Testing Out Multiple Possible Options

A second useful analogy is one between the behavior of electrons (or photons) and the value of testing out multiple possible options when making possible business decisions. Danah Zohar and Ian Marshall, authors of popular books on quantum theory and its social implications, write:

> The atom may become unstable for no apparent reason . . . quite suddenly, the electrons in a previously stable atom may begin to move into different energy orbits . . . there is no way of knowing by which path a particular electron may travel . . . Indeterminacy—the lack of any physical basis for predicting the outcome of events—characterizes the quantum realm. The electron may go to the next highest state, it may leap over several intermediate states or even double back on itself . . . quantum physics tells us that the electron actually follows all these possible paths, all at the same time. It behaves as though it is smeared out all over time and space and is everywhere at once.
>
> In much the same way as we play with multiple possibilities in our imaginations, or launch "trial balloons" to see how something might work out, the electron puts out "feelers" . . . to see which path ultimately suits it best.[2]

Like the electron that "feels" before deciding its next move, we should experiment before settling on an important course of action. Imagine doing *a, b,* and *c,* and also doing *x, y,* and *z.* Neither you nor your firm is predestined to pursue one course of action. You have many possibilities, bounded only by your imagination. There is *always* another path, always another way of doing things, always someplace else to go. Create many options. Play with them in your mind.

Consult colleagues. Think the unthinkable. Narrow your choice, but don't fix yet on one course of action. Keep a few tricks up your sleeve.

Now put out feelers to collaborators and to the marketplace. Ask distributors, suppliers, customers, and trusted experts for their opinion. What do you think about *x*? Would you prefer *y*? What would be the reaction if we chose $w + z$ but also $- b$? Even now, do not make your final decision.

Launch test markets to see whether the concept, technology, and product variants can meet the product concept expectations, and whether the product is sustainable, whether there is a sufficiently high level of repurchase. See which trial balloons go up and stay up, which go down, which go nowhere. Experiment. Now revise your plans. Experiment again.

Never make a crucial business decision until you have behaved like an electron. Procter & Gamble is a good example of a business known for examining every possibility before launching a new product. Innovation in P&G follows a structured process. Ideas are brainstormed with P&G's advertising agency based on detailed consumer knowledge. When various concept options are developed, product ideas are put to consumers and their feedback is noted. A test market is then set up to see whether product concept expectations are met. For the few products that survive this far, P&G's manufacturing experts get involved to decide where the products should be manufactured and to check that the expected economics can be met. Then retailers are involved to get their comments and their total support when introducing the new products. The products are then launched with massive advertising support and sampling promotions to ensure that everyone knows about the product. Finally, there is continuous consumer research to aid in further product refinement and innovation.

Bill Gates is another excellent example of a leader who examines and reexamines every possibility before choosing or sticking to his path. The "Microsoft Campus" is his name for the company's center in Redmond, Washington; it seems more like a university than a head office. Gates insists on a system where different parts of Microsoft provide constant feedback to colleagues: his famous "feedback loops" are integral to Microsoft's operations. Advance copies of Microsoft new product launches are tested on selected customers who are willing to provide feedback. As with his U-turn on the Internet, Gates is always willing to reverse his position as a result of clear feedback.

Quantum Theory Used As a Battering Ram

Several writers have attempted to use quantum mechanics as a battering ram to attack the Newtonian world view and support what we may loosely term a "new age" philosophy of society and business, based allegedly on quantum physics.

I believe that the key insight that can directly be drawn from quantum mechanics is that, wherever possible, we should adopt a both/and approach to business, escaping the tyranny of either/or. And here it is deeply ironic that expositions of quantum thinking should take such pains to denigrate Newtonian, mechanistic thinking. The paradoxical implication is that we can have *either* "Newtonian management" *or* "quantum management." This is doubly inappropriate. The choice we have is not between Newtonian physics and quantum physics: we need them both. And we are not forced to choose between the Newtonian world view, or a so-called Newtonian view of management, and the perspectives given by quantum theory and other twentieth-century science. We can benefit from both.

The appropriate view, surely, is that quantum theory reveals another world, a parallel universe that we cannot directly experience, another set of viewpoints and language; a world from which we can draw insight and inspiration, but which cannot and should not replace the Newtonian world of rational thought, plans, objectives, solid engineering, numbers, budgets, and the quest for high returns. Quantum thinking has a valuable role in supplementing this approach, in drawing attention to its flaws, and in stimulating the imagination. But quantum thinking alone can't supply a way of managing a business organization, any more than it can build a bridge or send someone to Mars. We do quantum physics and quantum thinking no favors by exaggerating its reach or comprehensiveness, or by setting it up as a complete replacement for "Newtonian" methods. The insistence by some that the quantum way is the true way runs directly counter to the more tolerant and inclusive wisdom of Niels Bohr, probably the greatest quantum physicist ever, who insisted that "the opposite of a great truth is also true."

The quantum world is not better or worse than the Newtonian world; it is just different.

How to Use the Natural Laws

- ***Pursue both/and.*** Don't believe that contradictions and trade-offs are inevitable. Be creative in seeking ways to defuse and defeat them, so that you can deliver the best of both worlds. Escape from the limitations of either/or thinking. Have it all.

- ***Experiment in thought and deed before you commit yourself to a major initiative.***

Part Two Concluding Note

In Part Two, we've examined two different types of physics, two different world views, and, by implication, two different views of organizations and management. It's interesting that the same physical science can give rise, sequentially, to such radically different views of how the world works. And, on reflection, the new world of quantum physics, with its fresh and subversive implications for how the universe works, supplements but does not replace its older cousin, the physics derived from Isaac Newton.

Chapter 6 celebrated the Newtonian model and the power of numbers, analysis, and simple ratios comparing two key relationships. Here lie the origins of accounting systems, profitability analyses, and two-by-two matrices. Their power is not to be sneered at. We examined one such powerful relationship: that between profitability and the distance from competitors and their relative size. While the extent to which the relationship works mathematically is unproven, we explored the intuitive appeal of the concept of the "gravity of competition," where competition from near and similar business units depresses returns. We posited that the way to earn very high returns on capital was to establish the maximum possible distance from competitors, along the dimensions of customer type, product type, geography, and the type of value-added provided.

Chapter 7's review of relativity concluded that time should not be thought of as a separate dimension of business. Time must be a key, integral part of any business offering. We also saw that objective reality is a mirage. If reality is a construct without objective underpinning, the way we think, our business endeavors, and our markets may determine our success or failure just as much as the other attributes we bring to bear.

Chapter 8's fascinating journey into the microworld revealed how strange and difficult to understand are the most minute portions of matter.

In concluding our review of physics, we have refused to let quantum mechanics overshadow Newtonian mechanics. The new does not replace the old. Apart from the world of very small—subatomic—matter, Newton's theories still work. And in business, it's quite possible to be very successful using Newtonian tools and disregarding everything else. However, the most important lesson from quantum theory is that apparently irreconcilable positions may just be two sides of the truth: that we should accept great truths as complementary even when they appear to be opposite. This means that in business, as in physics, there is room for the old view *and* the new one: for rational truth, numbers, cause-and-effect reasoning, and the mechanical view of the world; and also for unpredictable, probabilistic, experimental, unfolding, and paradoxical patterns of reality—which we shall learn a great deal more about in Part Three, as we look into the world of nonlinear systems in nature and society.

PART III

The Nonlinear Laws

Interdisciplinary Science

9 The Third Great Scientific Breakthrough

Chaos and Complexity

Chaos is when any system is so complex and irregular that it appears to be random unless you know a lot of hidden information about it. Chaos is lovely, it is absolutely wonderful. It is full of all sorts of intriguing forms and behaviours.

IAN STEWART,
Does God Play Dice?

Chaos and *complexity* are probably the most important scientific innovations of the late twentieth century. They are interdisciplinary concepts and fields of study, drawing on mathematics, biology, physics, economics, and many other disciplines. Although it is too early to be sure of their place in the history of science, many believe that they rank alongside or just behind relativity and quantum theory, comprising the third great scientific breakthrough of the last century. Chaos and complexity also provide insights that are very congruent with, but also complementary to, those already provided by relativity and quantum theory. As one physicist comments:

> Relativity eliminated the Newtonian illusion of absolute time and space; quantum theory eliminated the Newtonian dream of a controllable measurement pro-

cess; and chaos eliminates the Laplacian fantasy of deterministic predictability.[1]

Chaos

As suits its Alice-in-Wonderland nature ("whenever I use a word it means what I want it to mean"), "chaos" in this context means "the concept or field of study of chaos." Very few scientists working on chaos call it "chaos theory," and chaos is not necessarily or even usually "chaotic" in the ordinary sense of the word. Chaos is a severe misnomer because the processes studied often reveal beautiful and intricate patterns. The processes are only superficially chaotic; underneath there is a deep, if irregular, order.

Chaos is the search to identify and understand nonlinear patterns that have been ignored by traditional science. The paradox of chaos is that the structures in nonlinear systems are very similar, regardless of the phenomenon—from the weather to the economy, from snowflakes to coastlines, from stars in the sky to a series of stock exchange prices.

Chaos has its roots in quantum theory and in mathematical work on chance and probability performed during the nineteenth and early twentieth centuries. Quantum theory tells us that very small things like atoms and photons do not behave in a linear or predictable way. They really are chaotic. The brilliant French mathematician Henri Poincaré wrote in 1908: *"A very small cause, which escapes us, determines a considerable effect which we cannot ignore, and then we say that this effect is due to chance."*[2]

Chaos helps us to find the patterns that really determine so-called "chance" occurrences: these patterns may exist at several removes from the results we observe, and may appear too difficult or far back to trace. But chaos can help us do so, and therefore realize that "chance" and "luck" are often too simple explanations. Chance and luck always exist, but within a certain framework which is not purely random, and which need not be elusive.

Sensitive Dependence on Initial Conditions

Poincaré is really the intellectual forerunner of chaos, whose central insight is that of *sensitive dependence on initial conditions.* Many physical systems are very sensitive to arbitrary initial conditions, and are therefore essentially unpredictable. The classic example is the weather. It used to be thought that, with enough data and computing power, it would be possible to predict the weather reliably, perhaps months in advance. We now know that this is impossible, because of a phenomenon called the "butterfly effect."

The Butterfly Effect

In 1972 Edward Lorenz, a meteorologist at the Massachusetts Institute of Technology, gave a paper provocatively entitled "Predictability: does the flap of a butterfly's wings in Brazil set off a tornado in Texas?"[3]

The question, he said, was unanswerable, but it illustrates the nature of the weather. For many years Lorenz had used computers to model the weather, hoping to improve long-term forecasts. His pioneering work showed that eddies and cyclones obeyed certain mathematical rules, yet never repeated themselves. Long-term weather forecasting, he concluded, was impossible, because although he could model the influences on weather, minute changes in a couple of variables, extrapolated over a month or beyond, could produce radically different results.

Lorenz's insight was not just that small effects can have huge consequences—this is an old story, embodied for example in the Prussian verses about a kingdom being lost for want of a horseshoe nail. His real breakthrough was to demonstrate that the future of weather was literally uncertain, even if we knew everything there was to know about all the influences on it. The weather makes itself up as it goes along, as does evolution, and as do vibrant economies.

The search was on to understand complex, nonlinear systems.

Chaos in the Physical World

One milestone in the emergence—and naming—of chaos was the work of mathematician James Yorke around 1970. Yorke and some of his colleagues realized that when confronted with nonlinear systems, like weather, cities, economies, and insect colonies, the typical response of mathematicians was to attempt to explain them by substituting linear approximations. Yorke demonstrated that even nonlinear systems that were very sensitive to initial conditions could be modeled. For example, a scientist could input seemingly random biological data relating to fish populations into a computer and produce a graph that would show the fish population alternating between strikingly regular patterns and completely random "chaotic" ones. Yorke showed that beyond a certain mathematical point any population or similar system would exhibit both patterns at different times. Though inexplicable, the patterns would generate graphs that kept repeating themselves with remarkable faithfulness.

What's the Connection Between Cotton Prices and the Nile?

At about the same time, Benoit Mandelbrot, also a mathematician, was working in IBM's pure research department and using its most powerful new computers to analyze cotton price data. He showed that there were patterns for daily and monthly price changes that, when drawn on graphs of different scales, matched each other perfectly. In other words, the shape of the squiggles on the daily and monthly and yearly charts resembled each other perfectly, and the degree of variation had remained constant over a turbulent sixty years, which had included two world wars and a depression. This was a stunning conclusion, because logically one would expect the small-scale ups and downs during a day's trading to be insignificant and totally unrelated to monthly or annual data, which one might think related to macroeconomic variables. In other words, there was a statistical order within the disorder: the system had its own integral magic that seemed independent of the vagaries of mankind and nature. Mandelbrot found the same patterns in all the data he analyzed, including variations in the level of the river Nile over several millennia.

As more research was done in meteorology, biology, economics, and many other sciences, it became apparent that there were regular patterns that could be observed through the relationship of large scales to small scales.

Mitchell Feigenbaum, a physicist at the Los Alamos National Laboratory in New Mexico, conducted a series of calculations to measure the size difference between converging sets of data, such as Mandelbrot's cotton prices. His calculator repeatedly came up with the same number: 4.669. Feigenbaum had stumbled across one of the most startling properties of chaotic systems: universality. Universality means that, on some dimensions, different systems will behave identically. At a conference at Los Alamos in 1976, one of Feigenbaum's colleagues joyfully remarked: *"It was a very happy and shocking discovery that there were structures in non-linear systems that are always the same if you look at them the right way."*[4]

Fractal Similarities

Mandelbrot coined the very useful word "fractal" to describe things that are very similar to each other, yet not identical—coastlines, clouds, cotton prices, earthquakes, or trees. Patterns are endlessly repeated, yet also with endless and unpredictable variety. Plotting data from nonlinear systems reveals strikingly similar patterns regardless of the actual data being plotted. For example, the year-to-year graph of cotton prices is shaped similarly to the graph depicting the month-to-month cotton price variations.

Business is fractal: no situation is quite like another, but there is a limited set of key factors that always resemble each other. Business outcomes are utterly unpredictable, which is why the quest for a deterministic science of management—if you do *x* and *y*, then *z* will result—is futile and naïve. Yet there are always recurring patterns that are worth studying. The fact that business is fractal is the best justification for the case-study method used in business schools, although this would be much more useful if we could map the different fractal patterns for different types of businesses, something no one has yet done.

Chaos, Chance, and Business

The concept of chaos is that although the world is comprised largely of nonlinear systems, there are patterns discernible within the irregularities. Disorder in the universe is constrained. Chaos and chance do not lend themselves to tracing simple, causal links, which is what most of us in business look for. Yet there are many very useful applications of this theory that we can use in business:

- There is always some pattern or order in apparently random or disordered data.
- Patterns exist. The only question is whether we can detect them. All markets generate patterns of behavior and response.
- Analysis may not be the best way of finding the hidden order.

Analysis may be incapable of finding the pattern, if the system is reasonably complex and interdependent. With some flexibility and imagination, though, you can understand a market by immersing yourself in it, and waiting for inspiration to come.

A vintage example of the virtues of immersion in a market over analysis of it is provided by Honda's unexpected success in conquering the U.S. motorcycle market in the early 1960s. When Honda landed its bikes in the United States in 1959–60, they had four products: the very small 50 cc Supercub motor scooter (very popular in Japan), the 125 cc small bike, and the 250 and 350 cc motorcycles. All the effort went into selling the larger bikes, both because Honda executives believed that "everything was bigger and more luxurious" in the U.S. market and also because Mr. Honda himself felt that the fact that the 250 and 350 cc machines had their handlebars shaped like the eyebrows of the Buddha was a major selling point.

The Honda executives used the very small Supercub motorscooters to run errands around Los Angeles, but made no attempt to sell the machines in America. A senior buyer from Sears Roebuck noticed the scooters being used and expressed interest in the machine, but as this was contrary to the plan the lead was not followed up. By the spring of 1960, the bigger bikes had begun to sell, but their clutches and head gaskets began to break when driven long and fast by U.S. bikers. Desperate for some cash flow while the bigger bikes were sent back to Japan for repairs and redesign, the Honda executives made do with selling the Supercub scooters, the only machines that didn't break down. They were sold to sporting goods stores and eventually to catalogues. They sold extremely well, but were dismissed by Honda bosses as a sideline.

For another three years, Honda persevered trying to sell its larger bikes. Then, in 1963, a student at UCLA on a class assignment dreamed up the slogan, "You meet the nicest people on a Honda." Honda executives rejected a large advertising campaign with the slogan, but grudgingly tried it out on a small scale. It was an instant success. In 1964, half the motorcycles sold in the United States were Hondas—and they were mainly the smaller machines. Honda sales rose from $500,000 in 1960 to $7.7 million in 1965. A whole new middle-class market had arrived serendipitously.

Honda eventually listened to the market. The company could have won faster and with less anguish if it had discarded its preoccupations, immersed itself in the messy reality of its U.S. markets, and realized that unexpected successes are the best guide to strategy. Honda's tardiness in appreciating the market didn't really matter in the long run, but if the company hadn't had such a great Supercub product, and no competition, it could have.

Simple Systems Do Complicated Things

There may be three of four key factors that, combined with "chance" (better called "sensitive dependence on initial conditions"), lead to incredibly complicated and unpredictable results.

Imagine that a company, any company—IBM, Amazon.com, or a

company that you know personally—has had a great run of success but now appears to be floundering. What has happened? To solve the problem, you'll want to try to isolate the key variables that interact with each other, but also resist the temptation to reduce everything to one main cause or effect. List all the plausible explanations. Then think how they might be connected. You will soon realize that there is no simple way back to past glory. You will need to do several different things simultaneously to reverse decline, and you'll need to be mindful of how new initiatives could have negative effects elsewhere in the system. Because simple systems do complicated things, you may need to experiment with changing *everything* to discover what new permutations will work. Discovering causes may be less productive than trying out a whole new raft of remedies.

Complex Systems Can Give Rise to Simple Behavior

Behavior is a better and easier guide to a complex system than complex structural analysis. When looking at complex systems such as markets, customers, or competitors, look for reliable patterns of simple behavior. For example, if a competitor always follows your price changes, this is all you need to know to make pricing decisions.

Chance—The Role of Luck

Most markets, companies, and business units are complex systems that are sensitive to initial conditions. Therefore expect the unexpected, and expect it often to be due to minute and undetectable causes. There are several corollaries:

- Don't expect to be able to control everything. Don't be thrown totally off course when the unexpected happens.
- Build flexibility into your plans. If *x* happens, do *y*. If *w* happens, do *z*.
- When something goes wrong, don't waste enormous effort investigating what went wrong and punishing the wrongdoers. There may be no wrongdoers. Or the "wrongdoers" may

have behaved impeccably, as per your instructions. Get on with working out what to do next.

- When something goes right, remember that it may not be at all due to your skill or that of your firm. It may be sensitive dependence on initial conditions that happened to suit you brilliantly. Exploit the trend for all it is worth, but don't believe your own propaganda. The next "sensitive dependence" may better suit a competitor.

Chance—The Need for Multiple Strategies

Where there is major uncertainty about how an industry may evolve, it may make sense to have more than a single strategy.

Eric D. Beinhocker[5] comments that in 1988, when he wandered around COMDEX, the computer industry's trade show, there was something very odd and ambivalent about the Microsoft booth:

> While most booths focused on a single blockbuster technology, Microsoft's resembled a Middle Eastern bazaar. In one corner, the company was previewing the second version of . . . Windows . . . In another, it touted its latest release of DOS. Elsewhere, it was displaying OS/2 . . . [*and*] major new releases of Word, Excel . . . [*and*] SCO Unix . . .
>
> "What am I supposed to make of all this?" grumbled a corporate buyer standing next to me. Columnists wrote that Microsoft was adrift . . . [*and*] had no strategy. Reporters told stories of infighting at the company as one group . . . worked furiously on Windows and DOS while others poured their energies into OS/2, Mac applications, and Unix.
>
> . . . in 1988 it wasn't obvious which operating system would win. In the face of this uncertainty, Microsoft followed the only robust strategy: betting on every horse to win.[6]

Microsoft had *strategies* rather than a *strategy.*

Focus is a wonderful thing, but corporations in fast-moving and unpredictable markets may need to take some of their resources and have a few side bets at long odds: this is equivalent to spending money on financial "call options."

Beinhocker also said:

> A company should use most of its resources to build its current activities, but the resources devoted to riskier experiments further afield are critically important, since they could contain the seeds of success in a currently unimaginable future.[7]

The First-Mover Advantage

Since most complex systems are very sensitive to initial conditions, it makes sense to get in on the ground floor of any new development that may be important to your key markets. The idea of the *first-mover advantage*—that the first person in has an edge over other equally qualified later-comers—is well known in business, but the science of chaos reinforces its importance. A firm that, in an embryonic market, puts out a product that is, say, 10 percent more attractive than any other offering, may end up with a 100 or 200 percent greater market share, *even if competitors later provide something better.* The first-mover advantage "locks in" standards and makes the market behave in ways that are tilted to favor the first mover.

Consider how clocks behave. Why should nearly all clocks exhibit 12 hours and move to the right ("clockwise")? This was not inevitable. Why not a 24-hour face and have the clock hands move to the left? There is, in fact, a cathedral in Florence whose clock moves counterclockwise through 24 hours. The cathedral and clock date from 1442. At that time the options were open. Shortly after, clockmakers standardized "our" 12-hour, clockwise method. Yet if 51 percent of clocks had ever been like the one in Florence, we would now be reading a 24-hour clock backwards, and the clock in the first line of George Orwell's *1984* could not have shocked readers by chiming thirteen.

The early bird gets the worm, and hence the competitive advantage. So get to market quickly, establish the standard, and grab competitive advantage while the field is still fallow.

Business Is Fractal

There is too much uncertainty and uniqueness in business—in the language of chaos, business is too fractal and too sensitive to initial conditions—to allow for "paint-by-numbers" strategies, to slavishly follow well-worn rules of thumb. This does not mean that we should make decisions by tossing a die. A large part of the difference between successful and unsuccessful executives and entrepreneurs is the ability to recognize fractal patterns and to make decisions accordingly.

If you spend your lifetime looking at clouds or coastlines, you will make a better guess than most people at whether it is going to rain or which way the coast will run beyond the point you can see. If you have many years' experience and track record at making good decisions in a particular industry and market, the odds are that you will continue to make good decisions by recognizing recurrent patterns—as long as you stay in the same industry and market.

One of the sad things about corporate life today is how often operating managers, who know their markets well, are overruled simply because they are unable to explain or rationalize their instincts to their corporate bosses. A more sensible setup would not require explanations; it would just judge by results.

Recognizing that business is fractal gives you many very important warning and encouraging signals:

- Experience and intuition will usually win over analysis, because the analysis can never be precise enough or conclusive. Analysis, of course, is useful as a supplement to intuition, and, as we have seen earlier, the intuition/analysis dichotomy is in some ways a false one. Good intuition is the compilation of previous accurate analyses, and good analysis is often the exploration, by collecting data, of intuitive hypotheses. Yet so great is the importance of recognizing fractal patterns and previous results—realizing, for example, that your position now is more similar to previous situation A than it is to previous situation B, and that situation A led to disaster—that a great young manager and analyst may well lose out to a cunning old hand.

- At the very least, recognition that business is fractal, and that slight differences in inputs can lead to totally different outcomes, should teach us to be careful when we enter apparently adjacent but new markets. These may look the same as the old markets, and yet be subtly different—with shocking results! Look at the terrible track record of most retailers the first time they venture beyond their home country. I experienced this when I was director of Filofax, the personal organizer company. Although it is a global brand, Filofax originated in Great Britain. For decades, the British management tried to get its American subsidiary to sell in the same way and through the same type of stationery stores that worked for Filofax in Britain and most other countries. For decades, the local American management argued that these approaches would never work. For decades, they were ignored: not out of high-handedness, but because the local American executives could never explain *why* the tried-and-tested formula would not work there, nor why an alternative approach should logically work. For decades, Filofax made losses or tiny profits in America but high profits almost everywhere else. We would have been better advised not to worry about why the standard approach didn't work, and to realize that business is fractal. A fractal approach would have led to experimentation by local management, until they found an American strategy that worked.

- Whenever you face an important decision, try to find the nearest equivalent situation in your experience or that of colleagues or friends. Do not leap to conclusions. Engage in sober debate about the possibilities. Unless you are very certain, draw up a "top-three" list of possibly similar situations and what could happen next.

- Once you have headed down a particular path, look for the early signs that you are on or off the expected path, just as you would when following a map. If the early signs are not what you expect, you have probably chosen the wrong "fractal comparison."

Because there are so many different types of business, where different rules apply, specialized businesses always have an advantage over generalized ones. A specialized unit, company, or market will generally win over an undifferentiated one. Where possible, therefore, form specialized teams, new business units, new divisions, and, above all, new companies. Most company owners are reluctant to split their company in two, yet if business is fractal, and part of the skill in business is recognizing fractal patterns, a specialized company will be much better placed to recognize the right patterns and make the right responses.

Complexity and Emergence

Most of the radical scientific innovators that discovered the secrets of chaos have now moved on to the study of *complexity*. Complexity is the study of nonlinear systems that manage to produce their own brand of order. Sometimes the same simple yet baffling patterns emerge in completely different types of complex systems: an economic slump looks very much like a hurricane, with similar feedback causes and effects; a developing city is very like a growing embryo.

Complexity builds on the insights gained from chaos, but adds three new theories. First, complexity focuses on complicated feedback systems and shows that these usually have surprising results. Second, as Philip Anderson—widely regarded as the founder of complexity—urged, complexity is about *emergence*, how groups or "wholes" behave quite differently from the aggregation of their individual characteristics. In combining individual units—individual customers, water molecules, body cells, business units—and groups—markets, steam, a butterfly wing, a company—we may emerge with something completely unexpected and different from what we started with. Third, what complexity is really interested in is "self-organizing systems": systems that start in a random state but somehow organize themselves, quite spontaneously, into a large-scale pattern.

Self-organizing Systems

Spontaneous self-organization is a fascinating thing, especially when the individual components are numerous and apparently unrelated to each other. Adam Smith (although he didn't know it) was an early exponent of complexity when he talked about the "invisible hand" that seemed to direct the self-interested intentions of millions of producers to satisfy the self-interest of millions of consumers.[8] Think of the billions of interconnected neurons in your brain, producing a result that surely an individual neuron could not envisage, and yet organizing effectively to ensure that you can understand my words. Think of the way that a city that starts out by being racially integrated soon divides itself into racial (or social, or lifestyle) groups. Think of the way that a stock-market crash, or a hurricane, organizes itself from its constituent parts, or how atoms combine into molecules by forming chemical bonds with each other; the molecules are quite different from, and more complex than, the atoms from whence they came.

Or think of the Internet. Nobody planned its evolution from a government and university research tool into a global network of information that has triggered the biggest and fastest change in industry and corporate structures ever seen. The Internet has a life of its own and decides what it will become as it goes along.

Complex Systems Are Adaptive

Self-organizing systems that are complex are also adaptive. They adapt to their surroundings and try to turn what is happening to their advantage. The brain develops and learns. Species evolve. Cities respond to new inputs. Markets become larger and more specialized, and adapt to pressure from important distant markets.

John Tyler Bonner has shown how this self-adjusting complexity evolves by natural selection.[9] A termite colony, for example, adjusts the numbers of its different castes by cascades of chemicals activated in the termite larvae. If there are too few "soldier termites," the smell given off by them in a colony falls below a certain level, and then the "larvae nursery" automatically produces more soldier termites, which differ physically from other termites. If this happens in nature, is it fanciful to see the emergence of complex systems such as cities and economies as part of the same process of evolution by natural selection?

Complexity theorists such as John Holland explain that complex adaptive systems typically have many niches, each with a specialized role and place. And new niches are always unfolding: niches for new predators, for new prey, for new symbiotic partners, for new parasites. As new niches open up, the system changes. It can never be in equilibrium.

The Edge of Chaos

Complex systems are perched on the *edge of chaos,* a curious state between order and disorder, between stability and transformation. Note that complex systems have a combination of order and randomness; they always operate within an ordered structure. You can't have self-organization without also having boundaries. When a complex system moves over the edge of chaos, then it crosses a boundary and becomes something different. This is what led John Horgen to claim that "everything interesting happens at the edge of chaos."[10]

Biologists use the "edge effect" to describe the tendency for a greater variety and density of organisms to cluster in the boundaries between communities. In complexity theory, the "edge of chaos" describes complex systems, because they possess both elements of order and elements of fluidity. A crystal is not a complex system, because it possesses perfect internal order and there is nothing left to change. At the other extreme, a boiling liquid is a chaotic rather than complex system; there is very little order. By way of contrast, a complex system such as amoebas, the stock exchange or an economy has both order and enough fluidity to change. In the words of biologist E. O. Wilson: *"The system that will evolve most rapidly must fall between, and more precisely on, the edge of chaos—possessing order, but with the parts connected loosely enough to be easily altered."*

The brilliant economist Paul Krugman has shown that cities behave in many different ways like complex, self-organizing, adaptive systems. One of his arguments concerns the size of American cities.[11] It turns out that they obey *Zipf's rank/size rule,* by Harvard professor of philology George Zipf, which says that the population of a city in any country is inversely proportional to its ranking. In other words, the second largest city would have half the population of the largest; and the third largest would have one third the people of the top city, and so on.

We should not expect a perfect fit; this never happens with data and laws. And you might protest that Los Angeles has well over half the population of New York. But as you go down the rankings, a pattern emerges. City number 10 in the United States is Houston, with 3.85 million people. City number 100 is Spokane in Washington State; this has 370,000 people, fractionally under one-tenth the size of Houston. Krugman tells us:

> If you regress the log of rank on the log of population, you get a coefficient of –1.003, with a standard error of only 0.01—a slope close to 1 and very tightly fitted. We are unused to seeing regularities this exact in economics—it is so exact that I find it spooky.

The same pattern emerges if we analyze relative city sizes in 1940 or 1890.[12]

Zipf's natural law works when applied to cities, but it also works in the same way for earthquakes, meteorites, and species. The frequency of earthquakes is inversely proportional to their size. Similarly, the frequency with which a meteorite hits Earth is (happily!) inversely proportional to the meteorite's size. And if we plot the number of animal species that exceed a particular size, we uncover the same relationship.

Cities, the economy, earthquakes, meteorites, and quite likely evolution too, are self-organizing systems that behave in clear and similar patterns, and that produce order from instability. The whole mysteriously assembles; we are back to Adam Smith's "invisible hand," although this paw stretches around far more than the economy. The constituent parts surely cannot "know" what they are doing. Or can they? In biology, how do we explain how cells arrive in their allotted places? Krugman comments:

> An individual fruit fly cell does not think to itself, "I am part of a wing," yet cells collectively seem in effect to decide to become different parts of the organism. Experiments suggest that cells indeed behave as if they knew their own polar co-ordinates.

In the business world, think of how teams sometimes magically gel together and define, without the need for words, each individual's role. Or, more darkly, how easily a crowd can turn into a frenzied mob, acting in perfect accord to destroy something. The whole is more fundamental and purposeful than the parts. Self-organization and the emergence and adaptation of complex systems are deeply rooted in the universe, and we had better notice, respect, and take account of them.

One man who did take note of organizations' self-organizing characteristics—although the concept of self-organization had not yet been invented—was C. Northcote Parkinson (1909–93). In 1958 he published *Parkinson's Law:* "work expands to fill the time available."

Parkinson's thesis was that bosses increase the size of their departments because there is more work to do and because they like to have large empires, not because they need to in rational economic terms. "An official wants to multiply subordinates, not rivals," he comments, noting also that "officials make work for each other." The fact that there is work to do justifies and masks the real objective, which has nothing to do with economic logic.[13]

Parkinson himself was an official in the British Navy during the Second World War. He pointed out in his book that whereas the number of officers and men in the Navy itself fell by 31 percent between 1914 and 1928, and the number of ships fell even more sharply, by 61 percent, the Admiralty administrators yet contrived to increase their ranks by 78 percent! In complexity terms, the Navy administration was self-organizing, fulfilling objectives that were quite independent of the original intention.

Complexity and Business

As we've discovered, complexity theory is about complicated feedback systems, how groups or whole entities "emerge" from quite different parts, how complex systems poise themselves on the "edge of chaos," and how they organize themselves spontaneously and deliberately into large-scale patterns.

Look for and Practice Emergence

Complex systems come together from the bottom up. They emerge. They come together from many constituent parts. Structure comes from no structure, or from lesser structures.

Markets and economics, and business strategy, are emergent phenomena. Therefore, as businesspeople our goal is to look for the signs that the "invisible hand" is at work. Ask yourself this: How did the most successful corporations from, say, 1750 to 1960 arrive at their successful strategies, before we knew how to plan them? Or ask another question: Who knows better what direction a firm should take, its bosses or the market? The leaders or the troops?

Japanese businesspeople and professors talk about "middle-up-down management" and suggest that the role of middle management is to develop a consensus between top management's intentions and the market reality observed by front-line executives. Tadashi Kume of Honda explains that listening to bottom management is crucial:

> I continually create dreams, but [we also need] to interact with reality . . . Top management does not know what bottom man-

> agement is doing. Middle management is charged with integrating the two viewpoints emanating from top and bottom. There can be no progress without such integration.

Many American corporations follow precisely this practice to great effect: Hewlett-Packard, Johnson & Johnson, and Mars are examples that spring to mind.

If we reflect on emergence, we realize that experiments of great strategic value often occur as we go along in the normal course of business. We open a small restaurant and it is successful beyond our expectations. A dull and low-status business unit invents a minor new product that suddenly is all the rage. We botch a formula but stumble onto the Post-it note. Things come together. Success emerges. But the best laid plans of mice and men . . .

The lesson is not to do nothing and hope for the best. The lesson is to spot emergence and then give it one almighty push on its way. It is better to observe the market than to plan it. It is better to see what is emerging from the lower reaches of the firm than to dictate from on high.

The Role of Self-Organization in Your Organization

Almost the only class of complex system in the universe that is not purely self-organizing is the modern business corporation and other hierarchical organizations modeled on it.

A laser organizes itself: photons (light particles) spontaneously organize themselves into a beam. A hurricane organizes itself. A living cell manages to self-organize. Cities organize themselves. So do economies—when left alone. So why do so many businesspeople preach laissez-faire for the economy, but never for the structure of the firms within it?

I'm not advocating that you automatically leave your organizations to organize themselves. The cost of self-adjustment could be much higher than that of intervention. Just because organizations *can* organize themselves does not mean that they *will* organize themselves the way you want them to. Resources will probably be wasted by self-organization.

But you should recognize the tendency toward self-organization. Sometimes you might try to stand aside and allow a team to work out a strategy on its own, without your direction. You should be extremely vigilant and aware that a system that is not controlled or watched will develop its own agenda. Sometimes you'll find that if you go with a simpler system your team is more likely to do what you want. If you double the size or increase the complexity of your organization, it will very likely do unwelcome new things. That's self-organization. Keeping systems simple and keeping tabs on organizations' tendency to self-organize will lead to higher profits and fitter corporations.

View Your Firm as a Living Organism

The organization has a life of its own, more than the sum of its parts and more than a set of economic transactions. It is more than the people who work in it, and even more than the set of relationships that it builds. The organization belongs to its own species. It can breed and it can die. It can be bought and sold, just as if it were property, yet each time it is bought it becomes something new—subtly or not-so-subtly different, yet always recognizably similar to its previous incarnation. As Peter Senge says:

> Is it that we think life starts and ends with us [humans]? Surely, simpler organisms are alive. Why then can't we regard more complex organisms, like families or societies or companies, as being alive as well? Is the tide pool, a teeming community of life, any less alive than the anemones, mussels or hermit crabs that populate it?[14]

Here are eight benefits in treating the firm as an organism rather than a machine:

- ***It takes away the illusion of control.*** A living thing is more difficult to control than a machine. An organism is unpredictable and headstrong, with a mind of its own.

- ***It stresses the role of growth and innovation.*** Machines don't grow. Organisms can't do anything else or they die.

- ***It reminds us that organizations, or parts of them, can be self-starting.*** A machine needs to be started, switched on and switched off. Machines suffer from entropy: they run down unless they are regularly maintained. Organisms can start themselves and renew themselves, they grow new cells and regulate their own metabolisms. Take the case of CEMEX (Cementos Mexicanos), the Mexican ready-mix cement business that has renewed itself and transformed its industry through tapping into self-organization. The Mexican industry used to have an on-time delivery rate of less than 35 percent, with traffic delays, tardy contractors, and poor roads blamed for the failure of cement to arrive when needed at construction sites. CEMEX changed all that, promising to deliver cement faster than pizza. If the load was more than ten minutes late, CEMEX guaranteed you a 20 percent discount.

  CEMEX uses technology to the full: each truck has real-time location signals. But what really matters is that the information is fully available to CEMEX's drivers and dispatchers, and that they have full authority to act on the information. CEMEX lets the drivers themselves schedule deliveries as they drive around. If a contractor calls in with a specific order, the closest available truck to the contractor's site makes the delivery. On-time delivery is now 98 percent instead of 35 percent.

  Whole industries can organize themselves better when central decision-making is removed. Take Hollywood. The days are gone when giant film studios really made movies. Today the big studios still brand the output, but small firms, linked in loose networks, do nearly all the work. Cyberpunk author Bruce Sterling explains how to make a movie: "Pitchfork a bunch of free-lancers together, expose some film, use the movie as the billboard to sell ancillary rights, and after the thing gets slotted to video, everybody just vanishes."

- ***Organisms are part of systems.*** An organism is a complex whole composed of many subsystems and part of many "super-systems" above it. The corporation is going to be affected by a change in its subsystems—for example, by the recruitment or retirement of individuals—and by super-systems—its market and competitive environment. Machines are not affected like this.

- ***Organisms can build networks and relationships.*** Machines can't. Humans can. Admittedly, the parallel is not perfect. It is not the organization which builds the networks and relationships, but rather the humans inside the organization building these relationships. The organization doesn't comprise its people, nor is it an extension of them. The people are not owned by the organization or compelled to remain part of it. Even when they are in it, the people have a life outside it. The networks and relationships that are built are not just with other humans, but with other organizations and with society as a whole. Networks and relationships are valuable because they can lead to new deals, new ideas, and improved ways of doing things without anyone having to organize the process. With networks and relationships, economic progress is easier, faster, and greater.

- ***Organisms have their own purpose.*** Machines have the purpose prescribed by their builders or owners. Organizations have purposes that evolve as a result of their founders' characteristics and what happens along the way. Does Microsoft have a purpose aside from making money for its owners? Or the Disney Corporation? Or McDonald's? Of course they do. You couldn't imagine any of these organizations swapping purposes, even if the owners wanted to.

- ***Organisms learn.*** Only living things can learn. Clearly, organizations can learn: Greenpeace can learn better ways to promote environmental responsibility, a rock band can learn new music, a baseball team can learn better technique, Microsoft can learn Internet technology (even though the company's founders were skeptical). Knowledge exists as a function of working together within the human players, not in the organization independent of its members.

As Peter Senge notes,[15] it is not just organizations that learn, but also the global business community. Technologies and ways of doing business get copied and extended. Self-service, the multidivisional corporation, the multinational corporation, hostile takeovers, leveraged buyouts and buyins, and spin-offs are invented in America and exported to most other economies. Total quality management is elaborated upon in Japan and then reimported into the United States, and, within a few years, it's ubiquitous. (As we saw in Chapter 1, organisms mutate and species learn. Improvements are diffused rapidly because there are only those that learn and those that die.)

- ***Finally, organisms can have their own character and uniqueness.*** A machine that has its own characteristics rather than those intended by its designers is probably not a very good machine. On the other hand, sophisticated organisms do exhibit their own character. Humans, and possibly other organisms, have emotions, which lead organizations to have their own cultures that are the product of history and accident as well as human design. A firm is sui generis, of its own species, and each member of it develops its own unique way of doing things.

How to Use the Natural Laws

- ***Exploit the fractal nature of business.*** Gain experience and skill in spotting the recurrent patterns that are peculiar to your own business space. Remember that it is experience at pattern spotting, not the time that you spend in a market, that is valuable. Don't expect the patterns to be the same as in other markets, even if they are very adjacent and appear very similar.

- ***Grab the first-mover advantage.***

- ***Be flexible and have strategies, not just one strategy.*** Realize the role of chance and apparently trivial events. Build flexibility into your plans and actions. Be willing and able to change tack halfway. Allocate some of your resources to "long-odds" bets: experiments that will probably come to nothing but could contain the seeds of major success if market conditions change radically.

- ***However unfavorable the circumstances, look for the things that you can control.*** When things go wrong, don't invent the excuse of a large and uncontrollable market change. Look for all the small things that could have gone wrong and that you could influence.

- ***Practice emergence.*** Identify emergent trends and unexpected successes, and go with their flow.

- ***Don't overorganize, but don't let self-organization scupper your plans.*** Be vigilant for evidence of corporate self-indulgence.

- ***Expect nonlinearity.*** Don't expect simple cause-and-effect relationships to dominate. Find hidden, recurrent patterns within apparently senseless data. Immerse yourself in the data and the action and leave your brain to sort out useful patterns.

10 Achieving More with Less

The 80/20 Principle

For a very long time, the Pareto law [the 80/20 Principle] has lumbered around the economic scene like an erratic block on the landscape: an empirical law which works and which nobody can explain.

JOSEF STEINDL, ECONOMIST, in *Random Processes and the Growth of Firms: A Study of the Pareto Law*

A microchip's physical content isn't very valuable. Silica is the cheapest and most abundant raw material on the planet—sand. But a microchip—its shape, its design, its unseen artistry—is extremely valuable. Yet it comes from a source that seems almost unlimited—the knowledge and inspiration that we draw from the human mind and spirit. This is the most valuable resource and the most abundant.

TACHI KIUCHI, CHAIRMAN, *Mitsubishi Electric America*

The history of civilization is the history of achieving more with less, the happiest nonlinear relationship. The development of agriculture nearly seven thousand years ago moved mankind beyond Stone Age hunter-gathering. The progress of science since the seventeenth century enabled fantastic and sustained leaps in agricultural and industrial productivity that have enabled the earth to support quite unprecedented numbers of people, hundreds of millions of them at or beyond living standards historically reserved for a tiny élite.

Science and technology have enabled us to do things—produce food and shelter, conquer disease, travel, build monuments, communicate, create art, enjoy ourselves—to progressively higher standards using only tiny fractions of the natural resources and time that used to be necessary. Reflect that two or three centuries ago 98 percent of the labor force was employed on the land, producing food, and now 2 to 3 percent of the workforce produces far more food for far more people with far less effort. Then think of how much is produced by computers and the Internet, and how few natural resources go into the process. A century ago there were no computers. And as Diane Coyle comments,[1] a single birthday card weighing less than a gram with a microchip that plays "Happy Birthday" when you open it contains more computer power than existed on the whole planet fifty years ago.

More for less, the hallmark of progress and wealth creation throughout the ages. More for less is always possible. It's also, happily, quite inevitable. Sooner or later, in anything, we will get more for less. And however much more you get for however much less today, you can be absolutely confident that tomorrow you will get even more than today's more for even less than today's less.

Furthermore, it all boils down to science and technology, to intelligent use of knowledge.

A myriad of specific applications and improvements incarnate science's forward march. But it is also worth asking whether there are general laws that underpin the process, that can help us extract more from less in any application or task.

It so happens that there are, and this chapter explores them.

Language, the Movies, and the World Wide Web

What do language, movies, and the World Wide Web all have in common? Many things, perhaps, but one key commonality is that they are all highly pronounced examples of an extremely useful natural law, one that can always point the direction to achieving more with less.

One example is everyday language. Sir Isaac Pitman invented shorthand after finding that just seven hundred words made up a staggering 70 percent of conversation. Including derivatives of these words, Pitman found, the proportion went up to 80 percent. The *New Oxford Shorter English Dictionary* lists more than half a million words. What this means, then, is that fewer than 1 percent of words make up 80 percent of word usage.

In 1999, two Xerox corporation researchers[2] found that a tiny proportion of sites on the World Wide Web command most of the traffic: 119 sites—fewer than one tenth of 1 percent—received 32 percent of all visits (the top site was Yahoo!). The top 5 percent of sites in the sample, comprising about 6000 sites, received 75 percent of the visits.

The same pattern of a few important winners and a mass of unimportant losers is evident in the movies. In 1997, two economists studied the revenues and life spans of 300 movies released over an eighteen-month period. They found that four movies earned 80 percent of the box office, while the other 296 movies had to make do with a miserable share of the remaining 20 percent.[3] In other words, 1.3 percent of the total number of movies accounted for 80 percent of the revenue: an even more extreme example than the World Wide Web, but the same general skewed distribution.

Pareto's Law

What speech, the Web, and movies have in common is a profound imbalance in how the spoils are divided. The first person to spot the prevalence of such patterns was the Italian economist Vilfredo Pareto in 1897, as he studied the distribution of wealth and income across the working population.[4] Pareto found a small minority earned a substantial majority of total incomes (or enjoyed a predominant share of wealth). What really fascinated him was that the distribution followed almost exactly the same pattern whatever the time period and whichever country he examined. In the last half century, Pareto's law has come to be generally known as the *80/20 Principle* (or 80/20 rule), based around the rough observation that the top 20 percent of any distribution usually accounts for about 80 percent of its power or impact.

In business, many studies have shown that the most popular 20 percent of products account for approximately 80 percent of sales; that the 20 percent of the largest customers also account for about 80 percent of sales; and that roughly 20 percent of sales account for 80 percent of profits. Likewise, it is a safe bet that about 80 percent of crime will be accounted for by only 20 percent of criminals, that 80 percent of accidents will be due to 20 percent of drivers, that 80 percent of wear and tear on your carpets will occur in only 20 percent of their area, and that 20 percent of your clothes get worn 80 percent of the time.

"80/20" is not a magic formula. The actual pattern is very unlikely to be precisely 80/20. Sometimes the relationship between results and causes is closer to 70/30 than to 80/20. Sometimes, as in the three examples above, the pattern is even more extreme than 80/20. For the World Wide Web, there is a 75/5 relationship: 5 percent of sites attracted 75 percent of visits, and about 7 percent of sites receive 80 percent, so in this case it is 80/7 rather than 80/20. For movies it is 80/1 (to the nearest round number): 1 percent of movies make 80 percent of the box office gross. The use of words also displays an 80/1 relationship: fewer than 1 percent of words is used 80 percent of the time.

The point is that *the relationship between causes and effects is very rarely 50/50 or anywhere near it.* In this sense, the universe is not very democratic, as proven on the World Wide Web, despite hopes that it would allow a large number of contestants to compete on a level playing field. The power of the 80/20 principle lies in the fact that it is not fully intuitive. Although we do expect some things to be more important than others, we don't expect the differences between the important things and the less important things to be anywhere near as great as they usually are.

The universe is predictably unbalanced—roughly along 80/20 lines. To a much greater extent than we expect, few things really matter. *Truly effective people and organizations batten on to the few powerful forces at work in their worlds, and turn them to their advantage.*

Less Is More

"Less is more" was made famous by Ludwig Mies van der Rohe (1886–1969), the "minimalist" German architect. The phrase actually comes from Robert Browning's 1855 poem, "Andrea del Sarto."

"Less is more" is a useful catchphrase because it reminds us that much of what we do, when closely analyzed, has negative value. Many activities, customers, products, and suppliers actually *subtract* value, which helps to explain why their very positive counterparts produce such a high proportion of net value. So here's another even more useful motto for businesspeople, courtesy of Bill Bain, founder of consultants Bain & Co.: "The best way to start making money is to stop losing money." The best way to become more effective is to stop your negative activities.

Juran's Rule of the Vital Few

One of the great heroes in business of the last century—better known in Japan than in the United States, the land of his adoption—was Joseph Moses Juran. More than anyone else,[5] Juran pioneered the quality revolution that made the second half of the twentieth century a time of unprecedented, and increasingly global, advances in the quality of consumer products from cars to computers. In 1951, Juran published the *Quality Control Handbook,* which made what he alternately identified as the Pareto principle and the *rule of the vital few* synonymous with the search for dramatically higher product quality.

Juran said that our key quest should always be to isolate the "vital few" causes of anything—in his case, of poor quality—as opposed to the "trivial many." Quality losses were not, in general, due to a multiplicity of causes. In each case, a small number of critical problems could be singled out.

Juran's theory made little headway in the United States in the two years after he published his great work. But his 1953 lectures in Japan caused a sensation. He stayed on to work with several major Japanese corporations, helping them to approach, then to catch up with, and finally to exceed the best American quality standards. It was only in the 1970s and 1980s, when Japanese competition menaced Europe and the United States, that Juran and his movement were taken seriously in the West. He moved back to do for U.S. business what he'd achieved in Japan.

Giant Strides in Computing Using the 80/20 Principle

In 1963, IBM realized that about 80 percent of a computer's time was spent on a maximum of 20 percent of the operating code. This insight immediately led the company to rewrite its software to make that most popular 20 percent much more accessible, fast, and user friendly than previously, giving it a significant advantage over competitors. In the 1990s, Microsoft took the 80/20 approach even further, devoting obsessive energy to simplifying the most popular uses of the PC.

Throughout the industry, most software writers and computing executives became aware, implicitly or explicitly, of the 80/20 principle. Is it a coincidence that, of all high-tech products, the PC is the easiest for technically challenged people (like me) to master?

Winner Take All ("Superstar") Principle

One illustration of the 80/20 principle is in the massive and increasing gap between the returns of the top earners—whether these are Steven Spielberg, Bill Gates, Rupert Murdoch, Oprah Winfrey, Pete Sampras, Luciano Pavarotti, or the top trial lawyers, writers, and other professionals who are the stars of their own worlds—and those who are just below the top rank. The superstars take an amazing proportion of the total, and their popularity becomes self-reinforcing.

Whenever markets operate freely, they tend to divide the world into a few very fortunate people on the one hand and everyone else on the other. During the 1980s, an astonishing 64 percent of the total increase in salaries in America went to the top 1 percent: a 64/1 principle! This may be neither healthy for society, nor sustainable, but it does illustrate how free markets, and the universe, generally operate.

The Ubiquity, Universality, and Usefulness of the 80/20 Principle

Of all the natural laws in this book, the 80/20 principle is one of the most universal. It seems to apply to almost anything. It is built into the fabric of the universe. Even evolution by natural selection can be viewed as one tremendously important subset of the 80/20 principle. (The theory of natural selection actually follows much more directly from the 80/20 principle than it does from Malthus's theory of competition among individuals for food.[6])

In evolution, in business, in society, and in life generally, there are always a few powerful influences, a few things that really matter—and also an enormous amount of background noise, which is best ignored. In paying attention to this distracting noise, which we often mistake for something important, significant, and urgent, we limit our effectiveness and squander the energy that we should be using to observe and co-opt (or avoid) the powerful forces around us. Nothing is more difficult, I find, than to keep remembering that, beneath the hurly-burly of ordinary life—when we are continually assaulted by demands on our attention and time—that the 80/20 principle is still operating.

Virtually all businesses do more than they should, own more than they should, acquire more than they should, and try to exert influence where they shouldn't. Nearly all executives overextend their managerial reach, get involved in too many projects, spread their resources too thin, and focus too little on the few details that will determine their success or failure. So do the great majority of managers in nonbusiness organizations, civil servants, and politicians. So do almost all of us in our private lives: we spend time, energy, and money on things that will only marginally affect our happiness and value to others; we fail to give due weight to the few people, events, and objectives that give our lives meaning.

How to Use the 80/20 Principle in Business

There are many helpful *tactical* uses of the 80/20 principle to help your organization or your career. It can be used in negotiations, including for a pay raise, and also in your personal life. But to avoid repeating what I've said in an earlier book,[7] I'm going to concentrate on the *strategic* ways to use the principle in business.

The key insight is that your firm almost certainly does too much.

The hypothesis is that 20 percent of what it does leads to 80 percent of the benefit. If this is true, it follows that the firm should do more of the 20 percent (or similar activity), but very little of the 80 percent.

Too abstract? Let me be more concrete. Your firm should do less, but more profitably. Whichever way you cut it, the firm should concentrate on its most productive and profitable elements and activities, and forget or farm out the rest.

So what should it do less of? For starters, the firm should:

- Own less.
- Acquire less and divest more.
- Participate in fewer stages of the value chain.
- Have fewer products.
- Have fewer customers.
- Have fewer suppliers.
- Have fewer employees.

Own Less

Managers like to own things that might go up in value, and it's generally believed that ownership enables us to control what is owned. Unfortunately, in business as in life, the reverse is often true: our possessions end up controlling us. In business, it is now clear that the obsession with owning things is passé. We don't need to own assets and infrastructure to control revenue and profit streams. In addition, there are severe disadvantages to ownership, when compared to the nonownership options.

By definition, half of the world's total business assets destroy value. They fail to earn the average return on capital. Having them therefore destroys value.

If this sounds too much like a theoretical construct, look at the following examples of value creation and capture without very much ownership.[8] Canon, a very successful player in global markets for copiers, laser printers, cameras, and image scanners, has two power alleys; research and development—especially its skills in optics, imaging, and microprocessor control—and marketing. In all other business activities, Canon partners with other companies and does very little independently. Most of its products are made from components manufactured by hundreds of small suppliers; Canon adds value by standing in the middle, designing the products and controlling the whole process, while owning few assets. In turn, Canon's products are sold through outside global trading companies, themselves working through independent dealer networks. Canon is able to earn high returns through others' capital because it confines itself to areas where it has unparalleled technical expertise—for example, no other corporation has such a mastery of the inner workings of fax machines.

Microsoft is extremely profitable because it has established Windows as the arbiter of PC operating system standards. Microsoft dominance in software—which accounts for only 2 percent of the computer industry's total costs, but a great deal more of its value—gives it profit margins several times the industry average. Microsoft does not own much, but what it owns is essential.

McDonald's follows the same path in a much lower-tech industry. It controls a whole network of suppliers and owns as few assets as possible. The hard slog is done by others. What McDonald's does is bind the whole system together, defining standards of customer service and organizing the machine like clockwork.

These are examples of what is increasingly referred to as the "virtual company."[9] Branded "manufacturers" of autos and PCs are usually nowadays nothing of the sort; they often contract out not just manufacturing, but often large chunks of design and subassembly. They don't own, yet they do control. Some airlines approach virtuality: they lease their planes, they contract in their engineering, maintenance, catering, ground support services, ticket sales, and in some cases even their pilots and cabin crew. You trust that they control these activities—because you trust the brand. Whole industries like oil exploration and production are becoming increasingly virtual.

Even government is discovering that it can control the delivery of welfare services without having to own the delivery service.

There are four advantages to controlling without owning. One is that the arrangement requires less cash, so return on capital can go up and, in some cases, reach astronomical levels. The second advantage is that you can concentrate your efforts on becoming a leader in your narrow specialty. Third, by outsourcing you have access to people who are best in their field. Try comparing other services to what you can get in-house. Often, the outside supplier can deliver a better product cheaper than the in-house alternative. Finally, and perhaps most importantly, controlling without owning results in flexibility and speed, and you can avoid paying unnecessary surpluses to internal staff. Inflexibility is also apparent when owning assets that are based on obsolete technology or high-cost labor, which can actually prevent firms from giving their customers the most up-to-date and efficient service possible. Ownership may enable you to control today's processes at the expense of missing out on tomorrow's.

Since knowing how to serve customers better and cheaper is the only way for companies to survive and profit, and since knowledge resides ultimately in people, it is impossible to own the most important components of corporate success in any case. Similarly, many activities that appear to involve ownership need not actually do so. Buildings, materials, computers, communication lines, manufacturing equipment, and almost everything else that appears to give physical substance to companies can be leased or hired.

Own only the 20 percent that contributes 80 percent of effective control. And if possible, don't own anything.

Acquire Less

It is a paradox that profits can be made by a company that owns nothing, yet managers spend enormous amounts of money to acquire other companies. A partial explanation for this is that access to a stream of profits is worth paying for. But this doesn't explain why managers prefer to acquire rather than build businesses from scratch (where much less capital can generate much more cash in the long run), or why the prices paid for acquisitions (as measured by price/earning ratios) have skyrocketed beyond the businesses' worth. Nor can "stream of profits" explain why you should sacrifice scarce capital to buy an existing business when you could earn a higher long-term return and spend less by expanding your own business.

The paradox can only be explained by what I call the "false market in acquisitions." Acquisitions are more expensive than is economically justified only because managers prefer to buy than to sell, and because managers have tighter deadlines than is good for the owners of the businesses (or anyone else). Building companies from the ground up takes too long for managers to reap the benefit personally.

I don't mean to imply that all acquisitions are stupid or too expensive; only that the average acquisition is (and all the below-average ones are). Conversely, not all divestments add value, but well over half do.

Mergers and acquisitions (M&A) are still growing, despite spin-offs, demergers, and unbundlings. But the alternative form of combinations—corporate alliance—has grown even faster.[10] Corporate alliance is often a better alternative to acquisition.

The global auto market now resembles a tangled mass of spaghetti, a complex network of relationships. Alliances are the dominant trend in the global auto market, in the financial services industry, in computers, and in telecommunications. Coca-Cola, McDonald's, and Disney have a global alliance that benefits them all, combining Coke's brand and marketing, McDonald's distribution strengths, and Disney's branded characters. Virgin uses its brand to enter other businesses, including its book and cola ventures in the United Kingdom. Whereas Richard Branson pays close attention to his international airline business, many of the other ventures benefit simply from the Virgin brand—everything else is organized autonomously from Virgin. This enables Virgin to take a financial interest without using any capital and virtually without any management; it avoids the expense and value destruction that come with acquisitions, while ensuring that value is added via the Virgin brand.

It is often easier, and nearly always much cheaper, to get what you want from another company via alliance rather than acquisition.

Participate in Fewer Stages of the Value Chain

The "value chain" is all the activities that lie between the conception of a product or service and its arrival in the hands of the customer. It involves research and development; product design, component manufacture, assembly, and processing; branding and marketing; selling, physical distribution, and delivery; after-sales service; and any other stages that are relevant to your own industry. If, like most businesses, you participate in more than one of these stages, you are unlikely to be equally good, when compared to the best competitor, at all of them.

Many very successful businesses focus all or nearly all their energies on one or two stages of the value chain. Companies that just do oil exploration, or production, or marketing have tended to be more profitable than the integrated majors. Firms like Filofax that used to undertake substantial aspects of product manufacture are more profitable now that they have focused only on product design, branding, and marketing. Companies that just brand and market baby buggies and strollers, *or* that just manufacture them, are more profitable than the firms that do it all. Hotel corporations are dividing themselves into units that own and manage the hotel property, and units that operate hotels. The profits of the Coca-Cola Company leapt after it divested its bottling and physical distribution operations to a large number of local bottlers around the world.

Concentrate on the 20 percent of activities which earn you 80 percent of the value.

Have Fewer Products

Examine your product profitability. A good hypothesis is that 20 percent of product will generate 80 percent of profits. Generally, the bottom half of products are depressing your average return on capital. It's also likely that the bottom half of products don't meet your required rate of return, and possible that a good chunk of them are actually loss-makers.

In the early 1980s, I was part of a consulting team that helped Baxter Travenol reduce its health care product line and increase the attention given to very profitable lines; profits soared as a result.

In 1990, I organized a rescue bid for the Filofax Group. One of the major issues was that the product line had proliferated wildly. The same basic personal organizer binder was available in a bewildering variety of sizes and a huge assortment of skins. Name a creature, and I am sure that Filofax had binders made of its skin. We didn't know what a karung was, but we inherited an awful lot of its hide in 1990. Similarly, name a subject: bridge, chess, photography, bird watching, windsurfing—inserts for all kinds of users were available. We were quickly able to establish that 85 percent of the product line was loss-making. Out it went. We focused on a small number of very profitable products. Within three years, losses had been turned to strong profits and the shares had multiplied ten times.

If your products conform to the typical pattern, a 20 percent increase in sales of the most profitable products would lead to an 80 percent increase in profits. Even a 10 percent sales increase, if concentrated in the most profitable products, will probably lead to a 40–60 percent profit increase. Conversely, a 10–20 percent drop in the least profitable products is likely to lead to an increase in profits, even if no overhead is cut. If overhead can be cut in line with sales, then over a year or so you may be able to cut sales by a third and increase absolute profits, as well as dramatically increase the return on capital.

Have Fewer Customers

The same logic applies to customers. Sometimes customers are more (or less) profitable because of the kind of products that they purchase or because they are willing to pay higher (or lower) prices. Very frequently, though, it's because they take different amounts of energy and cost to serve. In most businesses today, the majority of internal cost lies in "overhead." Overhead is very rarely allocated to customers, yet when this is done it becomes apparent that some customers require a great deal more overhead cost than others, relative to the sales that they produce.

Generally, the most profitable customers are those that have been customers for a long time. Gaining new customers is very expensive. If they are not suitable in the first place, or if they are lost quickly, the cost of acquiring these customers, through advertising, coupons, or discounts, may be much greater than the benefit from having them. Retaining and selling more to the most profitable existing customers has an enormous value that will never be apparent from conventional accounting reports.

Losing your worst customers means that you can provide a better service to your best ones and others like them.

State Farm is a highly successful insurance company that bases its success on identifying and retaining its profitable customers. It's a mutual company owned by its policyholders, and it has gained market share relentlessly, now insuring more than a fifth of U.S. households. Whereas growth by many insurance companies can only be funded by debt, State Farm has generated more than $20 billion of internal funds at the same time as it has grown so impressively—so State Farm is highly profitable. State Farm has lower sales and distribution costs than its competitors, yet it pays its agents more than the going rate. *Fortune* magazine hails State Farm as "one of the nation's great businesses."[11]

State Farm's success derives from its careful customer (and employee) selection and retention systems. Customers receive great rates and terrific service, so customer retention exceeds 95 percent—that is, fewer than 5 percent of customers in one year are not customers the following year. State Farm's retention rate is far higher than the industry norm and the best performance of any insurer that sells through agents.

How does State Farm do this? The answer is that it genuinely takes care of its customers. For instance, in 1992–93, Hurricane Andrew produced such large claims in Florida that many insurance companies disputed liability, paid the minimum possible, and then refused to reinsure their clients. But when State Farm found out that its policyholders had their roofs blown off because contractors had not anchored them properly to their frames, the company's response was in marked contrast to its competitors'. State Farm actually paid its customers *more* than required, so that they could secure the roofs properly: "We will be insuring the homes in the future, and we don't want them damaged," said State Farm's general counsel. This is how to generate loyalty, systematically raise revenues, and cut costs over the very long term.[12]

Another case of loyalty at work is Leo Burnett, the Chicago-based advertising agency, creator of the Jolly Green Giant, the Marlboro Man, and the Friendly Skies. Leo Burnett makes customer retention a religion, and has the highest retention rate in the industry: typically, 95 percent to 99 percent of Leo Burnett's revenues each year come from repeat clients. Leo Burnett is unusual in its industry in that senior account managers dedicate nearly all their time to one client, whose people and business they get to know intimately. Productivity at Leo Burnett is the highest in the industry, 15 to 20 percent higher than its competitors.

Very successful direct marketers like Lands' End and L. L. Bean also measure customer retention carefully, which is unusual in their industry. It helps to explain why they have grown faster and are more profitable than their peers. In this case, superb customer service is the key to generating loyalty.

Have Fewer Suppliers

We're generally more concerned with customer or product profitability than with supplier profitability, but supplier profitability is just as important. For example, ten suppliers each charge you $1 million a year for supplies; the 80/20 principle hypothesizes that 80 percent of the real value is contained in 20 percent of the supplies. If we assume that your return on sales is 10 percent, and that this applies equally to bought-in and in-house activities, it follows that the real value to you of the $10 million of bought-in goods and services is actually $11 million. Hypothetically, therefore, $2 million of the supplies are worth $8.8 million (80 percent of $11 million), and the remaining $8 million of supplies are worth only $2.2 million.

Wouldn't it be nice to identify the supplies where each dollar buys you $4.40 worth of value? Wouldn't you tend to buy more of these supplies? Wouldn't you have a strong incentive to sell more of the products and services that are particularly intensive in their use of the profitable supplies, and stop taking large losses on the majority of supplies bought in?

There have been thousands of studies of customer and product profitability that have reproduced the rough 80/20 pattern. But because it is much more difficult to measure supplier profitability, both conceptually and practically, than it is to measure customer or product profitability, I can cite no empirical studies to back up my point about suppliers. I am confident, however, that some supplies are much more profitable than others. There have been studies showing that firms with fewer suppliers are more profitable than comparable firms with more suppliers.[13] One reason for this is that simplicity has high value, but another reason is that firms with fewer suppliers are likely to have deliberately picked the most profitable ones.

Have Fewer Employees

This is a touchy subject, but it has long been apparent—both to objective academics and to reflective managers—that in every organization some employees add a great deal more value than they extract, whereas for others the reverse is true. In this case, because we can measure individual productivity easily, the 80/20 principle has been validated: both 80 percent of sales, and 80 percent of the profits from sales, are generated by roughly 20 percent of salespeople.

What is true of individuals in any function or activity is also true between groups. In every organization there is a small corps of individuals, in one particular type of function or activity, who generate the most spectacular profits relative to their cost, and a majority of people in other functions and activities who add little value beyond their cost, or who cost more than they are worth. In the consulting firms where I worked, for example, the real value was added at the top and the bottom of the firm—at the level of the best partners, and at the most junior professional level, where young analysts were cheap, bright, and incredibly hardworking. The partners sold and came up with workable ideas; the young analysts did most of the grunt work. The run-of-the-mill consultants in between pretended to do something useful, and were expensive.

In most pharmaceutical companies, it's a few geniuses in the labs who add most of the value. In Microsoft, the stars are Bill Gates, probably a few of his very top executives, and a few of the most creative software nerds. In investment banks, the real profits are generated by the few traders who consistently call their market right, the few analysts who pick excellent investments for the bank's own balance sheet, and the few rainmakers who bring in the mega-deals. In all these organizations, every other cadre and every other individual is seriously overpaid, just because they're there and the organization can afford to overpay them.

Keep the 20 percent (or fewer) of employees who add most of the value, and work out how to export the rest, whether by outsourcing, through spin-offs, natural wastage, or mass firings. If this is impossible, form a spin-off company comprised of the most valuable cadre of individuals.

The Simple Firm

The firm that owns less, acquires less, divests more, reduces its scope in terms of value-added activities, trims its product line, and reduces its number of customers, suppliers and employees, will find itself much less complex than when it started. Complexity adds cost, and it also encourages executives and the whole firm to be slow, inward looking, and deaf to customers. Simplicity changes the firm's ratio between useful cost and useless cost, to the customer's benefit.

The firm that does more with less is not necessarily a small firm. Because it does more, the firm may end up being very large indeed, or at least very valuable. The world's most valuable firm is Microsoft. Relative to its stock market value, it is still a small firm. And it *feels* like a small firm. "Size works against excellence," Gates comments. "Even if we are a big company, we cannot think like a big company or we are dead." Gates splits the company into units with no more than two hundred people in each. But the main reason why Microsoft avoids the pitfalls usually associated with size is that it is a *simple* company. It has one major product line. It hires one sort of person: exceptionally smart, young, energetic, and in love with technology. It is a meritocracy in one sense, with no status symbols and respect dependent on achievement, and an autocracy in another sense, with Gates as CEO enjoying unrivaled power. Everything conduces toward simplicity.

Return On Management Employed (ROME)

Simplicity is important because management expertise is becoming more important than capital. Probably the defining, most important business concept of the twentieth century was ROCE, *Return On Capital Employed.* The defining business concept of the twenty-first century could prove to be ROME,[14] *Return On Management Employed* (or *Return On Management Effort*), which refers to focused, insightful, value-adding executives, not capital. Ideas, brains, knowledge, technical skills, and the sheer ability to get sensible things done—these have more value and rarity than cash.

Whether it knows it or not, the simple firm has worked this out. It is trying to maximize ROME, not ROCE.

More complex firms would do well to classify all their business segments on a two-by-two matrix, looking at ROME and ROCE. Only businesses with high ROCE and high ROME should be retained as part of the core; the rest should be spun off or sold. *Even businesses with high ROCE are not really as profitable as they look if they also have a low ROME, because they are hogging the scarce resource (management) which, if used, elsewhere, could raise profitability.*

Focus on the 20 percent of businesses that have high ROCE and high ROME, the few that really do offer great returns on what is truly scarce. If there is a conflict between ROCE and ROME, give priority to the latter.

The Power of Weak Ties

A weak tie is one where there is no direct ownership, financial interest, control, contract, or affiliation, but where there is some connection as a result of knowledge, indirect links ("a friend of a friend"), geography, professional group, or some other accidental or incidental conduit. One example of the power of weak ties is how people find out about jobs. Apart from advertisements and headhunters, the main source of information is not from close friends and family or existing employers, but via informal networks, friends of friends, and information randomly accessed from other sources.

Another example might be two communities that were threatened with disruption by major road projects. In one community, there were plenty of strong ties within monolithic organizations, like the church, a few large organizations, and the local council, but few links across the boundaries of these strong ties. Each group kept to itself. In the other community, there were few strong ties, but many weak ties between smaller clusters of interest groups, none very strong or influential. In the first community, the monolithic groups each kicked up an enormous fuss but could not mobilize across a broad front because each group ignored the others. In the second community, the weak ties gradually produced a groundswell of united protest that was successful in blocking the road project.

Silicon Valley epitomizes the power of weak ties. Here are a large number of independent, fiercely competitive businesses and yet there are ties between the firms and the people. Executives swap jobs frequently, they gossip in bars, they go to industry conventions, they occasionally collaborate on projects, they play sports together, they share information. By way of contrast, Route 128 outside of Boston has the same industrial structure—many competing firms—but far fewer of the informal, weak ties; people are much more secretive and insulated from each other, and engage far less in a wide range of social contacts.[15] Sharing information and experience is important because learning doesn't have to take place within one firm. Ideas in Silicon Valley are cross-pollinated quickly to raise productivity.

The power of weak ties is closely related to another natural law we examined in Chapter 5, Jared Diamond's principle of intermediate fragmentation, which states that you don't want excessive unity and you don't want excessive fragmentation. Instead, you want your human society or business to be broken up into a number of groups that compete with each other but that also maintain relatively free communication.

The power of weak ties illuminates both the 80/20 principle and the way in which influence can be exerted across boundaries. If weak ties will do, you can forgo strong ties, ownership, and control over people. You can achieve 80 percent of your objective with only 20 percent of the ammunition. In fact, strong ties may be less effective than weak ones, because strong ties encourage a sense of internal identity that removes the appetite for, or the ability to digest, a whole range of weak external ties.

The 50/5 Principle

Another theory parallel to the 80/20 principle is the *50/5 principle.* Typically, 50 percent of a company's customers, products, components, and suppliers comprise a mere 5 percent or less of sales and profits. Therefore, if you eliminate the low-volume customers, products, components, and suppliers, whether or not the numbers show it, you will experience an increase in real profits.

For instance, in the early 1990s, Corning conducted 50/5 analysis at two plants which produced ceramic substrates for auto exhaust systems, one in Greenville, Ohio, and the other in Kaiserslautern, Germany. True to the 50/5 principle, out of 450 products made at Greenville, half produced 96.3 percent of total sales. The other 50 percent of products yielded just 3.7 percent. At the German plant, the bottom half of products produced only 2–5 percent of sales. In both plants, the lower 50 percent of products were responsible for most of the losses. These products were eliminated, resulting in much simpler businesses, and, before long, a 25 percent reduction in engineering overhead.[16]

Because it is less radical and less threatening, 50/5 analysis is a good precursor to 80/20 analysis.

Control Theory

The 80/20 principle implies that we should reduce the number of variables that we are trying to control. There are a few cases, however, in which it may be appropriate to exercise extremely tight control.

Control theory can help here. In physics and biology, control mechanisms are used to regulate dynamic processes to achieve the controller's objectives. The basic idea is simple: monitor your experiment and if the system doesn't perform as expected, force it back on course via repeated corrections called "negative feedback."

Many biological processes exemplify negative feedback, such as when the population of a species rises. As a result, food becomes scarce and the population then falls back to a sustainable level.

Thermostats and air conditioning are based on control theory. Attempts are now being made to use it to control complex systems such as irregular heartbeats, nerve impulses, or artificial satellites. Whereas many attempts by humanity to exert control over the environment have proved disappointing, control theory, because it is part of natural patterns, may prove to be an extremely effective tool. According to Ian Stewart:

> In the future we may well use it [control theory] to control the flow of turbulent air past an aircraft wing, the population of codfish off the coast of Newfoundland, or the migration of locusts in North Africa. And we may use it to send supplies to our newly constructed Moonbase using only half the fuel now required.[17]

Control theory can only work if it is possible to define the outputs you want precisely, and to measure them precisely, too. Budgeting is a form of control mechanism; the accounting systems that reduce business to a few figures that can be measured and monitored are a good example of the value and limitations of control theory. The system of budget monitoring works quite well, but only if we all believe in the validity of the numbers presented. In reality, the information presented is necessarily distorted and only part of what should really be monitored, yet alternative systems have proved too complex and unworkable.

Sometimes, when a company launches a new product, it sets up a system to measure how often customers decide to try it. Therein lies the mistake, because what matters is not trial but repurchase rates after trial. Because repurchase is much more difficult to track, the wrong measure is often used—and the whole effort has no value.

Only use control theory if you are sure that you are going to measure the really important thing and that it can be measured precisely. Then:

- Define precisely what you are trying to do and how you will measure the output.
- Measure the output.
- Expect the output to differ from the plan.
- Correct the output to achieve the plan by applying feedback, or, if the market is telling you clearly to do so, change the plan.
- Keep repeating the process until the output is in line with the plan.

Fermat's Principle of Least Time

The French mathematician Pierre de Fermat (1601–65) discovered that a ray of light traveling between two points will go the way that takes least time, not the physically shortest route. His mathematical proof of the *principle of least time* led to the laws of reflection and refraction.

In going the quickest way, light is minimizing its scarcest resource: time. We can apply the same principle in business by thinking not about time, but about what is the scarcest resource. Business plans should be organized so that the scarcest resource is used most parsimoniously; things should be arranged for the convenience of the scarcest resource.

Reflect on what's really the scarcest resource in your business. If it is the time of a person, learn to make the most of this. In other words, learn to delegate.

Trichotomy Law

The final natural law which can show you how to achieve more with less is the *trichotomy law.* This states that every real number is either zero, or negative, or positive.

In organizations and in life, we tend to focus on the value that is created, ignoring the value that is subtracted. For example, the management hierarchy clearly has value in helping the top people achieve the organization's objectives. Or individual executives clearly add value in the course of their jobs. Or an organization benefits from having a sister division that is able to share some costs, such as a joint sales force.

The problem is that every activity, unit, or person that adds value probably subtracts value as well. The management hierarchy may demotivate people down the line, insulate them from the business, or lead them to pay more attention to their bosses than to customers. Individual executives may have great strengths, but great weaknesses too, that require clean-up or damage limitation exercises all around them. The sister division may share the cost of the sales force, but limit its effectiveness in selling your most profitable products, which may require a focus on a different sort of customer.

For every plus, there's likely to be a minus. What matters is the net result. We nearly always err in looking at the positive side and neglecting the negative.

One reason that we can achieve more with less is that we can decide not to do things that actually have negative value. Here we benefit twice: once because cost is removed, and again because we remove a negative effect that is greater than the positive effect.

The easiest, and often the best, way to add to personal or orga-

nizational effectiveness is simply to stop doing things that subtract net value. If you can't see what you routinely do—or what the organization routinely does—that subtracts value, ask your colleagues. Be prepared for a long list.

How to Use the Natural Laws

- ***Achieve more with less.*** Make this your resolution every year, month, week, and day.

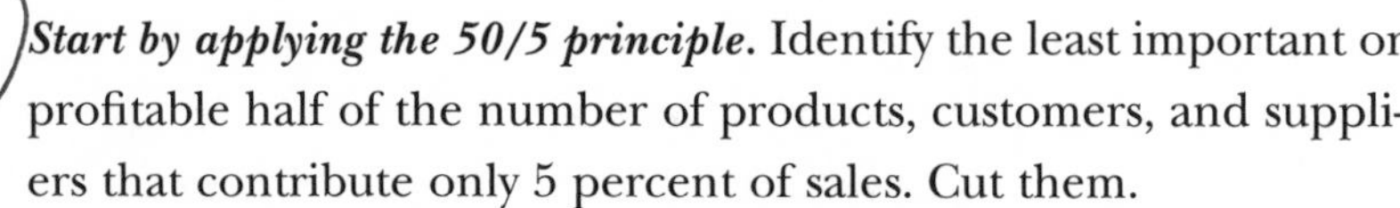

- ***Start by applying the 50/5 principle.*** Identify the least important or profitable half of the number of products, customers, and suppliers that contribute only 5 percent of sales. Cut them.
- ***Move on to the 80/20 principle.*** Identify the 80 percent of products, customers, suppliers, and employees that contribute only 20 percent of value. Make them much more profitable or productive, if this is possible, or, if it isn't, remove them over time.
- ***Focus all your energies on increasing the 20 percent of business***—whether defined by customers, products, or any other measure—**that contributes 80 percent of the value.** Try to sell more of the same or similar products to the relevant customers or others who share similar characteristics.
- ***Be extremely sparing in what you own,*** the capital you use, the acquisitions you make, the number of stages of value added in which you participate, and what you try to control. Over time, make your company more virtual and more focused on the minority of activity that delivers most of the value.
- ***Make your firm as simple as possible.***
- ***Develop skill in managing and exerting influence beyond your organization's boundaries.***

- ***Identify the scarcest, most valuable resource in your organization,*** and arrange everything else to make the best use of this scarce resource.

- ***Think about and measure value subtracted as well as value added.*** Identify whatever activities or links subtract more value than they add, and cut them. Stop any activity that you or others engage in if the value subtracted is nearly as great as, or is greater than, the value added.

11

Punctuated Equilibrium, the Tipping Point, and Increasing Returns

Punctuated Equilibrium

First there is a mountain
Then there is no mountain
Then there is.

ZEN PROVERB

At the start of Chapter 4, we looked briefly at *punctuated equilibrium,* the theory that evolution consists of long periods of stability, interrupted by short periods of rapid transition. Conditions can be stable for several million years. Then, suddenly, the environment changes. The dominant species dies out to be replaced by another species. Or new species altogether emerge. Evolution proceeds by a series of lurches, and everything is different.

Here we will explore this key natural law in more detail, with particular stress on changes in technology and the way it follows the pattern of punctuated equilibrium.

Technological change is *the* main determinant of long-term growth everywhere. Besides opening up new possibilities and creating new needs, technology provides more for less. Besides driving up standards, it lowers costs dramatically. Indexed to one hundred in 1930, the cost of air transport per mile and per passenger had fallen to around seventeen dollars by 1980. The charges for using satellites fell from one hundred dollars in 1980 to about fifteen dollars in 1990. The cost of a three-minute phone call from New York to London fell from around one hundred dollars in 1940 to about two dollars today.

The most important technological changes are the "general purpose" or "enabling" technologies that transform economies and societies, that punctuate the equilibrium. The inventions of the nineteenth century, such as railroads, gas, electricity, and automobiles, marked a punctuation point. Another one occurred in the twentieth century with the surge in computing power, telecommunications, genetic engineering, and the Internet. The historical highlights of enabling technology include domestication of crops and animals, writing, bronze, iron, the water wheel, the windmill, the three-masted sailing ship, the printing press, automated textile machinery, the steam engine, electricity, the internal combustion engine, and the computer. Growth is very largely a function of the extent and speed with which enabling technologies are used, adapted, and spread.[1]

Recall Joseph Schumpeter's insistence that capitalism proceeds via "creative destruction" brought about by technological change. A punctuated point will bring great opportunity to some, and disaster to others. A traditional farmer, determined to plant, grow, and harvest his crops the way his ancestors did for centuries will be threatened by the development of genetically modified crops. A forward-thinking farmer will see the chance to triple productivity, while also raising resistance to agricultural disease, as a financial opportunity and a chance to improve upon an antiquated system.

The "Warning Period" of Embryonic Pre-change

Punctuated equilibrium has some potentially profitable characteristics, though technology may lie latent or largely unexploited for several years before suddenly taking off. The potter's wheel, for instance, was invented before 1500 B.C. but was only adapted for spinning wool thread two and a half millennia later. Eyeglasses were invented in the thirteenth century, but were only recently produced on a mass scale. Leonardo da Vinci designed prototype helicopters and many other advanced machines, but the power mechanisms needed to make them run wouldn't exist for another five hundred years.

Capitalism's advance in the eighteenth century greatly shortened the period between invention and rapid deployment of new technologies. Steam power was applied within decades to every conceivable use: factories, steamships, railroad locomotives. Markets supplied incentives to introduce and diffuse new technologies.

Even today, however, new technologies like cell phones, video recorders, or the Internet do not take off immediately after their invention. They often spend time lurking in the profitless limbo of the enthusiast and the pioneer before exploding into mass markets. For instance, you could buy a fax machine in 1965, but it cost a thousand dollars and could communicate with only a few other machines. Today a fax machine costs only two hundred dollars and connects to 18 million other faxes. Somewhere along the way—in the late 1980s and early 1990s—there were enough fax machines in the network, at a low enough price, to encourage a self-feeding explosion in the purchase of faxes. The process is slow-moving: a prolonged period of stability followed by a much shorter but significant period of embryonic change, followed by the punctuation, and then rapid transition to the new equilibrium. Change does not come from out of the blue. There is a warning period when the embryonic change is apparent to those who are watching for it, even though the full effect of the change has not yet been felt.

Plague Theory

It turns out that the spread of new technologies can be accurately predicted using, of all things, plague theory, which charts how infectious diseases spread. The progress of any disease, from the Black Death to AIDS to less serious infections, can be projected fairly accurately by calculating the proportion of the relevant population that has been infected at a few different time points (years, months, or days) and then extrapolating what will happen if the rate of growth of the disease, as measured by the ratio of the infected to the not yet infected, remains constant.

It is reasonable to assume that the rate of infection will be roughly constant, if we adjust for the proportions of the population that, at any given time, are infected or healthy. It is worth explaining the formula, because it is also useful in estimating how fast any new technology or new business method will spread. Assume that in the first month, 100 people have the plague out of a population of one million. So 999,900 don't have the plague. By the second month, 500 people have the plague and 999,500 don't. In the third month, 2,500 are infected and 997,500 are healthy. With just three data points like this, there is a good chance that we can predict how many people will have the plague in months four to forty-eight. By the fourth month, about 12,300 people are likely to have the plague and 987,700 to be uninfected. The formula for the projections is:

$$x = \frac{f}{1-f}$$

where:

x = the factor by which to measure growth

f = the percentage of the relevant population with the plague

And $1-f$ = the percentage of the population not infected with the plague.

The theory holds that the rate of growth in *x* will remain constant. What typically happens is that the proportion of the population affected by the plague will grow rapidly and at an accelerating rate, then will reach a point of inflection and slow down, and then decelerate rapidly: a typical *S* curve. The fast initial growth comes when the number of people who are infected and can therefore infect other people reaches a certain critical level. The rate of increase in infection slows down when most of those susceptible to infection have been infected and the disease runs out of new people to colonize.

The Tipping Point

If action can be taken to keep the disease below a certain critical level, then it may never reach the point of rapid acceleration, and the proportion of the population affected may end up being a fraction of what it would otherwise have been. The point at which rapid acceleration begins is known as the "tipping point," when the disease "tips over" from being a low-level outbreak to a full-blown public health crisis. We can think of it also as the time when the disease acquires critical mass.

The tipping point is therefore very similar to the time of "punctuation" in punctuated equilibrium. The idea can be applied to any new product, fad, or trend. A new social habit such as taking Ecstasy, in-line skating, or following a new rock group, may initially be a small movement, staying confined to a small subculture or area. Suddenly, it may begin to gather momentum. If it crosses an invisible line, it will eventually embed itself in the culture. If it doesn't cross the line, it will remain a small minority interest. That invisible line is the tipping point.[2]

All new technologies that punctuate an existing equilibrium, and then replace it with another equilibrium, must pass their tipping point. If they don't, they will never become dominant or cause significant change to a business system. The idea of the tipping point is enormously valuable if you are trying to launch a new technology or product, or trying to assess what impact someone else's innovation will have. What's important to realize is that effort or expense is never proportional to results. In the early stages, a terrific amount of cash and energy may be invested, with little apparent payoff. It's at this juncture that many pioneers cut their losses. Yet if you can reach the tipping point it's all downhill from there. Sales and profits snowball, with relatively little incremental investment.

Microsoft's profits were tiny for its first ten years. But once the tipping point was reached, around 1985, they exploded. So too for Federal Express. Following its tipping point, in the early 1980s, it was impossible not to compound profits.

The idea of the tipping point does not tell you how to reach it.

Microsoft's profits exploded because in developing software there is a huge fixed cost; once the software can be sold in large quantities revenues soar without any corresponding increase of costs. Moreover, once Microsoft became accepted as the standard operating system, its revenues rose dramatically. A similar thing happened with FedEx: once the network to deliver everywhere was in place, increasing volume led to much higher revenues but not correspondingly higher costs (a lot of costs like rent, marketing, and other overheads are fixed and do not increase with volume). Moreover, once the FedEx system of reliable overnight delivery was in place, more people used it.

A common characteristic of all systems reaching the tipping point is that there is a snowball effect—what analysts call a "virtuous circle" develops, where one "good thing" leads to another which reinforces a third which in turn increases the initial "good thing." For both Microsoft and FedEx increasing volume lowered unit costs, which both lowered prices and also increased profits, and hence further investment to make the product or service better. Lower prices and better products further increased demand, which further decreased costs and prices and increased profits . . . and so on.

So if you want to know how to reach the tipping point, imagine what it would take to cause a huge upsurge in demand via a virtuous circle. How could you generate a snowball effect, an epidemic? If everything went right, what would happen? Then how can you nudge events on to some such path? This might require heavy investment, but take heart: if the investment is in a direction that nobody has taken yet, it will probably be worthwhile. Before long you may have a success of epidemic proportions on your hands.

The Power of the Unexpected

Peter Drucker, the preeminent management theorist, points out that the easiest and simplest innovation opportunity often lies in the unexpected.[3] In the late 1940s, everyone knew that the only sensible use of computers was for advanced scientific work. Then IBM picked up an unexpected source of interest: certain large business firms, who were not then users of computers at all, indicated that they might want a machine that could run the payroll. IBM was much smaller than UNIVAC—the UNIVAC (UNIVersal Automatic Computer) was the first general-purpose electronic digital computer designed for commercial use, including payroll management—but by providing a machine specifically for payroll applications, IBM overtook UNIVAC within five years. Unexpected successes can transform an industry and overturn competitors' rankings.

Drucker also demonstrates that unexpected *failures* may be just as fertile a source of insight as successes. The Ford Edsel was the best planned and designed car in automobile history, yet it stunned the industry by being its biggest failure. Ford very wisely wanted to find out why: what was happening in the industry that ran counter to everyone's assumptions? Ford discovered that customers were no longer buying cars according to income, but by lifestyle, so that designing new cars for people in a certain income group no longer worked. Hence Ford developed the Mustang, a personality-based car that restored the company's fortunes.

The unexpected is often a tremendous clue to developments that are reaching their tipping point. It is very much cheaper and more effective to latch on to social trends that are already developing, rather than to try to create them from scratch. If something unexpected is happening, this means that an unplanned trend is at work. Exploit it to the fullest!

Crossing the Chasm

In the 1950s, marketing theorists proposed a useful model of how new technologies and products are adopted—first by innovators, then by early adopters, then by the early majority of users, then by the late majority, and finally by the laggards. An original and useful twist to this general model was proposed in the 1990s by Geoffrey Moore, a California-based high-tech marketing guru.

In his brilliant book *Crossing the Chasm*,[4] Moore points out that in the early days, it is easy for a new technology or product to sell itself, since the people who will try it will be "innovators" who love technology or something new for its own sake. Typically, the founder of a high-tech company will be a "techie," an enthusiast and evangelist of the new way. For him, selling to innovators is natural and there is no need to reframe the message.

But when it comes to selling to the early adopters, and still more to the early majority of users, there is a major barrier or gap to be crossed, what Moore calls the "chasm." The chasm exists because the mainstream market is not impressed by technology per se; if anything, the mainstream market is intimidated by technology. The mainstream market wants better performance, lower cost, and all the normal boring purchase criteria; and it wants to be sure above all that the new product and technology is reliable, here to stay, and an integral part of the mainstream market, rather than a plaything for technophiles. This requires a different marketing and selling approach than that of the early days: technological enthusiasm becomes counterproductive—the message must be functional benefits and superior performance. This is the chasm that many incipient technologies and very young companies cannot cross. If they can't cross the chasm, they disappear into it, never to be heard of again.

Moore's model helps to explain what I call the "warning period," during which the new technology is evident but not yet prevalent. The model also gives the astute observer the tools with which to predict whether or not the new technology will make it, and some insight as to when. Unless the technology can sell itself to mainstream customers, which is very unlikely, it requires particularly careful product design and marketing to make it very user-friendly.

The technology will only cross the chasm if it is dressed up to look much less innovative and subversive than it really is. The technology needs the Trojan horse of mainstream marketing to persuade mainstream customers to let it into their lives. Until this happens, the new technology will languish. Cars must appear like horse-drawn carriages (hence "horseless carriage"). Airplanes have to look like trains (with aisles and windows and an engine at the front), not like birds or bats. The PC has to resemble a typewriter. The Internet has to seem like an extension of earlier software tools, linked to the well-established PC.

Exponential Growth

Albert Einstein, when asked what was the greatest force in the world, replied without hesitation: "compound interest."

Try this puzzle. One lily pad, covering one square foot, sits in a pond with an area of one hundred thirty thousand square feet. After a week, there are two lily pads. After two weeks, four pads. Estimate how long it will take to cover the entire pond.

After sixteen weeks, half the pond is covered. Now estimate again: how long before the whole pond is covered with lilies?

It has taken the lily sixteen weeks to cover half the pond. Yet the right answer is that it will take only one more week to cover the whole, since the lily pads are doubling their domain every week—seventeen weeks in total.

There is a fable about an Indian king who wanted to reward the inventor of chess. All the inventor requested was a few grains of rice: one for the first square on the chessboard, two for the second, four for the third, and so on for all the squares. The king thought this was modest—until it was computed that for the last square alone, some 9,223,372,036,000,000,000 grains would be required, about 153 billion tons, more than two and a half million big cargo ships packed to the gunwales with rice. This is because of "exponential" growth, in this case the doubling of rice on every square.

An exponent is a number saying how many times something should be multiplied by itself. For example, if the exponent is 3, and the number is 4, then the expression 4^3 means $4 \times 4 \times 4$, which equals 64. In the mathematical expression y^2, 2 is the exponent, and it means $y \times y$.

How is exponential growth different from linear growth? In linear growth, something increases in size by the same *amount* at each step, not by the same *multiple*. If I start out owning $1,000, and increase it by $100 each year, after ten years I will have doubled my money to $2,000. This is a linear increase, the same amount each year. But if I start with $1,000, and increase it by 10 percent each year, after ten years I will have $2,594. This is exponential growth, a constant multiple (1.1) of growth each year. If I carried on for another ten years, linear growth would give me a total of $3,000, but exponential growth $6,727.

Any market or business that grows at 10 percent or more for any significant stretch of time will have a far greater effect in terms of value creation than we might intuitively estimate. Some businesses—such as IBM or McDonald's in the period from 1950 to 1985, or Microsoft in the 1990s—managed to grow at more than 15 percent per annum, producing fantastic increases in wealth. A slightly higher gain in percentage terms makes a large difference in your potential earnings.

For example, American stock picker William J. O'Neil ran a fund for his Harvard Business School classmates that started with $850 in 1961 and ended up with $51,653 in 1986, after all taxes had been paid.[5] Over twenty-five years, this is an average increase of 17.85 percent each year, producing a total that is 61 times the original stake. Thus, 15 percent per annum for twenty-five years produces 33 times the stake, but adding fewer than 3 percentage points to the growth rate, at just under 18 percent, produces a 61-times increase.

Exponential growth changes things qualitatively as well as quantitatively. For example, when an industry grows quickly—Peter Drucker says when it grows by about 40 percent within ten years—its structure changes, and new market leaders often come to the fore. Markets grow fast because of innovation, discontinuity, new products, new technologies, or new customers. Innovators, by definition, do things differently. The new way of doing business rarely fits the habits, ideas, procedures, and structures of established firms. Innovators may plow forward with their new ideas for several years before traditional leaders counterattack, and then it is often too late.

Big Bang

An extreme form of exponential growth was probably responsible for the start of the universe. Astronomers and physicists now generally accept the *big bang theory,* according to which the universe started at an unimaginably small size and then doubled one hundred times in a split second, enough to make it the size of a small grapefruit. This period of "inflation" or exponential growth then ended, and linear growth took over, with an expanding fireball creating the universe that we know today.

Creation of any sort involves exponential growth. The important lesson here is that, with exponential growth, you don't need to start big. In fact, the initial size of a new business is totally irrelevant. The key requirement is a period of exponential growth, followed by a longer period of linear growth.

Say's Law of Economic Arbitrage

In 1803, French economist Jean-Baptiste Say (1767–1832) produced a remarkably modern work titled *A Treatise on Political Economy.* It contained many surprising innovations, including coining the word "entrepreneur," and the first theory of economic arbitrage: *"The entrepreneur shifts economic resources out of an area of lower productivity into an area of higher productivity and yield."*

Long before the notion of return on capital was promulgated, Say identified one of the most important engines of economic creation and progress. Resources are essentially finite, so growth depends not so much on the discovery and exploitation of natural resources as on making each unit of resource go further. This is partly a function of better technology and methods, but also the entrepreneur's skill in moving resources to where they can be most productive. *All* that is needed to add to human wealth is to take a given set of resources and shift them from areas of low productivity to areas of high productivity. All economic progress rests on economic arbitrage of this type. Arbitrage is easier than creation. Everyone should be capable of thinking of something that could benefit from economic arbitrage, of identifying resources that could be used more effectively.

Creation and entrepreneurship require the supply of new ideas, new methods, and unreasonable approaches. In insisting that automobiles should be bought by workingmen, and not just by the rich, was Henry Ford being reasonable or unreasonable? He certainly was not following demand, since there was no demand for cars except from the rich. Ford refused to accept the world as it was; he persisted in trying to adapt the world to his vision. By using the assembly line and maximum standardization, Ford cut the cost of a Model T from eight hundred and fifty dollars in 1908 to three hundred dollars in 1922 and succeeded in his mission of "democratizing the automobile."[6]

True entrepreneurs don't expect market research to tell them what to do. They have a vision of how to do something better and differently, they work out how to do more with less, they shift resources from low- to high-value uses, and they are persistent and unreasonable until the world has conceded their point.

The Law of Diminishing Returns

One of the most influential and long-running ideas about how markets and businesses operate is the *law of diminishing returns*, developed around 1767 by French economist Robert-Jacques Turgot.

This law says that after a point, increases in effort or investment result in diminishing returns; that is, the incremental value declines. To a hungry woman, a loaf of bread has high value. The second loaf has less. The tenth may have very little value. If you hire additional peasants to till the same plot of land, beyond a certain point diminishing returns set in.

A century after Turgot, the British classical economists, led by Alfred Marshall, extended this idea to markets and firms: products or companies that lead a market run into diminishing returns. The value of being bigger in business—having a larger market share, a bigger factory, a larger product range—reaches a peak and then declines.

The classical economists then claimed that a predictable equilibrium of prices and market shares would be reached, and that perfect competition and diminishing returns should eventually operate to ensure that super to normal returns would be impossible. This theory justified government regulation of markets: if high returns were being made, it could only be because monopolists were rigging the market and obstructing perfect competition.

An Attack on Microeconomics by Heretical Consultants

For almost a century, Marshall and his school dominated economic thinking. It was left to a few business mavericks, such as Bruce Henderson and his Boston Consulting Group (BCG), founded in the early 1960s, to challenge the consensus. BCG demonstrated that:

- Firms typically do not have equal costs. The costs of the market leader are usually significantly lower than those of followers.
- Costs and prices do not reach a static equilibrium. In competitive markets, costs and prices continually shrink. These decreases are particularly characteristic of high-growth markets.
- A firm with high relative market share should, and usually does, have both higher return on capital and intrinsic competitive advantages, compared to other firms in the same market. Far from being subject to diminishing returns, high market share makes it possible to reinforce competitive advantage, by providing better products and services at lower prices, while still earning higher returns than competitors. High market share can lead to a virtuous circle, which further compounds advantage for the leader.

Moore's Law

At about the same time that BCG was publishing its ideas, Gordon Moore, the cofounder of Fairchild Semiconductor in 1957 and Intel in 1968, claimed that computing capacity would double every year at no extra cost, as semiconductor density doubles. He explains:

> I looked at the first few integrated circuits that Fairchild [produced] . . . and just happened to see that we had about doubled the number of components on an integrated circuit every year.

> So I blindly extrapolated that for 10 years, from about 60 to about 60,000 circuits on a chip—a long extrapolation—and it was amazingly precise.[7]

Moore's law was updated in 1975 to say that the number of components on the chip would double every two years, and that has also proved accurate. In 1999, Moore predicted that the gradient would change again and that "it will double every four or five years for quite a long while."

Moore's law was consistent with a more general natural law enunciated in the late 1960s, BCG's experience curve, which said that costs come down by 20 to 30 percent every time the accumulated production of an item doubles. The change in the slope of Moore's law—where initially value doubled every year, then every two years—just reflects the change from hypergrowth to high growth, or an increase in the months needed for industry production to double.

Some industry observers began to suggest that the "IT economy" was different from the rest of the economy, because it did not appear to be subject to diminishing returns. BCG, however, had an intellectual framework suggesting that the world of information technology was just a faster-growth version of the whole economy. BCG's views did not, however, reach their tipping point; they remained largely ignored.

BCG lacked two things: the professional academic credentials to be taken seriously by economists, and a snappy name to encapsulate its new version of economics.

The Law of Increasing Returns

Then, around 1980, along came W. Brian Arthur, an economist from Northern Ireland working in the United States, who was heavily influenced by the ideas of chaos.

Brian Arthur had both professional credentials and the bright idea of branding his thinking as "increasing returns." He also had the good sense not to take on the economic establishment head-on. His *law of increasing returns,* he said, should be seen as a supplement to Marshall's ideas about diminishing returns, not as a replacement for them.

Brian Arthur asked what if products and businesses that got ahead thereby got further ahead?[8] In the early 1980s there were three contenders for the market for operating systems in PCs: CP/M, Microsoft's DOS, and the Apple Macintosh system. CP/M had the advantage of being first. The Mac was probably the best, and certainly the easiest to use.

But operating systems for PCs exhibit increasing returns; if one system gets ahead, more hardware manufacturers and software developers will adopt it, causing it to get further ahead. The turning point happened in 1980 when IBM gave Microsoft an exclusive deal to write the operating system for the IBM PC. Although the latter was not a great machine, the growing base of DOS/IBM users attracted independent software houses, such as Lotus, to write for DOS. Once DOS/IBM had established a clear lead, it was bound to get further ahead because the costs to switch to another system were too high. Microsoft then benefited from economies of scale, being able to spread its costs over a larger user base than competitors, thus enabling Microsoft both to enjoy fatter margins and also to spend more to improve its system.

Increasing returns, says Arthur, are characteristic whenever markets have the following attributes:

- ***High up-front costs,*** especially in R&D rather than production. The first sale of Windows cost Microsoft $50 million; the second $3. These economics make leadership extremely valuable and difficult to challenge.
- ***Network effects.*** Many high-tech products must be compatible with a network of users. Therefore a popular product or system is likely to become the standard. Also, network economics are different from traditional economics.
- ***Customer groove-in.*** High-tech products are difficult to use and also have several generations of product. Users have to invest in training. This training "grooves" or locks customers into the leading product.

Metcalfe's Law

Networks comprise an increasingly important part of our world, and they have their own peculiar economic characteristics. This is easiest to see in communication products like the telephone, fax, a PC operating system, the FedEx courier system, or the Internet. One phone, fax, or e-mail address is useless. Two have some value. Thereafter, any increase in the network size has a more than proportionate increase in value to each user.

Bob Metcalfe, the inventor of Ethernet, a localized networking technology, noticed that small-scale networks were not viable, but that putting together small local networks sharply multiplied their value. In 1980 *Metcalfe's Law* was born: the value of a network equals n squared $(n \times n)$, where n is the number of people in the network. Thus a 10-person network is worth 100, but a 20-person network is worth 400: you double the network and quadruple its value. A linear increase in membership means an exponential (to be more precise, geometric) increase in value.

Network economics therefore exhibit an extreme form of increasing returns, both for all members of a network and for leading suppliers to the network. An expanding network becomes a self-reinforcing virtuous circle. Each new member increases the network's value, which in turn attracts new members.

Networks typically spend quite a while reaching their tipping point, and then there is no stopping them. For twenty years, fax machines struggled to reach their tipping point. Then, from about 1985, almost everyone was installing them.

With networks, value comes from openness and from proliferation. Traditionally, value comes from having a closed, proprietary system and from scarcity. No more. Ask Apple whether keeping the Mac system proprietary was such a smart idea. Ask banks whether cash machines should be proprietary or shared. The more networks ally with other networks, the more valuable they become. The gain in coverage and value creation far exceeds the loss in the exclusivity of value capture.

Economist Paul Krugman observes that "in the Network Economy, supply curves slope down instead of up and demand curves slope up instead of down." The more you have, the more you want: the exact opposite of diminishing utility. The more we make, the easier and cheaper it becomes to make more. This is the beauty of network economics. It is both deflationary—prices come down forever—and expansionary—more and more useful things are created and used.

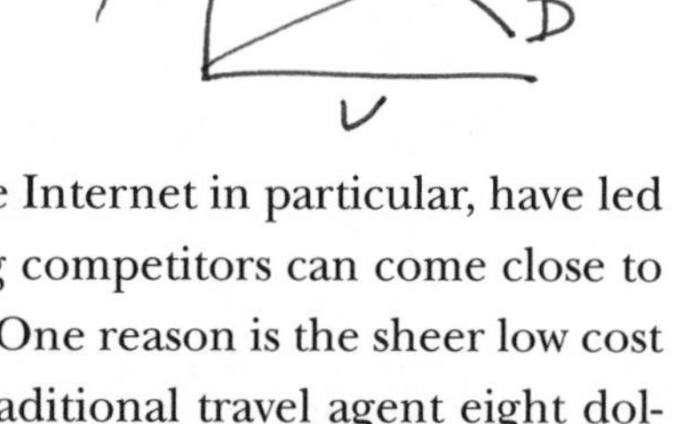

Is There a "New Economy" and a "New Paradigm"?

The possibilities of networks, and the Internet in particular, have led some observers to claim that leading competitors can come close to generating virtually infinite returns. One reason is the sheer low cost of Internet transactions: it costs a traditional travel agent eight dollars to process a typical airline ticket versus just one dollar on the Web; a typical bank transaction costs one dollar, but through the Web it can cost as little as one cent.

As the marginal value of a network increases with scale, so the average cost of software declines, since marginal cost is almost zero. Nonnetwork businesses may have high fixed costs, but the marginal cost of meeting customers' demands never falls near to zero: sales, marketing, and customer service are all expensive operations. Traditionally, there has been a trade-off between high-volume standard business and customized business. The latter has required extra expense, and thus has only been viable if customers pay more. But, post-Internet, the cost of customization can be trivial, and if customization greatly increases volumes, it could actually lower average cost.

For instance, Dell Computer offers customers the chance to create their own personal computer by mixing and matching hundreds of components, so that there are (through the power of permutations) millions of "different" machines that can be created. The cost of doing this is very low, since Dell already has all the components in stock and it has created a very efficient process to create whatever is asked for. In fact, the extra cost of creating each customized computer is less than the savings in cost that results from the extra demand generated by customization. The extra volume means that the costs of marketing and fixed overheads like rent and administration are spread over more units, so that the average cost is lower: and yet the customer satisfaction is very much higher.

The Internet also separates information flows from physical flows. A supermarket or a book store is both a physical entity—a warehouse—and a source of information to the shopper—what is on the shelves is what is available and what may be inspected. But the Internet separates the two. Amazon.com initially supplied the information (the book) without involvement with physical flows (stocking and delivering the book). It could therefore have huge stock with zero inventory, escaping the traditional trade-off between cost and choice.

Web economics also create the possibility that *consumers* of information also become unpaid *producers* of information, as when Amazon.com users add book reviews to the site.

Note finally that the cost of cross-selling different products decreases dramatically with the Internet. If you are selling an airline ticket, you can very easily and cheaply sell hotel rooms, travel insurance, car hire, and many other services. The value of a loyal customer base can hardly be exaggerated.

But Internet and network economics generally do not offer a bonanza for everyone. Though the amount of new value created can be enormous, most of it goes to a few players in the industry. There is a further reinforcement of the normal tendency for returns to be distributed unevenly because of the emergence of "sweet spots" in the total industry chain.

Industry Sweet Spots

The Internet's separation of physical flows from information flows makes vertical integration unnecessary and tends to divide industries into a large number of "layers," separate stages of the value-added chain where independent firms specialize. But whereas traditionally it was an industry or segment leader that made high returns, now it is the leader in *certain layers only,* probably just one or two, who will make high returns—and everyone else in the industry, including leaders in the nonfavored layers, may struggle to cover the cost of capital. The Boston Consulting Group calls the favored layers *sweet spots.*

An excellent instance where the sweet spot in an industry takes a quite disproportionate share of the industry's total profits is the case of Microsoft in PC operating systems. Microsoft's near-monopoly of the software layer gives it a very large share of total industry profits, despite Windows comprising only 2 percent of the total industry cost structure. The actual production of PCs comprises 75 percent of the industry cost structure and capital employed, but only a small percentage of total industry profits.

Establishing Dominant Standards in Sweet Spots

Establishing competitive advantage in the new environment requires recognition of the strategic layers in an industry, the sweet spots, and then their domination, if necessary in alliance with another powerful industry player. To establish dominance in the sweet spot, in turn, requires establishing a dominant standard. Thereafter, it requires a careful "orchestration" of players in the other industry layers: the suppliers and users of the sweet-spot products. To stop the orchestrated from becoming powerful, you have to divide and rule, and ensure that no one else can supply a differentiated and valuable product. Otherwise, the orchestrated will bite back.

This, after all, is what happened when Microsoft was orchestrated by IBM in the 1980s, when IBM outsourced the design of its operating system software to Microsoft. Later, the balance of power shifted decisively, because Microsoft's market size and value increased faster than IBM's (because of open architecture, which allowed Microsoft to supply IBM's competitors), and because there was no attractive alternative to Microsoft's products.

Competitive Advantage May Be Temporary

Because competitive advantage becomes based more on dominant standards than low costs, it may become more difficult to sustain. There is always the risk that an innovative competitor may find the next sweet spot in the system. Microsoft can't rest on its laurels. Netscape and its friends are promoting network computing, where any PC operating system, including Windows, is subordinated to a new high-value strategic layer controlled by a Java-enabled browser. To defend its dominant position, Microsoft has scrambled to incorporate browser technology into its operating system.

Changes in the "New Economy"

To sustain extraordinary returns requires eternal innovation. The system dynamics have become richer, the inequality in returns has become greater, and choosing where to compete has become even more important. But leadership remains crucial. From a macroeconomic viewpoint, a long period of high growth—while the new enabling technologies become fully used—may be possible. Industrial structures and leadership may be transformed, returns on capital may rise, and temporary monopolies may become essential for the public good. The "new paradigm," however, is not really new—it just represents one more punctuation point within mankind's long history of economic punctuations.

Are There Two Economies and Two Sets of Economics?

Brian Arthur argues that there are really two different economies, and that different economic and management theory is applicable to each:

> We can usefully think of two economic régimes or worlds: a bulk-production world yielding products that essentially are congealed resources with a little knowledge, and operating

> according to Marshall's principles of diminishing returns, and a knowledge-based part of the economy yielding products that essentially are congealed knowledge with a little resources and operating under increasing returns . . .
>
> Because the two worlds of business—processing bulk goods and crafting knowledge into products—differ in their underlying economics, it follows that they differ in their character of competition and their culture of management. It is a mistake to think that what works in one world is appropriate for the other.[9]

Arthur goes on to ask why the new management ideology of flat hierarchies, missions, flexible strategies, reengineering, and "re-everything" have emerged. His answer is that they are not fads, but correspond to the high-tech world of constant reinvention, and that hierarchies and old-style management are appropriate to smokestack industry: *"Marshall's world tends to be one that favors hierarchy, planning, and controls. Above all, it is a world of optimization."*[10]

Arthur goes on to propose that there is a middle ground between the old world and the new. As for service industries such as insurance, restaurants, and banking, they have a foot in each camp. On the one hand, most services are low-tech, consist of "processing," and are subject to regional limits on demand—all characteristics of the diminishing-returns economy. On the other hand, most services can be branded and are subject to network effects—McDonald's or Motel 6 franchises attract more than their fair share of customers because the brand is well known and reliable. Over time, though, services are moving to the new economy. Information is key, and is now processed more by software than by people. So "service providers become hitched into software networks, regional limitations weaken, and user-base network effects kick in."[11]

Brian Arthur's examples of the new world are spot-on. Yet is there really an "old" economy that fits Marshall's diminishing-returns economics? Shouldn't we consider the possibility of a "standard" economy and a "new" economy, both subject to differing degrees of increasing-returns economics?

Do Marshall's Economics Work at All?

The whole of microeconomics is an impressive intellectual edifice, constructed with mathematical elegance and, within the terms of its system, consistent and coherent. The problem is that it does not correspond to the real world, not even to Marshall's world. The technological innovations of steam, railways, electricity, gas, and motorcars were at least as transforming as our own high-tech industries, and subject to network effects and increasing returns.

What was the Ford Motor Company if not the Microsoft of its day? Every time Ford made a new Model T, in increasing quantities, the cost of each unit went down. Every time the cost went down, more people could buy one. Every time more Model Ts were bought, the cost of making the next went down. Every buyer increased the need for new roads, motels, and roadside restaurants, and mobilized support for initiatives that would make the motorcar yet more popular. When government began to build freeways, this network effect accelerated the car's spread. Plainly, autos manifested increasing rather than decreasing returns.

If classical economics has any validity at all, it is in the preindustrial world, related to commodities and to agriculture before it was mechanized. Gold, silver, iron; potatoes, wheat, cotton—these may be subject to diminishing returns. When supply goes up, price goes down, but costs do not, so increasing supply is bad for producers. And as long as all producers use the same means of production, and there are no economies of scale or experience, then markets will behave as Marshall predicted and come to an equilibrium point where capital cannot earn any differential superprofits. Classical economics does not work, however, when any of the following conditions applies:

- There are economies of scale or experience, so that the largest producer has lower costs, and increased supply lowers prices, resulting in higher demand and still lower prices in a circle that can go on forever.
- There are differences of technology used, so that one

technology may come to have lower costs than another—another reason that competitors may have different costs.

- Any competitor finds a better or cheaper way to do something, again contributing to unequal margins between suppliers.
- Goods cease to be commodities, because one manufacturer adds extra value by means of branding, product differentiation, or better service.
- There are high fixed costs in production.
- There are substantial barriers to entry for new suppliers.
- There are network effects.
- Human ingenuity can make more out of less, so that the material costs become a very small part of the total (as with the silicon chip, made with sand).
- Resources—such as information—are enhanced rather than used up as production expands.

Most business since the nineteenth century has had at least one of these characteristics.

The "new economics" is a new description of something old. It is just a better description than classical economics of how the market economy has always worked.

Different Management Styles for Different Types of Business

A final note on Brian Arthur's hypothesis that the "new economy" requires new management structures such as flat hierarchies and "re-everything." This hypothesis is not new. It is essentially a restatement and updating of the argument in Tom Burns and G. M. Stalker's classic book *The Management of Innovation,* published in 1961. The book "identified the 'organic' organization characterized by networks, shared vision and values, and teamworking."[12] Burns and Stalker also argued that it was precisely high-tech and high-growth organizations that required the new management approach, and that slower-growth firms in more predictable environments were more suited to command-and-control methods.

But are Arthur, Burns, and Stalker correct? If there are, in fact, only gradations of the "new economy," and nearly all businesses in fact belong, to a greater or lesser extent, to that "new economy"—which is not really new, but just a better description of the world after the Industrial Revolution—then different types of company may not need very different styles of management. Don't all firms need "observation, positioning, flattened organizations, missions, teams, and cunning"?

Equally, don't *all* organizations need hierarchy, and have it? Microsoft is a meritocratic dictatorship run by Bill Gates, and it would be worth much less otherwise. What creates value is insight plus hierarchy.

Microsoft is an ideal model for any type of business: a dictatorship of ends, a meritocracy of execution, and a collegiate, "democratic" style that respects intelligence and insight at every level, so long as it does not challenge the basic strategy.

Insights on Networks, the "New Economy," and Increasing Returns

Traditional microeconomics was always a poor guide to the real economy of business.

Whenever products cease to be undifferentiated commodities, whenever one competitor has and can retain a cost or product/service advantage over other suppliers, whenever brands or standards are important, whenever there are high fixed costs in a business and low incremental costs, whenever there are substantial barriers stopping new players coming into a market—whenever one or more of these conditions holds, we are in a dynamic economy where equilibrium is elusive and advantage goes to the leader, who may enjoy and compound high returns.

Though for a long time nearly all businesses have been part of the dynamic economy, the extent to which they have been subject to the laws of dynamism has been steadily increasing. Fixed costs have risen. The cost of overhead, in the form of highly qualified and expensive professionals, has steadily increased; the cost of materials and unskilled labor has steadily declined; and incremental costs have declined. Technology and know-how also have become increasingly important; the risks and returns of business have increased; and the value of leadership in high-growth markets, which was always substantial, has increased still further.

The shift toward winner-take-most economics has been most pronounced in network businesses, and, at the extreme, in electronic business. Here the stakes are raised. The few winners may make fantastic returns, grabbing most of the industry value-added despite participating in only a thin strategic layer, the industry sweet spot. The many losers will be stuck in their cash traps.

Two long-standing rules of business strategy have only become more important: Do whatever is necessary to move ahead of competitors, and cut your losses when someone else has reached that point. To these we may add two new rules: (1) Identify and dominate the industry sweet spots by establishing new standards there, orchestrating others to do the donkey work in the bulk of the industry, and (2) Defend the dominance by dividing and ruling the orchestrated, and by continual innovation to find the next industry sweet spot.

How to Use the Natural Laws

- ***Identify sweet spots in emerging networks and dominate them by creating a new standard of value.*** Find the best possible ally or allies and strike a deal with them before anyone else. Confine your part in the industry to the chosen sweet spots and orchestrate suppliers carefully. Ensure that no supplier can develop its own distinctive standard on which you become dependent.

- ***Don't play in network markets unless you can win,*** or unless you have a fair chance of winning and are using other people's money to punt with.

- ***Find a high-growth market that you can dominate,*** even if it isn't a network market. Start by identifying a technology or superior way of doing business that is approaching, but has not yet reached, its tipping point. Become the best exponent of the new approach.

- ***Find an undervalued resource and apply it to a new market.***

- ***Cut your losses if you can't overhaul the market leader,*** especially in markets with high fixed costs and low incremental costs.

The Paradox of Enrichment, Entropy, and Unintended Consequences

The Natural Laws of Caution

Nothing fails like success.

RICHARD PASCALE[1]

In just thirteen years between 1970 and 1983, one third of the 1970 Fortune 500 top U.S. firms vanished into the corporate Bermuda triangle. Few of them actually went bust—most were taken over or merged with other companies. Still, it's a remarkable attrition rate.

In 1982, the most successful business book of all time was published: *In Search of Excellence* by Tom Peters and Bob Waterman, in which the authors identify eight management principles common to the most successful companies of their time. Two years later, *Business Week* ran a cover story under the headline "Oops," gleefully chronicling the fall from grace of many of the seventy-five "excellent" companies heralded in the book. Later on, one of the most apparently impregnable and successful of the companies, IBM, nearly went under.

The average life expectancy of a multinational company, according to Arie de Geus, a former Shell executive, is between forty and fifty years.[2] A study of firms of all sizes, including Japan and most European countries, showed an average life expectancy of just twelve and a half years.[3]

What these stories indicate is that it's difficult to sustain success, and that even very successful corporations suffer from the occupational hazard of all corporations—they live and die by the market and competition, not just for customers, but also for corporate control via takeovers. No other major institution is as susceptible to failure as the corporation.

And so it should be. If corporations were not exposed to failure, we would not enjoy high living standards. And the fruits of sustained success are so high—especially for investors and top executives—that it should be difficult to keep ahead.

Can systems thinking help us here? There is no simple or overarching recommendation. Instead, we have to piece together insights from a number of "natural laws of caution."

- ***The Paradox of Enrichment***
- ***The Law of Entropy***
- ***The Law of Unintended Consequences***

The Paradox of Enrichment

Studies in ecology have confirmed that the number of predators and prey in any targeted area tend to fluctuate at the same time fairly regularly. For example, the Hudson's Bay Company has kept tabs on the number of lynxes and hares since 1850, and graphs of these records show remarkable symmetry.[4]

The prey depend on the predators as much as the other way around. Without the predators, the prey will become too numerous and starve. Both populations benefit from a "swinging cycle," where their numbers swing up and down but never reach unsustainable peaks or troughs. The cycle moves around a central point, or "swinging equilibrium."

The paradox of enrichment reveals itself when nature literally gives a population too much of a good thing. If some apparently benign environmental change allows the population of the prey to go up substantially, it isn't necessarily any more beneficial for the predators. A large increase in prey leads to an even larger increase in predators, who before long find that they don't have enough prey to eat. The number of predators zooms up initially and then plummets, and the number of prey follows the same pattern—deprived of predators, there are soon too many prey, and not enough food to sustain them. So a stable cycle, the swinging equilibrium, turns into an unstable cycle, which may end in disaster for both prey and predators if one of the cycles pushes their numbers too low, and the entire population of one or the other is wiped out.

Another example might be trees sprayed with insecticide intended to kill harmful insects. If too much is sprayed on the leaves and it rains, the excess insecticide is washed from the leaves to the ground, where it kills the insects' predators. Result: more insecticide leads to more insects.

The paradox of enrichment parallels classical economic theory in that when a market is very profitable, it will attract new entrants, and profit will be driven back down to zero until a new equilibrium is found. Where once there were too few firms in a market, before long there are too many. But as we discovered in the last chapter, classical economics very rarely corresponds to real-world markets. Equilibrium rarely happens. There are cycles, however, which can be divided into three types: swinging equilibrium, virtuous cycles, and vicious cycles.

Swinging Equilibrium

Swinging equilibrium is the closest to the classical economists' dream. Equilibrium is rare, but the system swings up and down in predictable and functional ways just as control theory says it should. We see evidence of a swinging equilibrium in the Hudson Bay Company's records of hares and lynxes, in a room where the temperature is controlled by a thermostat, and in the stock market's bull and bear oscillations.

In my experience, only small segments of the business world like commodity prices, follow this pattern. For the pattern to exist, markets must have very low barriers to entry and exit, undifferentiated products and services, and no possible advantages from scale, technology, or innovative thinking.

Virtuous Cycles

A virtuous cycle occurs when a player differentiates his product or service so that he can enjoy a higher margin than competitors yet have a larger market share; or when he achieves the same effect through having much lower costs than competitors (and therefore higher margins despite lower prices) as a result of superior scale, technology, cunning, or defensibly lower input costs. The player with higher margins can make further investments to consolidate and increase his lead; he can pay more to get the very best people or the most productive systems. He can afford to advertise or market at lower cost and higher efficacy. He can provide even better value and make the gap between himself and competitors almost unbridgeable.

Successful, very profitable companies operate within this world of increasing returns. Firms with virtuous cycles always account for the majority of profits in a sophisticated economy.

Vicious Cycles

Vicious cycles are the flip side of virtuous cycles, as seen from the viewpoint of the unsuccessful challengers. Those who are behind fall further behind. Returns diminish. St. Paul was a great advocate of virtuous and vicious cycles: "Whoever sows sparingly will also reap sparingly; and whoever sows generously will also reap generously."[5] Successful firms can afford to sow generously, less successful ones have to be more sparing.

When Virtuous Switches to Vicious

The danger for successful firms is when something happens in the system to turn a virtuous cycle into a vicious cycle. One way is via the paradox of enrichment—having too much of a good thing.

Too much success can make a business owner arrogant, complacent, or greedy. You ignore a new technology that has the potential to provide a better or cheaper service because your success is built on the old technology. You make such fat profits that your managers or your unions raise the firm's costs beyond those of rivals. You stop listening to customers—you already know what they want. You stop hiring new talent, or you hire talented people but stop them from doing anything new. You make the firm bigger, more complex, more heterogeneous, less manageable, all thanks to the paradox of enrichment.

The Law of Entropy

"Entropy" was coined by the German physicist Rudolf Julius Emanuel Clausius to mean the tendency of things to run down and wear out. People grow old. Houses fall down. Stars burn out. Cliffs slide into the sea.

The law of entropy is a restatement of the first two laws of thermodynamics, developed before 1850 in the quest to build better steam engines. The First Law of Thermodynamics, arrived at separately by British physicist James Prescott Joule and German scientist Julius Robert von Mayer, states that energy can neither be created nor destroyed—it can only change form. Then in 1850, Clausius gave us the Second Law of Thermodynamics: any chemical system, be it solid, liquid, or gas, will tend toward maximum disorder. Energy flows in one direction only, toward thermal equilibrium. Heat is transferred from one body to another, and this transfer cannot be reversed. Heat can only be used up once—it flows into the cooler body and cannot be retrieved from it (without adding yet more energy). The law of entropy has parallels to two biological concepts that we examined in Part One: the Red Queen effect, or the evolutionary arms race in which there is constant improvement on two sides but no change in their relative position. The world changes, and to preserve what we had before we have to do more than we did yesterday. Things can be maintained, or even improved (paint from a house may fade, but it can be painted again better than it ever was), but it requires new action. A system's energy is discharged and lost to it, so life requires infusions of new energy.

To maintain success requires constant effort. The natural condition is not equilibrium: it's entropy. A company's competitive position rests on a bundle of unique resources and relationships that are alive and restive; like all systems and all relationships, if they are not tended, reinforced, and renewed, they'll falter and fall apart. It is entirely possible to counter entropy—how else could we have accumulated wealth in the remarkable way we have over the past two hundred fifty years?—but it requires constant innovation and improved use of the energy that is available.

Murphy's Laws

Closely related to entropy are the laws attributed to "Murphy." They have no scientific validity, except perhaps as examples of entropy, but they certainly have resonance. They're useful to any successful organization by helping to puncture complacency and prepare for contingencies.

No one is sure who Murphy was, or even if he ever really existed, but there is now a very large number of *Murphy's laws*. Here's a useful selection:

- If anything can go wrong, it will.
- If several things can go wrong, the one that will cause the most damage will go wrong first.
- If anything just cannot go wrong, it will anyway (for example, the *Titanic*).
- If you realize that there are four ways in which something

could go wrong, and circumvent them, then a fifth way will promptly develop.

- Left to themselves, things go from bad to worse.
- If everything is going well, you have overlooked something.
- Nature always sides with the hidden flaw.
- Nothing is as simple as it seems.
- Everything takes much longer than you expect.
- It's impossible to make anything foolproof; fools are so ingenious.
- If the experts have spent a huge amount of time and failed to find the answer, it will be immediately obvious to the first unqualified person asked.
- When things go wrong somewhere, they go wrong everywhere.
- Whatever you want to do, you have to do something else first.
- Figures that are obviously correct will contain errors. A decimal will always be misplaced. The error will cause most damage to the calculation.
- If you get the premise right, but the argument wrong, you'll get the wrong answer; while if you get the premise wrong, but the argument right, you'll also arrive at the wrong answer. You are unlikely to get both the premise and the argument right.
- The probability of anything happening is proportional to the damage it will cause.

The Law of Unintended Consequences

The third common way in which success turns to failure is through the unintended consequences of well-intentioned actions. It's usually caused by simple miscalculation, based on a failure to understand how systems operate.

In his book *The Logic of Failure,*[6] Dietrich Dörner, professor of psychology at Germany's University of Bamberg, explores why intelligent people and institutions can proceed with care and goodwill and yet often produce disastrous results. He says that the problem lies in our linear patterns of thought; we take one thing at a time, always thinking in terms of cause and effect. Because we don't think in terms of systems and their interrelationships, we miss the big picture, pile small error on small error, and end up with spectacularly unintended and often tragic consequences. Dörner's ideas derive from systems thinking and clearly relate to ideas that we explored in relation to quantum mechanics (Chapter 6) and chaos and complexity (Chapter 9).

Dörner gives many examples of disasters. Why did the well-qualified engineers who planned the Aswan Dam, and whose simple aim was to bring cheap electricity to Egypt, not realize that they would eradicate the annual floods that had kept the Nile Valley rich and fertile for millennia? Why do planners of health programs in poor countries not take into account that increasing the numbers alive will also increase demand for food, and that without extra food production, improved health care will just lead to malnutrition and sometimes famine? Why did the operators of Reactor 4 of the atomic energy plant at Chernobyl, who had just won a safety award, end up with the ghastly explosion of April 26, 1986?

On a less horrific scale, what about the mayor and city council who dealt with traffic congestion and air pollution in a city by installing speed bumps and a twenty mile-per-hour speed limit? The cars now had to travel in second gear, so they were noisier and produced more exhaust. Shopping trips took longer, and the number of cars in the city center actually increased. After a while, fewer people shopped downtown, preferring the convenience of the big new mall on the edge of a neighboring town. That solved the noise and pollution problems, but led to many shops in the city closing. Tax revenues plummeted, so taxes had to be raised on the remaining businesses, which just reinforced the cycle of decline. All this havoc was caused by the installation of a few speed bumps in a noble cause.

The Theory of the Second Best

The example of the speed bumps links nicely to a theory beloved of economists, especially those in the area of public policy. This is the *theory of the second best,* which says that reaching an optimal outcome in individual markets may lead to a suboptimal overall outcome. For example, if free markets led to an optimal position in all individual product markets, but left an economy with 40 percent unemployment, this would not really be optimal. The theory therefore says that instead of seeking optimality in each part of the economy, we should go for the best overall solution, which may imply "second best" solutions in individual markets.

Stripped of economists' usual obsession with equilibrium and optimality, two very elusive goals, the theory of the second best is really just saying that the economy is a system, and that actions in one area may have unintended consequences in another. It is a useful idea because it tells us that we may have to compromise, and that pursuit of one objective may be myopic, like the speed bumps.

System Dynamics

Jay Forrester of MIT was a computer pioneer who developed "system dynamics" in the 1960s and 1970s (an elaboration of systems thinking that had developed since 1950). Forrester was one of the first to call attention to the unintended consequences of well-intentioned policies on issues such as urban decay or the environment. Typically, he said, the policies attacked the symptoms of the problems, alleviating the symptoms but often exacerbating the fundamental problems that were "systems" rather than individual issues.

Systems thinking also has much in common with the concepts of chaos and complexity. The intention in all cases is to identify the underlying system in order to find long-term solutions rather than short-term palliatives.

Avoiding Unintended Consequences

Dietrich Dörner suggests the following prescriptions:

- ***Set clear, explicit, positive, and multiple goals.***

- ***Pursue several goals at once.*** If you focus on one goal alone, you will produce all kinds of unintended by-products. You may object that to pursue several goals at once may bring conflicts between the goals. This is true. But the conflict is constructive, because it forces us to consider the relative priorities and trade-offs implicit in the goals.

  For example, would we rather have speed bumps and a clean, quiet, pollution-free city center, or a thriving retail and business center at the expense of some congestion and exhaust fumes? Perhaps we can think of a realistic way to have most of our cake and eat most of it too.

  We can't always realize all our goals at once because the goals may partly conflict with each other. We must be prepared to compromise. We should always have a clear set of priorities, but be willing to change them if it's clear that they'll lead to results we don't really want.

- ***Construct hypotheses and test them.*** If we do *x*, it will result in *a, b,* and *c*. If we like *a, b,* and *c,* we should try out *x*. Even if it doesn't have the expected result, at least we'll have more data. Wrong hypotheses can be corrected.

- ***Use analogies to go from what you know to what you don't.***

- ***Think of everything as a system.*** Try to identify all the important system elements. Form a model of the system. Then focus on a single element but be sure to consider its context.

- ***Think about problems you don't have at the moment but which may emerge as side-effects of your actions.*** Think about what may happen over time. Imagine potential pitfalls.

- ***Don't hastily ascribe everything that happens to one central cause.*** This is rarely the case.

- ***Construct simulations.*** By playing games, with many variables affecting a system, you'll learn how systems work, and be able to make mistakes with no real-life penalties.

One thing that Dörner does not say but that seems apparent to me is that, ultimately, the most effective antidote to unintended consequences is human creativity and adaptability. Unintended consequences arise because we live in nonlinear systems and because we make changes, because we *do* things. We are restless, just like nature. Each action generates new instabilities, and will always do so, so unintended consequences can never be eliminated. We should therefore be prepared for them, ready to notice them before they can do too much harm. And we should be creative in correcting them—and aware that the corrections will lead to further unintended consequences, which will require further correction . . .

How to Perpetuate Success

Dietrich Dörner's model and suggestions are useful for those in charge of a successful business; they help us to think about what could go wrong. Consider this in three ways:

- ***What happens if something in the business system changes unilaterally?*** A successful system can only turn into an unsuccessful system if one of two things happens: either we do something differently, or something else in the system changes to our disadvantage.

  Therefore, if we're doing the same as ever and things start to go wrong, it must be because of a change (or changes) in other elements of the business system.

  So start by asking: What has changed? Have the customers changed what they want? Is a competitor gaining market share? Why? Is the technology or the business definition shifting? Has everyone else found a way of cutting their costs while ours remain the same?

Construct several hypotheses, both complementary and competing. Remember that it's unlikely there will be one simple cause. Even if there is, it will have second- and third-order effects that must be traced.

Test and refine the hypotheses until there's a reasonable chance you're right. Then act to restore your advantage. If this doesn't work, go through the whole cycle again.

- ***What new actions that we've taken in the current business system could have had unintended consequences?*** What are we doing differently? If you know the answer, fine. If not, ask other people. Introspection will not be accurate or complete.

  Map out all elements of the business system, including (but not necessarily confined to) all of your customers, suppliers, distributors, other collaborators, colleagues, cost structures, technologies, and regulators. Imagine all possible impacts that the changes may have had on each part of the system, and the consequential results, particularly negative results, that might have arisen.

  Construct and test hypotheses. Be suspicious of pat solutions involving just one variable. For the system to have changed fundamentally, several aspects of the system are likely to have shifted.

  Then act, and if it doesn't restore the system to your advantage, start the cycle over.

- ***How do we plan new initiatives that will be as successful as current ones and won't have unintended consequences?*** The truth is that new initiatives probably won't be as successful as existing ones, unless they use the same formulae, skills, competencies, technologies, and any other key attribute (such as a fantastic proprietary client base) that drives the success of the existing business.

  It's also unlikely that the new business won't have unintended consequences, so the following questions should be considered:

- *What unintended consequences could the new business have on the existing one?* Think through all elements of the system and their relationships to each other.
- *What other unintended consequences could your presence in the new business have?* Again, trace through all components of the new business system.
- *If there do turn out to be negative consequences, construct hypotheses and test them (as discussed above) until you have an answer that works.*

How to Use the Natural Laws

- ***Sustain success by creating new value every day.***
- ***Keep yourself and your firm humble, service-oriented, focused, lean, and hungry.*** Eschew corporate complexity. Root out arrogance, greed, and complacency.
- ***Expect and correct unexpected consequences.*** Learn to anticipate and deal with them. Think of business as a system whose components are always shifting, where a major shift in just one component can change the entire system, where there will always be unintended consequences, and where continual monitoring, adjustment, and creativity must be deployed to detect and overcome them.

Part Three Concluding Note

One common theme in Part Three, shared with Parts One and Two, is the wonkiness of the world. We expect and search out linear relationships and rejoice when we find them, but we tend to ignore the more frequent nonlinear relationships because they are inconvenient and perplexing. The message of Part Three is that nonlinear relationships can be understood and be extremely useful.

The concept of chaos is very helpful because it highlights the importance of "initial conditions": markets, relationships, and corporations evolve as they do because of early, chance events, and quickly get frozen into the patterns formed at the outset. Chaos also illuminates the fractal nature of business.

Complexity theory demonstrates how systems emerge and organize themselves into something different from their component parts: a phenomenon at once constructive and destructive.

The 80/20 principle is also a fantastically useful natural law enabling us, almost infallibly, to extract more from less.

The nonlinear, jerky nature of market growth and technological change is also something that, when appreciated, can help us separate the fad from the trend, tell us whether we can drive a new product or business over its tipping point, and enable us to spot a possible mega-success. Insight into the nature of networks can also tell us when there is scope to create enormous new value, and how to profit from whatever value is created.

Finally, the paradox of enrichment, the law of entropy, and the law of unintended consequences all highlight the pitfalls of success and how to avoid them.

A second common theme of Part Three is the tension between laissez-faire and intervention. In nonlinear systems we deal with some extremely powerful natural forces, and many different kinds of "invisible hands" can produce extremely pleasing results or they can defeat our best-laid plans. As with the forces of biology and physics, however, we must strike a balance between automatically accepting the natural laws on the one hand, and ignoring them on the other. The laws do exist, but nature is not infallible or inherently virtuous, and neither are markets, high-growth phenomena, successful corporations, or self-organization. Progress requires us to channel nature and its forces, to use them for our own ends, and to intervene when they threaten civilization and its achievements.

We now know that business, and the forces operating within and around it, are not essentially different from the rest of "life, the universe, and everything." All the natural laws apply to life generally; they apply to business because business is part of life. Hence, we can apply the insights gathered beyond the walls of commerce. But it also follows that the view of business as a separate terrain—an enclave with its own conventions and laws, a field of study that requires its own schools, a landscape that can safely ignore more general insights on how to live a happy and fulfilled life and behave responsibly to others—is deeply flawed. Business is an intrinsic part of the messy reality governed by nonlinear forces.

Now it is time to see where the science of the past four centuries has taken us, and what that means in regards to business and all other parts of our life.

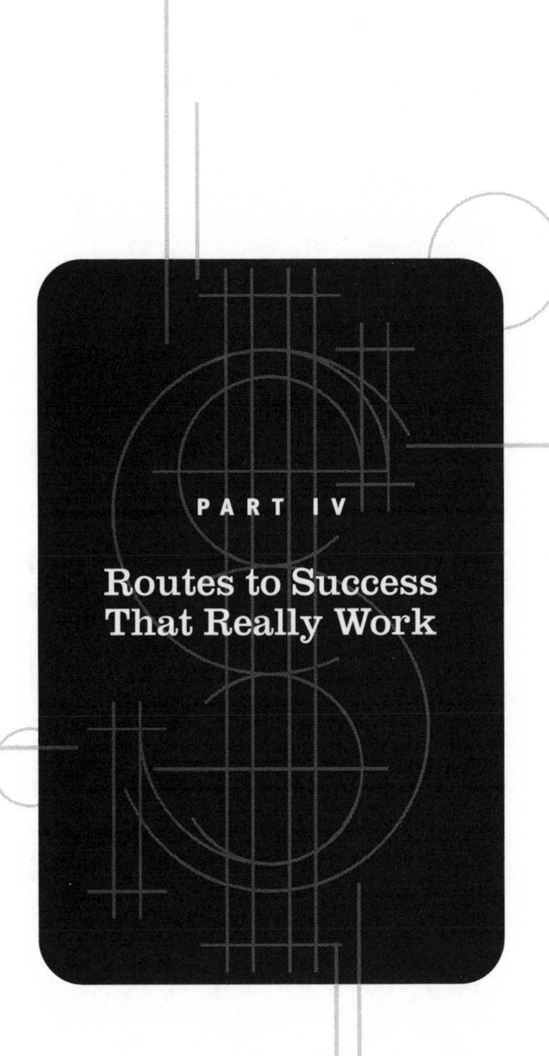

PART IV

Routes to Success That Really Work

Finale: **The Gospel According to the Natural Laws**

The Scientific Laws Driving Progress

We are better at predicting events at the edge of the galaxy or inside the nucleus of an atom than whether it will rain on Aunty's garden party three Sundays from now, because the problem turns out to be different . . . It is the best possible time to be alive, when almost everything you thought you knew is wrong.

TOM STOPPARD, *Arcadia*

All aspects of business—all products, all activities, all methods—have an information structure at their core that has long been hidden, just like the genetic code of plants . . . executives will have to create new genetic structures for their businesses.

JAY WALKER, INTERNET ENTREPRENEUR

Darwin's account of evolution by natural selection is a marvel of inference and insight. God is gently shunted to the sidelines, and creation, from the first form of life to the rich complexity of countless species, is reduced to one simple, dialectical process: growth via sex, inheritance, variation, and a ratio of population increase so high as to lead to a struggle for life—and therefore to natural selection, divergence of character, and the extinction of less-improved forms. We know that genes replicate themselves by using organisms as vehicles, and suspect that our genes are not fully aligned either to our own objectives or to commercial, urban society. Human appropriation and creation of knowledge is an alternative and additional form of replication to that of genes, one that may enable humans to drive parts of the evolutionary process in the direction we want.

We've looked at the remarkable triumphs of physics, which have shown not only how the same rules of motion apply on heaven and earth, but also the astonishing way that the smallest parts of matter operate, and the awesome power that we can generate through our understanding of the process. We've seen that space and time are not two separate dimensions, but are intimately linked.

We have some insight into how complex systems can emerge from simple ones, how everything in the universe tends to organize itself into systems, and how even the most puzzling phenomena follow intricate and predictable patterns, at once similar to and different from each other. In any distribution of a population, whether of people, clouds, diseases, events, whether good or bad or neutral from our viewpoint, a small minority of the forces will have much more influence than the great majority, and we have learned how to distinguish the vital few forces from the trivial many.

Mathematics has given us dazzling insights into the power of exponential growth and how the same patterns recur in numbers, regardless of the phenomena being observed.

We know how new technology evolves in a lumpy fashion, and how to predict when we're likely to move from one dominant technology to another. The same tools enable us to observe, and often predict, how and when any phase transition will take place, whether it is a major social change, a trend or fashion, an epidemic reaching crisis proportions, or a company's profits taking off.

Although the attempt to discover general and useful scientific laws has been less successful in economics and social sciences than in the physical sciences, the last three centuries have taught us a few very useful things: how markets and organizations are self-structuring, dynamic systems with their own way of sorting things out; how wealth is created by the division of labor and trade, based on comparative rather than absolute advantage; how returns can increase over time, so that costs and prices can go down forever. We've seen, in addition, how networks increase value; how economic arbitrage creates more from less, as resources are shifted from low- to high-productivity uses; and how societies evolve by means of increased specialization, reciprocity, trade, technology, and ever greater levels of cooperation and interdependence.

Some Things We Don't Know

We also know more about the limits to our knowledge and perception. We understand that there is no objective truth, and that we are continually distorting and adding to reality. The most important things we can create are concepts, ideas, and hypotheses, which take on a life of their own: information and imagination are our evolutionary aces in our game with the inscrutable universe. Uncertainty is at the heart of the universe, and like it or not, chance is central to all life.

Humans sit in a very odd relationship to our environment: our genes are probably out of sync with the society we have created, and our emotions have not caught up with our reason. Are we controlling our genes, or are they controlling us?

We also don't know whether our universe is the only one with "intelligent life," whether there are other universes from which we may have branched out in space and/or in time, or how much longer Earth and the universe will last.

Oh, and yes, Tom Stoppard is right: we don't know whether it will rain at Aunty's garden party.

Darwin would have been amazed at how much we know, and at how little.

The Natural Laws Change Our Perspective

The most interesting modern science is that which unifies its different branches, enabling us to glimpse universal natural laws. But there is a more fundamental unification that is beginning to take place. As Harvard biologist Edward O. Wilson says: *"The greatest enterprise of the mind has always been and will always be the attempted linkage of the sciences and the humanities."*[1]

Wilson also argues for "a belief in the unity of the sciences—a conviction, far deeper than a mere working proposition, that the world is orderly and can be explained by a small number of natural laws."[2] Through study of our natural laws, we can see the links among the sciences, the humanities, and business.

The natural laws cast business in a new light. We can see that business operates in the same way as other complex systems, and is subject to the same operation of laws as other parts of the universe. We have described the most important of these laws, which apply to business because they refer to nature and life, and business is part of life.

The Natural Laws Present a Coherent View of Reality

The biological laws and the nonlinear laws complement each other and are also consistent with each other. Evolution is an extremely nonlinear process; it is an example of chaos theory in action. Species (and combinations of species) emerge as complex systems. Evolution is also the best and most important example of the 80/20 principle.

The other natural laws also cohere with the biological laws, the nonlinear laws, and each other. For example, relativity and quantum mechanics have many parallels with chaos and complexity; evolutionary psychology flows from theories of evolution and genetics; the Prisoner's Dilemma, and associated theories demonstrating the importance of cooperation, resonate strongly with evolution and other nonlinear systems. Punctuated equilibrium, moreover, is an evolutionary theory that has a clear parallel in the economic theories of growth via technological change and in the tipping point; the tipping point and the theory of increasing returns relate closely to the 80/20 principle; and the law of unintended consequences can be viewed as a corollary of chaos theory.

The knowledge embodied in the natural laws is itself "on the edge of chaos," poised between coherent theories with supporting data marshaled in good order on the one hand, and open-ended speculation with many loose ends on the other. Some order is necessary for a law to be useful, but some disorder is also necessary to allow us to improve the state of our knowledge and to reach out to other realities, both known and currently unknown.

What is most impressive about the natural laws is the consistency between their gestalt and value in a nonbusiness context, and their application to business itself. They help us understand "life, the universe, and everything," but they also simultaneously help us understand business, and show how business is not so very different from other aspects of life.

The Gospel According to the Natural Laws

In the beginning was information. Each day brought, and brings, more and better information. All business is information—the gathering, creation, refinement, combination, processing, and delivery of information. Information goes into products and services. But the information is not consumed; rather, new information is created. Information is retained and enhanced, alive and bubbling, in the brains of businesspeople and in the networks and vehicles set up to provide goods and services.

The universe is restless, dynamic, ever-changing, expanding. Information begets information—more information, better information; more diverse information, more specialized information, more accurate information. The universe is endlessly creative, endlessly destructive. It makes mistakes, corrects mistakes, and then corrects the corrections, which themselves contain mistakes, which require correction . . . in an endless cycle that always increases richness, but never reaches perfection. Information can never be complete, never be consistent, and never be absolutely true.

Business exists to satisfy and create human needs and wants, to create and enhance civilized conditions of life. Businesses thrive if they do this well and differently. But, happily, they will never do it perfectly. The business universe can therefore expand forever, because there is always room for something more and something better.

All progress requires improvement: a new product or service, or the delivery of existing ones in cheaper, better, or more convenient forms. Improvement requires experimentation, variation, and market exposure.

Successful businesses meet three conditions: they are different from all other businesses; they make better use of ideas and resources; and they continually improve, using myriad experiments to ensure that they remain different from any other business. You can't catch a moving target that is continually creating its own new space.

Most experiments fail. We should let them. We should concentrate energy on the few successful experiments. We should conduct new experiments on these successful experiments, so that there are always new variants of them. For continued success, this process must never flag.

Business is exciting and challenging because new and better information is always available. New ideas, new ways of doing things, new potential partners, new customers, and new demands from existing customers all create a kaleidoscope of potential change and improvement.

Technological change drives growth. Technological improvement is not just inventions and the application of sophisticated science, but also the use of all kinds of knowledge to make things better and cheaper. Every successful businessperson is a technologist, using and creating knowledge, which others then use for further improvements.

Technological change can be spotted accelerating along the runway, before the take-off. Innovators need keen eyes and quick reflexes, but they do not need to start rich.

Change is blocked by three things—the failure to recognize, collect, and use information; the inbuilt human reluctance to take risks; and the tendency to build corporate fortresses that are larger, more diversified, and more isolated than they should be. All three blockages create great opportunities for entrepreneurs.

A narrow canvas is usually better than a broad one. But the tighter the focus, the wider must be the window on developments elsewhere, and the network of weak ties. The ideal? Focus without high walls. Specialization without inflexibility. Differentiation without hubris. A unique stall in the bazaar, not a cathedral on the hill.

Business abounds with profitable asymmetry. A small minority of effort produces a large majority of value. Some things are *much* more profitable than others. It's much more valuable or economical to do things one way rather than another. It's much more productive to work with some individuals, some teams, and some networks than with others. The most productive resources are distinctive, and are committed to constant change and improvement.

These are the rules for business revealed by the natural laws. They are your route to success. They show that, always, entrepreneurial bonanzas lurk unexploited. There are always new combinations of ideas, technologies, fellow travelers, suppliers, distributors, customers, and partners that you can use to create a superior business system. There is always a way of doing something better, and of finding something better to do.

Now all you have to do is do it.

Notes

Preface

1 Edward Gibbon (1776–88; 1993) *The History of the Decline and Fall of the Roman Empire,* Volume I, Everyman, London.

2 Quoted in Danah Zohar and Ian Marshall (1993) *The Quantum Society,* Bloomsbury, London.

3 The new science of evolutionary psychology suggests that we're still "hardwired" for life on the savannah, and that our emotional responses, though well suited to life two hundred thousand years ago, are quite at odds with what is needed today. Yet there is also evidence that we can tamper with our own hardwiring; see Chapter 4.

Chapter 1

1 Thomas Hobbes (1651; 1973) *Leviathan,* J. M. Dent and Sons, London.

2 Quoted in Jane Jacobs (2000) *The Nature of Economies,* The Modern Library, New York.

3 See Stephen Jay Gould (1977) *Ontogeny and Phylogeny,* Belknap/Harvard, Cambridge, MA.

4 Charles Darwin (1859) *On the Origin of Species by Means of Natural Selection,* John Murray, London, Chapter III. My quotations are from the 1985 edition from Penguin, London, edited by J. W. Burrow: see pp. 115ff.

5 Ibid.

6 Ibid.

7 See Adrian Forsyth and Ken Miyata (1984) *Tropical Nature,* Macmillan, New York.

8 Charles Darwin, op. cit., Chapter X, p. 342.

9 See Jane Jacobs (2000) *The Nature of Economies,* Random House, New York. This is an excellent short study expressed in didactic dialogue, and I have drawn on many of its themes.

10 Jane Jacobs (2000) *The Nature of Economies,* The Modern Library, New York.
11 Carl W. Stern and George Stalk, Jr. (1998) *Perspectives on Strategy from the Boston Consulting Group,* John Wiley & Sons, New York.
12 This process is called "value innovation" and is extremely useful, but beyond the scope of this book. For an excellent introduction, see W. Chan Kim and Renée Mauborgne (1997) "Value innovation: the strategic logic of high growth," *Harvard Business Review,* January–February, pp. 103–12.
13 Al Ries (1996) *Focus,* HarperCollins, London.

Chapter 2

1 Darwin eventually settled on the (wrong) idea that cells throughout the body contribute instructions to the reproductive cells, thus enabling traits to be passed on to offspring.
2 Francis Crick and James Watson (1953) "Molecular Structures of Nucleic Acids," in *Nature,* April 1953.
3 Richard Dawkins (1976, revised edition 1989) *The Selfish Gene,* Oxford University Press, Oxford.
4 Ibid.
5 Ibid.
6 See Lee Alan Dugatkin (1998) *Cheating Monkeys and Citizen Bees: The Nature of Cooperation in Animals and Humans,* Free Press, New York; Lee Alan Dugatkin and Jean-Guy J. Godin (1998) "How females choose their mates," *Scientific American,* April 1998, pp. 56–61; and Lee Alan Dugatkin (forthcoming) *Guppy Love: Genes, Culture and the Science of Mate Choice,* Free Press, New York.
7 Richard Dawkins (1995) *River Out of Eden,* Weidenfeld & Nicholson, London.
8 Ibid.
9 Steven Rose (1997) *Lifelines,* Allen Lane/The Penguin Press, London.
10 Joseph A. Schumpeter (1942) *Capitalism, Socialism and Democracy,* New York, Harper & Row.

Chapter 3

1 R. H. MacArthur (1958) "Popular ecology of some warblers of northeastern coniferous forests," *Ecology,* 39, pp. 599–619.
2 Bruce Henderson in Carl W. Stern and George Stalk Jr. (1998) *Perspectives on Strategy,* John Wiley and Sons, New York.

Chapter 4

1 Edward O. Wilson (1998) *Consilience: the Unity of Knowledge,* Alfred A. Knopf, New York.
2 The real problem, evolutionary psychologists imply (although they are often coy about saying so bluntly), is not so much Stone Age woman as Stone Age

man. There is an unfashionable sexism that is implicit in evolutionary psychology, because one of its contentions is that sexual roles too are hard-wired and that we cannot totally escape them. The macho nature of Stone Age man is more inappropriate to today's conditions than the more passive and modest behavior of women. Objectively, therefore, women may be better suited to business than are men. But because men dominate organizations and set the rules, women may find it difficult to conform and break the glass ceiling. This may explain why there are plenty of examples of successful female entrepreneurs, yet few women at the helm of big business.

3 Robin Dunbar (1996) *Grooming, Gossip and the Evolution of Language,* Faber & Faber, London.

4 Robert Townsend (1970) *Up the Organization,* Michael Joseph, London.

5 Ibid., p. 9.

6 *The Antidote,* Issue 19, 1999, p. 10. The article is reporting on the views of Sumantra Ghoshal and Christopher A. Bartlett (1998) *The Individualized Corporation,* William Heinemann, London.

7 Richard Pascale (1990) *Managing on the Edge,* Simon & Schuster, New York.

8 Charles Darwin (1871) *The Descent of Man and Selection in Relation to Sex,* John Murray, London.

9 Matt Ridley, *The Origins of Virtue,* p. 193. (Penguin ed.) (1996) Viking/Penguin, New York/London.

10 John Kay (1999) "Total war and managers from Mars," *Financial Times,* August 4.

11 Report on a Strategic Planning Society conference, "Don't try to minimise risk," in *Strategy,* January 1999 (The Strategic Planning Society, London). See also Thomas A. Stewart (1998) *Intellectual Capital: the New Wealth of Organizations,* Nicholas Brealey, London.

12 This example and the endowment effect are taken from a charming book: Karl Sigmund (1993) *Games of Life,* Oxford University Press, Oxford, Chapter 7.

13 Philip Cohen (1998) "Song lines: singing lessons could affect the evolution of whales," *New Scientist,* 5 December, p. 15 (www.newscientist.com).

14 Lee Alan Dugatkin and Jean-Guy J. Godin (1992) "Reversal of female mate choice by copying in the guppy," *Proceedings of the Royal Society of London,* 249:179–84. See also Dugatkin's forthcoming book *Guppy Love: Genes, Culture and the Science of Mate Choice.*

15 See the forthcoming book by Jeffrey Schwartz and Sharon Begley, *The Mindful Brain: a New Paradigm for Understanding How the Mind Rewires the Brain.* See also Josie Glausiusz (1996) "The chemistry of obsession," *Discover,* June, p. 36.

16 Schwartz and Begley, *The Mindful Brain.*

17 See "Small but perfectly formed," *The Economist,* January 3, 1998.

18 Quoted in Stuart Crainer (1998) *The Ultimate Business Guru Book,* Capstone, Oxford, p. 43.

Chapter 5

1 Robert Axelrod was the organizer. See Robert Axelrod (1984) *The Evolution of Cooperation,* Basic Books, New York.

2 Matt Ridley, *The Origins of Virtue.*

3 Ibid.

4 Ibid.

5 See Jared Diamond (1999) "How to get rich," *Edge 56,* June 7, www.edge.org/documents/archive/edge56.html.

6 Matt Ridley, *The Origins of Virtue.*

7 See Richard Koch (1998) *The Third Revolution,* Capstone, Oxford.

8 See Robert Waterman (1994) *The Frontiers of Excellence,* Nicholas Brealey, London, Appendix 2. In North America the book is called *What America Does Right.*

9 The title of their book; see Barry J. Nalebuff and Adam M. Brandenburger (1996) *Co-opetition,* HarperCollins, New York.

10 Eric S. Raymond (1999) *The Cathedral and the Bazaar,* http://www.tuxedo.org/~/writings/-cathedral-bazaar/.

11 Jared Diamond, *op. cit.*

12 Ibid.

13 Matt Ridley, *The Origins of Virtue.*

Chapter 6

1 Although such discussion is beyond the scope of this book, Newton is a fascinating character, partly because of the contrast between the conventional view of him as the world's most influential scientist ever, the father of modern empirical science, on the one hand; and on the other, the more complex reality, that he was a brilliant synthesizer, but very far from a rationalist, a man who spent most of his later years poring over the Bible, inventing bizarre theological fantasies, and tending bubbling cauldrons to discover the secrets of alchemy. For good descriptions of the conventional view of Newton, see John Simmons (1996) *The 100 Most Influential Scientists* (where Newton tops the chart), Carol Publishing Group, New York; and the more populist and entertaining Melvyn Bragg (1998) *On Giant's Shoulders,* Hodder and Stoughton, London. For a scholarly and highly readable account of the complexities of Newton's character and intellectual influences, see Michael White (1998) *Isaac Newton: The Last Sorcerer,* Fourth Estate, London.

2 See Chapter 11 for a discussion of increasing returns to scale and their role in the so-called new economy.

Chapter 7

1 My account has borrowed extensively from the very useful essay on Einstein in John Simmons (1996) *The 100 Most Influential Scientists,* Carol Publishing Group, New York. Einstein is ranked second, behind Isaac Newton, and ahead of Neils Bohr (third) and Charles Darwin (fourth).

2 Quoted in *Oxford Book of Verse* (1961), p. 216.

3 Mark F. Blaxill and Thomas M. Hout (1987) "Make decisions like a fighter pilot," in Carl W. Stern and George Stalk Jr., editors (1998) *Perspectives on Strategy,* John Wiley, New York, p. 165.

4 I have written on this at more length in the chapter on "Time Revolution" in Richard Koch (1998, revised edition) *The 80/20 Principle: the Secret of Achieving More with Less,* Nicholas Brealey, London.

5 *Fortune,* July 7, 1997.

6 Marshall McLuhan (1964, 1965) *Understanding Media: The Extensions of Man,* revised edition, McGraw-Hill, New York.

7 The phrase "legacy mindset" comes from the Boston Consulting Group. See the excellent new book by Philip Evans and Thomas S. Wurster (2000) *Blown to Bits: How the New Economics of Information Transforms Strategy,* Harvard Business School Press, Boston. Evans and Wurster comment: "A greater vulnerability than legacy assets is a legacy mindset. It may be easy to grasp this point intellectually, but it is profoundly different in practice. Managers must put aside the presuppositions of the old competitive world and compete according to totally new rules of engagement. They must make decisions at a different speed, long before the numbers are in place . . . They must acquire totally new technical and entrepreneurial skills, quite different from what made their organization (and them personally) so successful. They must manage for maximal opportunity, not minimum risk. They must devolve decision making, install different reward structures, and perhaps even devise different ownership structures." Good luck!

8 The ways in which the Internet will transform business lie beyond the scope of this book, although some useful hints are given in Chapter 11. There are three books that you must read to understand what is happening: one is the BCG book quoted above. The other two are Alex Birch, Philip Gerbert, and Dirk Scheider (2000) *The Age of E-tail,* Capstone, Oxford; and Evan I. Schwartz (1999) *Digital Darwinism: Seven Breakthrough Business Strategies for Surviving in the Cutthroat Web Economy,* Broadway/Penguin, New York/Harmondsworth.

Chapter 8

1 True, Einstein did not say exactly what is universally attributed to him. Instead, he wrote to Max Born, "You believe in the God who plays dice, and I

in complete law and order." Quoted in Ian Stewart (1989) *Does God Play Dice?* Basil Blackwell, Oxford.

2 Danah Zohar and Ian Marshall (1993) *The Quantum Society,* Bloomsbury, London.

Chapter 9

1 Quoted in James Gleick (1987) *Chaos,* Little, Brown, New York.

2 Henri Poincaré (1908) *Science et Méthode,* Ernest Flammarion, Paris; quoted in David Ruelle (1991) *Chance and Chaos,* Princeton University Press, Princeton, also published (1993) by Penguin, London.

3 Although it quickly became famous, Lorenz's paper was initially not published, except as a press release of the conference of the American Association for the Advancement of Science, to which the paper was presented on December 29, 1972 in Washington, D.C. The butterfly paper was first published, along with other lectures, in Edward Lorenz (1993) *The Essence of Chaos,* University of Washington Press, Seattle.

4 Quoted in James Gleick (1987) *Chaos,* Little, Brown, New York.

5 Eric D. Beinhocker (1999) "On the origin of strategies," *McKinsey Quarterly,* 4, pp. 47–57.

6 Quoted in Michael Lissack and Johan Roos (1999) *The Next Common Sense: Mastering Corporate Complexity Through Coherence,* Nicholas Brealey Publishing, London.

7 Ibid.

8 Adam Smith actually identified several ways in which the economy automatically adjusted itself in accordance with what we would today call "feedback mechanisms." He showed that high prices stimulated production of those goods and low prices discouraged production, thereby matching supplies more closely to demand. He also showed how the prices of wages and capital triggered desirable adjustments.

9 John Tyler Bonner (1988) *The Evolution of Complexity by Means of Natural Selection,* Princeton University Press, Princeton.

10 John Horgen (1995) "From complexity to perplexity," *Scientific American,* June.

11 See the terrific little book by Paul Krugman (1996) *The Self-Organizing Economy,* Blackwell Publishers, Cambridge, MA.

12 Krugman notes that Zipf's law does not work so well in countries with a single preeminent "primate city" that combines the "normal" economic role with that of the political center—places like London or Paris. To the expected "economic" population, we have to add the employment provided by the bureaucracy and all those who cluster around power. Zipf's law then works with hypothetically adjusted populations. It also works in most countries where there is no primate city.

13 C. Northcote Parkinson (1958) *Parkinson's Law,* John Murray, London.

14 Foreword to Arie de Geus (1997) *The Living Company: Growth, Learning and Longevity in Business,* Nicholas Brealey, London.

15 Peter M. Senge (1994) *The Fifth Discipline: the Art and Practice of the Learning Organization,* Doubleday, New York, p. 4.

Chapter 10

1 Diane Coyle (1997) *The Weightless World,* Capstone, Oxford, page 1.

2 The researchers are Bernardo Huberman and Lada Adamic; see the *New York Times,* June 21, 1999.

3 "Chaos theory explodes Hollywood hype," *Independent on Sunday,* March 30, 1997.

4 Vilfredo Pareto (1896–97) *Cours d'Economique Politique,* Lausanne University. For a full explanation of Pareto's findings and how they can be used, see Richard Koch (1997, 1998) *The 80/20 Principle: The Secret of Achieving More with Less,* Nicholas Brealey, London.

5 With the possible exception of his contemporary, W. Edwards Deming.

6 See Chapter 1. Darwin's theory can be reduced to three observations: the struggle for existence among creatures resulting in the early death of most embryos and siblings (the insight from Malthus); the variations between and within species; and the inheritance of variation. Darwin then jumped to the conclusion that the variations facilitated selection, since nature could reward variations that were most suited to the conditions of life. If he had started with the 80/20 principle, Darwin could immediately have hypothesized that a small minority of the most powerful variants would eventually populate most of their species; and that a minority of siblings would leave a majority of descendants. Thus two out of three of the planks of Darwin's theory are at least implicit in the 80/20 principle (only the inheritance point is not implied).

7 See footnote 4 above. Since you've bothered to read the endnote, here's the 80/20 insight into negotiating a pay hike. It's likely that about 80 percent of concessions will be made in the last 20 percent of negotiating time. So don't peak too early in your demands. If you start the meeting at 5:30 P.M. and you know your boss has to leave the office at 6:30, the critical moments will occur around 6:20. Try not to allow things to get resolved before then. If proposals are made before then, look unhappy and keep your own suggestions until near the time when the supervisor has to rush off.

8 I am drawing here on pioneering work undertaken by the Ashridge Strategic Management Centre, and in particular one of its directors, Marcus Alexander, for which I am most grateful.

9 As Marcus Alexander points out, "virtual" can mean two different things. It can mean either lack of physical proximity, or, as here, lack of ownership. See

the article from which my examples are taken and which contains many more: Marcus Alexander (1997) "Getting to grips with the virtual organization," *Long Range Planning,* February, 30 (1), pp. 122–24.

10 Based on an unpublished paper by Marcus Alexander (1999) "The value in corporate alliances," draft prepared by the Ashridge Strategic Management Centre for the Singapore Chambers of Commerce.

11 Quoted in Frederick F. Reichheld (1996) *The Loyalty Effect,* Harvard Business School Press, Boston.

12 Ibid.

13 See, for example, a study of thirty-nine middle-sized German companies: Gunter Rommel (1996) *Simplicity Wins,* Harvard Business School Press, Cambridge, MA.

14 ROME for any business segment may be defined as the percentage of total profit before interest and tax (PBIT) divided by the percentage of total management effort (ideally weighted by the cost of that management effort) going into looking after that business segment. Thus we can express ROME arithmetically as:

$$\text{ROME} = \frac{\text{Percentage of Profit Before Interest and Tax}}{\text{Percentage of Management Effort}}$$

A ROME of more than1.0 indicates a segment of above-average profitability, and the higher the number the better. A ROME of below 1.0, and especially one below 0.5, should lead to one of the following actions:

- a reduction in management effort, and/or
- an increase in profits, and/or
- withdrawal from the segment.

The hypothesis derived from the 80/20 principle is that segments taking approximately 20 percent of total management effort (those with the highest ROME) will account for 80 percent of PBIT. These segments should be expanded.

15 Jared Diamond (1999) "How to get rich," *Edge* 56, June 7.

16 George Elliott, Ronald G. Evans and Bruce Gardiner (1996) "Managing cost: transatlantic lessons," *Management Review,* June.

17 Ian Stewart (1989) *Does God Play Dice?,* Basil Blackwell/Penguin, Oxford/London.

Chapter 11

1 See Martin Wolf (1999) "Putting the paradigm to the test," *Financial Times,* 10 November. The cost indices quoted are derived from OECD research by Professor Richard Lipsey of the Simon Fraser University, Canada.

2 Malcolm Gladwell (1996) "The tipping point," *New Yorker,* June.

3 See his classic article: Peter F. Drucker (1985) "The discipline of innovation," *Harvard Business Review,* May–June, reprinted in November–December 1998.

4 Geoffrey Moore (1991) *Crossing the Chasm: Marketing and Selling Technology Products to Mainstream Customers,* Capstone/HarperBusiness, Oxford/New York.

5 William J. O'Neil (1991) *How to Make Money in Stocks,* McGraw-Hill, New York, p. 132.

6 Henry Ford (1923) *My Life and Work,* Doubleday, Page & Co., New York.

7 Gordon Moore reported in John Naughton (1999) "No goodbyes for world's Mr. Chips," *Observer,* 8 August.

8 The best short summary is W. Brian Arthur (1996) "Increasing returns and the new world of business," *Harvard Business Review,* July–August.

9 Ibid., p. 103.

10 W. Brian Arthur (1996), "Increasing returns and the new world of business," *Harvard Business Review,* July–August.

11 Ibid.

12 See Stuart Crainer (1998) *The Ultimate Business Guru Book,* Capstone, Oxford, p. 271.

Chapter 12

1 Richard Pascale (1990) *Managing on the Edge,* Simon & Schuster, New York.

2 Arie de Geus, *The Living Company.*

3 Ellen de Rooij (1996) "A brief desk research study into the average life expectancy of companies in a number of countries," Stratix Consulting Group, Amsterdam, quoted in Arie de Geus, *op. cit.*

4 See Karl Sigmund (1993) *Games of Chance,* Oxford University Press/Penguin, Oxford/London.

5 *Second Letter of St. Paul to the Corinthians,* Chapter 9, verse 6.

6 Dietrich Dörner, *The Logic of Failure.*

Finale

1 E. O. Wilson (1998) *Consilience: the Unity of Knowledge,* Alfred A. Knopf, New York/Little, Brown and Company, London, page 6. Now available in an Abacus paperback (London).

2 Ibid.

Index

Richard Koch is an entrepreneur and investor who has started successful businesses ranging from restaurants and hotels to consulting and publishing. A former partner with Bain and Company, he currently advises venture capital groups in the United Kingdom and South Africa.

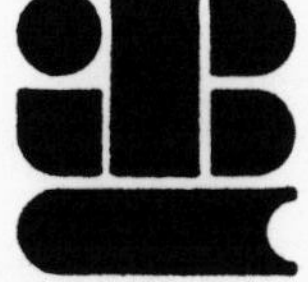